Communications in Computer and Information Science 429

Andrzej Dziech   Andrzej Czyżewski (Eds.)

Multimedia Communications, Services and Security

7th International Conference, MCSS 2014
Krakow, Poland, June 11-12, 2014
Proceedings

 Springer

Volume Editors

Andrzej Dziech
AGH University of Science and Technology
Department of Telecommunications
Krakow, Poland
E-mail: adzie@tlen.pl

Andrzej Czyżewski
Gdansk University of Technology
Multimedia Systems Department
Gdansk, Poland
E-mail: indect@sound.eti.pg.gda.pl

ISSN 1865-0929   e-ISSN 1865-0937
ISBN 978-3-319-07568-6   e-ISBN 978-3-319-07569-3
DOI 10.1007/978-3-319-07569-3
Springer Cham Heidelberg New York Dordrecht London

Library of Congress Control Number: Applied for

Typesetting: Camera-ready by author, data conversion by Scientific Publishing Services, Chennai, India

Printed on acid-free paper

Springer is part of Springer Science+Business Media (www.springer.com)

Preface

Welcome to the proceedings of the 7th Multimedia Communications, Services and Security Conference held once again in Kraków.

With so many security and safety topics, and a wide range of related disciplines, this well-established forum strives to raise many important questions for us to consider and to provide answers to in the field of state-of-the-art technological solutions. Running in parallel, privacy aspects of technological progress are to be guided by criteria and metrics determined by social and ethical experts and end users, establishing the characteristics that technology must fulfil in order for it to be an effective and integral part of privacy protection.

As in previous years, this conference also provided an opportunity for all of us who are concerned with the future of multimedia communications, services, and security to come together, collaborate, and share experiences. As organizers, we are delighted that you are joining us for this year's specialists gathering and participating in the discussions that will help us chart the future course of state-of-the-art technological solutions in the fields addressed by this year's MCSS conference.

The objective of the Multimedia Communications, Services and Security (MCSS 2014) Conference is to present research and development activities contributing to many aspects of multimedia communications, systems, and security. We have invited both theoretical and experimental papers, as well as ongoing research in the domain of audiovisual systems including novel multimedia architectures, multimedia data fusion, acquisition of multimedia content and quality of experience management, watermarking technology and applications, content searching methods, interactive multimedia applications, cybercrime countermeasures, cryptography, biometry, and many others. And of course we did not overlook privacy protection solutions ensuring the optimal use of technologies for the benefit of civil European security.

As during previous events, the above examples are just a brief overview of the rich scope of the 7th MCSS conference, and this year's program also included an exhibition of advanced technological achievements. Immediately after the conference, the final review of the FP7 INDECT ("Intelligent information system supporting observation, searching and detection for security of citizens in urban environment") project was held, which was coordinated by the AGH University of Science and Technology, hosting the conference. This expanded the exhibition programme even further: It presented the achievements of the project to the reviewers, while for the remaining participants it was an opportunity to learn the results of this project completed jointly by many European institutions.

Finally, we believe the participants made the most of the social program accompanying the conference, listened to exceptional musical performances, and enjoyed the beautiful city of Kraków at the threshold of summer.

June 2014   Andrzej Dziech
                                                                Andrzej Czyżewski

Organization

The International Conference on Multimedia Communications, Services and Security (MCSS 2014) was organized by AGH University of Science and Technology within the scope of and under the auspices of the INDECT project.

Executive Committee

General Chair

Andrzej Dziech — AGH University of Science and Technology, Poland

Committee Chairs

Andrzej Dziech — AGH University of Science and Technology, Poland

Andrzej Czyżewski — Gdansk University of Technology, Poland

Technical Program Committee

Alexander Bekiarski	Technical University - Sofia, Bulgaria
Fernando Boavida	University of Coimbra, Portugal
Jarosław Bułat	AGH University of Science and Technology, Poland
Eduardo Cerqueira	Federal University of Para, Brazil
Michele Colajanni	University of Modena and Reggio Emilia, Italy
Marilia Curado	University of Coimbra, Portugal
Andrzej Czyzewski	Gdansk University of Technology, Poland
Jacek Danda	AGH University of Science and Technology, Poland
Anne Demoisy	Skynet Belgacom, Belgium
Charalampos Dimoulas	Aristotle University of Thessaloniki, Greece
Marek Domański	Poznan University of Technology, Poland
Andrzej Duda	Grenoble Institute of Technology, France
Andrzej Dziech	AGH University of Science and Technology, Poland
Apostolos Gkamas	Research Academic Computer Technology Institute, Greece
Andrzej Glowacz	AGH University of Science and Technology, Poland

Michał Grega   AGH University of Science and Technology,
                                Poland
Nils Johanning   InnoTec Data, Germany
Eva Kiktova   Technical University of Kosice, Slovakia
Georgios Kioumourtzis   Ministry of Public Order and Citizen
                                Protection, Greece
Marek Kisiel-Dorohinicki   AGH University of Science and Technology,
                                Poland
Christian Kollmitzer   FHTW Wien, Austria
Bozena Kostek   Gdansk University of Technology, Poland
Zbigniew Kotulski   Warsaw University of Technology, Poland
Anton Kummert   University of Wuppertal, Germany
David Larrabeiti   Universidad Carlos III de Madrid, Spain
Mikolaj Leszczuk   AGH University of Science and Technology,
                                Poland
Antoni Ligęza   AGH University of Science and Technology,
                                Poland
Tomasz Marciniak   Poznan University of Technology, Poland
Augusto Neto   Universidade Federal do Rio Grande do Norte,
                                Brazil
George Papanikolaou   Aristotle University of Thessaloniki, Greece
Yogachandran Rahulamathavan   City University London, UK
Muttukrishnan Rajarajan   City University London, UK
Kamissety R. Rao   University of Texas at Arlington, USA
Thomas Sablik   University of Wuppertal, Germany
Irena Stange   U.S. Department of Commerce, USA
Nikolai Stoianov   Technical University of Sofia, Bulgaria
Piotr Szczuko   Gdansk University of Technology, Poland
Andrzej Szwabe   Poznan University of Technology, Poland
Ryszard Tadeusiewicz   AGH University of Science and Technology,
                                Poland
Manuel Uruena   Universidad Carlos III de Madrid, Spain
Vladimir Vasinek   VSB - Technical University of Ostrava,
                                Czech Republic
Joerg Velten   University of Wuppertal, Germany
Eva Vozarikova Kiktova   Technical University of Kosice, Slovakia
Jaroslav Zdralek   VSB, Technical University of Ostrava,
                                Czech Republic

Organizing Committee

Remigiusz Baran   Kielce University of Technology, Poland
Jacek Dańda   AGH University of Science and Technology,
                                Poland

Jan Derkacz	AGH University of Science and Technology, Poland
Sabina Drzewicka	AGH University of Science and Technology, Poland
Andrzej Głowacz	AGH University of Science and Technology, Poland
Michał Grega	AGH University of Science and Technology, Poland
Piotr Guzik	AGH University of Science and Technology, Poland
Magdalena Hrynkiewicz-Sudnik	AGH University of Science and Technology, Poland
Agnieszka Kleszcz	AGH University of Science and Technology, Poland
Paweł Korus	AGH University of Science and Technology, Poland
Mikołaj Leszczuk	AGH University of Science and Technology, Poland
Andrzej Matiolański	AGH University of Science and Technology, Poland
Piotr Romaniak	AGH University of Science and Technology, Poland
Krzysztof Rusek	AGH University of Science and Technology, Poland

Sponsoring Institutions

- Institute of Electrical and Electronics Engineers (IEEE)
- Intelligent information system supporting observation, searching and detection for security of citizens in urban environment (INDECT Project)
- AGH University of Science and Technology, Department of Telecommunications

Table of Contents

A Smart Camera for Traffic Surveillance

Remigiusz Baran[1], Tomasz Ruść[2], and Mariusz Rychlik[3]

[1] Kielce University of Technology,
Faculty of Electrical Engineering, Automatics and Computer Science,
al. 1000-lecia P.P. 7, 25-314 Kielce, Poland
r.baran@tu.kielce.pl
[2] Institute of Physics, Jan Kochanowski University,
ul. Swietokrzyska 15, 25-406 Kielce, Poland
tomasz.rusc@ujk.edu.pl
[3] University of Computer Engineering and Telecommunications
ul. Toporowskiego 98, 25-553 Kielce, Poland
mr.mariusz.rychlik@gmail.com

Abstract. An intelligent surveillance system based on visual information gathered by smart cameras, aimed at traffic monitoring with emphasis on traffic
events caused by cars, is presented in the paper. The system components and
their capabilities for automatic detection and recognition of selected parameters
of cars, as well as different aspects of system efficiency, are described and discussed in detail. Smart facilities for Make and Model Recognition (MMR), License Plate Recognition (LPR) and Color Recognition (CR), embedded in the
system in the form of their individual software implementations, are analyzed
and their recognition rates detailed. Finally, a discussion of the system's efficiency as a whole, with an insight into possible future improvements, is included in the conclusion.

Keywords: intelligent camera, surveillance system, vehicle recognition.

1 Introduction

The growth of the digital camera market can be said to have begun in the late 1990s
and early 2000s. Reasons for this growth are numerous technological advancements
in chip manufacturing, progress in embedded system design, the coming-of-age of
CMOS (Complementary Metal Oxide Semiconductor) image sensors and so on [1]. In
particular, the development of CMOS image sensors (CIS) - cheaper to be manufac-
ture than CCDs (Charge-Coupled Devices), boosted this growth. Together with digital
stand-alone cameras and camera phones, accessibility and demand for smart cameras
have also increased. The market for this category of smart devices grew 22% in 2012,
and is projected to climb at an annual average of 12% through 2017 [2]. In total, the
global CIS market is expected to increase from $6.6 billion in 2012 to $11 billion by
2017 [3]. For these reasons and because of the potential of CIS sensors to make smart
cameras smaller, cheaper and more widespread, their role development of digital
camera technology is of great importance at the moment.

A. Dziech and A. Czyżewski (Eds.): MCSS 2014, CCIS 429, pp. 1–15, 2014.
© Springer International Publishing Switzerland 2014

"While the primary function of a normal camera is to provide video for monitoring and recording, smart cameras are usually designed to perform specific, repetitive, high-speed and high-accuracy tasks" [1]. Machine vision or intelligent video surveillance systems (IVSS) are their typical applications. There are many different applications of smart cameras within these areas; therefore, only a few representative examples are described below to illustrate the "state-of-the-art" in the field.

One example of a camera dedicated for machine vision applications is the Matrox Iris GT from Matrox Imaging. As well as a CCD sensor, it integrates a CPU architecture with an embedded operating system pre-installed (Microsoft® Windows® Embedded CE or Windows® XP Embedded). This integration "enables the Matrox Iris GT to provide a PC-like environment for deploying fully custom application" [4]. Because of the embedded system, application development is fully supported within the range of communication protocols, including industrial ones, and can be done using the popular and widely known Microsoft Visual Studio IDE (Integrated Development Environment). In addition, "Matrox Iris GT is supported by the Matrox Imaging Library (MIL), a comprehensive collection of software tools for developing machine vision applications" [5].

In general, surveillance camera systems aim to observe a given area in order to increase safety and security. Solutions developed by the research team of Professor Anton Kummert from the University of Wuppertal are good examples of IVSS systems. In [6], for instance, a surveillance system for the detection of individuals within a dense crowd from a scene captured by a Time-of-Flight camera is presented. It enables detection and tracking of every person's movement as well as analysis of this movement in contrast to the behavior of the entire crowd. Dedicated software enhances these capabilities by adding for example analysis of the crowding situation. Another "state-of-the-art" application of this kind refers to self-guided and driverless transport vehicles which are being developed under the cooperative project SaLsA [7].

However, other applications of smart cameras also exist. They are widely used in traffic management and monitoring, automated parking garages, driver assistance and control access systems, etc. The most common and well-known application in the category of traffic management and monitoring is License Plate Recognition (LPR) [8]. However, due to growing demand other categories of vehicle classification have recently been added. Make and Model Recognition (MMR) of cars [9] is major and relatively new functionality, along with Color Recognition (CR) and the distinguishing of vehicle types.

The smart camera system presented in this paper also belongs to the category of traffic management and monitoring applications. In common with the solution reported in [10], the presented system also incorporates three functionalities mentioned above: LPR, MMR and CR. Development of the presented architecture as well as relevant performed research were motivated by the INSIGMA R&D project [11] in which the authors of this paper are currently involved. One of INSIGMA's objectives is to develop software which will be able to process video sequences registered by surveillance cameras in order to detect and extract selected features of cars, including those discussed above.

For clarity of presentation, the rest of the paper is organized as follows. Section 2 introduces the overall architecture of the presented smart camera system. Organization of MMR, LPR and CR modules is presented in Sections 3 to 5. In Section 6, the system's efficiency is reported and discussed. Conclusions with an insight to possible future improvements are drawn in Section 7.

2   General Assumptions and System Architecture

According to the INSIGMA project's objectives, it has been assumed that smart surveillance cameras will be positioned over every traffic lane, including highways, streets, parking lots, etc. It has also been assumed that the resolution of M-JPEG video sequences recorded by these cameras should not be less than 4CIF. In other words, the expected minimum resolution of processed video frames is 704 x 576 pixels. Taking into account the standard image sensor type (1/3, for instance) and the focal length of applied lens equal to for example 60 mm, the size of the camera field of view (FOV) from a distance of about 40 m is 2.35 x 1.76 meters. FOV of the same size can be also obtained from a distance of about 5 m, but with a focal length equal to 8 mm. These relationships are illustrated in Fig. 1.

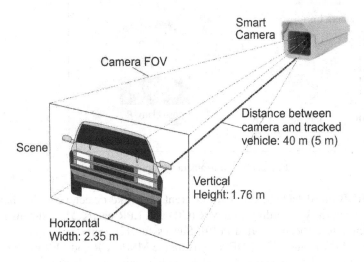

Fig. 1. Predetermined parameters of the camera's FOV

At its core, our smart camera implementation (known as the iCamera system), is a JVM-based system built using the Spring Framework [11]. It works on the Ubuntu 13.04 64 bit operating system. Despite this, to increase the system efficiency, its specialized modules (MMR, LPR, CR) have been written in C. To use their functionalities as well as to exchange data between them and the system backbone (the Camera Core), the Java Native Interface (JNI) framework has been used.

As illustrated in Fig. 2, the Camera Core receives the video stream from the Camera IP, and decodes and passes it on to subsequent modules. The decoded video frames are initially passed on to the Global Detection and Extraction (GDE) module. The task of this module is to detect (on a video frame from the camera) and then to extract (by cropping this frame) two Regions of Interest (ROIs). One of them - a sub-image containing the grill part of a car together with its headlights and indicator lights is for the MMR and CR modules. The other − a sub-image limited to the license plate area is for the LPR module.

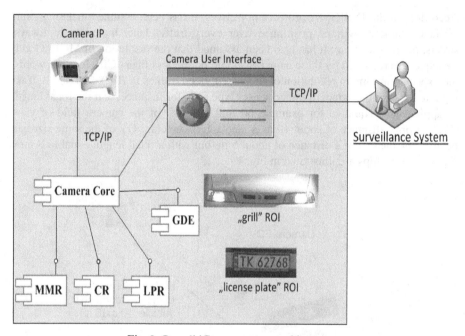

Fig. 2. Overall iCamera system architecture

Both ROIs are detected using two different Haar-like detectors, which have been trained concurrently according to MMR (CR) and LPR needs. More details of Haar-like detectors have been reported in [9]. Successful ROI detection (equivalent to car detection in FOV) causes the GDE to activate the MMR, CR and LPR modules. After activation, the MMR, CR and LPR modules individually process ROIs passed to them from the GDE, and send the results of this processing back to the Camera Core. These results are metadata depending on the module which generates them. In the case of MMR, for instance, the returned metadata contains an alias name identifying the make and model of the car, which have been predicted by the classifier built into the module. In the case of LPR however, the metadata contains the text read from the license plate by the embedded OCR tool. This information like that is passed as Exif fields [12] in the XML format. Selected examples of these fields are shown in Fig. 3.

```
<icamera_dcg:grill>
    <icamera_dcg:x>600</icamera_dcg:x>
    <icamera_dcg:y>451</icamera_dcg:y>
    <icamera_dcg:width>339</icamera_dcg:width>
    <icamera_dcg:height>74</icamera_dcg:height>
</icamera_dcg:grill>
<icamera_mmr:markAndmodel>astra_1</icamera_mmr:markAndmodel>
<icamera_cr:color>
    <icamera_cr:name>czerwony</icamera_cr:name>
</icamera_cr:color>
```

Fig. 3. Exif fields with metadata returned by GDE, MMR and CR modules, respectively

A more detailed illustration of threads and their activities initiated in the iCamera system is shown in Fig. 4.

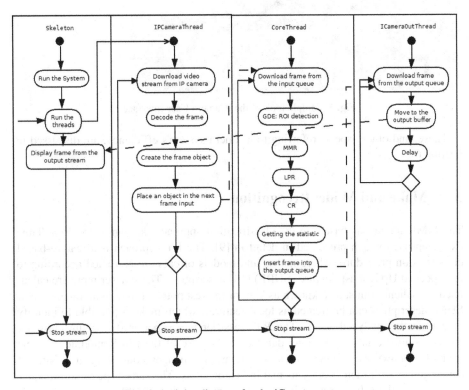

Fig. 4. Activity diagram for the iCamera system

Fig. 4 shows that the input video stream is supplemented by additional data during its passage through the iCamera system. The added data are the previously mentioned Exif fields. The video stream extended in this way is finally passed to the user interface, as illustrated in Fig. 2. The interface allows the user to control the iCamera system by for example stopping and starting the video streaming and enabling or disabling each of the specialized modules. Its current look is shown in Fig. 5. Fig. 4 also shows that the Core Thread aggregates the prediction/OCR results referring to the same vehicle from successive neighboring video frames to obtain statistics and finally increase the system accuracy. Final accuracy in this case is proportional to the camera frame rate. However, the greater the frame rate the shorter the frame processing time. Of course, there are also other factors, for instance the efficiency of the hardware platform used, which impact the system's performance as well as its accuracy.

Fig. 5. Sample look of the iCamera User Interface

These, and other aspects referring to iCamera system's efficiency, are discussed in Section 6.

3   Make and Model Recognition

The MMR module is based on the classification approach, known as the Real-Time (RT) approach which presented in detail in [9]. The RT approach is a feature-based classification procedure, where makes and models of cars are predicted according to the Speeded Up Robust Feature (SURF) [13] descriptors. These descriptors are calculated for salient points, also known as key- or interest points, found in an image. Their SURF descriptors can be treated as local features, which make it possible to identify objects in the analyzed scene. The RT classifier is a supervised learning classifier which requires a labeled training dataset. In the case of the MMR module, training examples known as reference images (RI) are sub-images containing grill parts of cars together with their headlights and indicator lights. The same type of sub-images, known as grill ROIs, are used in the testing phase, when the SURF descriptors are determined for the analyzed image, known as the query image (QI). Workflow of both training and testing phases is shown in Fig. 6. In the training phase, collection of RI's SURF descriptors, taken as a whole, is partitioned using a k-means clustering procedure into a given number of clusters, known as the vocabulary (Voc).

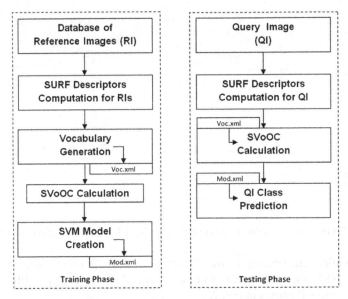

Fig. 6. Workflow of the RT approach

SURF descriptors related to a given photo from the training dataset (and in consequence to a given model name) are then assigned to the clusters' centroids, and a sparse vector of occurrence counts (SVoOC) is created. At the end of the training phase, the Support Vector Machines (SVM) algorithm [14] is used to construct, from the SVoOC vectors, a multi-dimensional hyper-plane which optimally separates the input space of SURF descriptors into predetermined number of classes. Support vectors closest to the optimal hyper-plane create the SVM model (Mod).

Both the vocabulary (Voc) and the SVM model (Mod) are loaded during the testing phase. SURF descriptors calculated for the Query Image are then assigned to appropriate Voc clusters, and a new SVoOC vector is created. Finally, according to this vector as well as the SVM model, the SVM classifier predicts a class to which the car model from the QI belongs.

Analysis of the classification accuracy for the RT approach was performed according to the Overall Success Rate measure (OSR), which is defined as follows [15]:

$$OSR = \frac{1}{n} \sum_{i=1}^{k} n_{i,i} \tag{1}$$

where:

n is the number of test images, k is the number of estimated classes and $n_{i,i}$ are entries of the main diagonal of a confusion matrix.

The classification accuracy of the RT approach depends on the number of reference images (RI) and the number of clusters (size of the vocabulary). Illustration of these dependences is shown in Fig. 7.

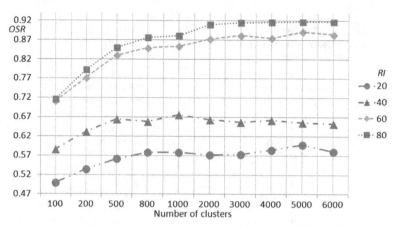

Fig. 7. OSR versus various number of clusters, for different RI values *(n = 2499)*

The classification accuracy of the RT approach depends on the number of reference images (RI) and the number of clusters (size of the vocabulary). Illustration of these dependences is shown in Fig. 7.

Fig. 7 shows that highest the OSR values (up to 0.92) are obtained for RI equal to 80 and for the number of clusters which range between 3000 and 6000.

The number of clusters impacts durations of both phases. Results related to OSR values and to the average duration of the entire testing phase, for RI = 80 and for the number of clusters greater than 3000, are given in Table 1.

Table 1. OSR and average duration of the testing phase (RI = 80, *n* = 2499)[1]

No. of clusters	3000	4000	5000	6000
OSR	0.916	0.917	0.918	0.918
Duration [ms]	37.93	40.51	42.58	45.64

4   License Plate Recognition

Automatic recognition of license plates is performed using the Tesseract OCR tool [16]. Tesseract is a powerful open source OCR specially designated to read text from various image formats. The ability to use custom-created training sets is a significant advantage of Tesseract. An OCR application can be oriented to a given specific font type thanks to this ability. As reported in [17], the recognition accuracy of Tesseract, when used to digitize antique books, is comparable with the well-known commercial ABBYY Fine Reader package. According to our tests, this accuracy is also comparable with that achieved by the OCR Reader – a part of Matrox Image Library.

Subsequent steps of the algorithm built in the LPR module are illustrated in Fig. 8.

---

[1] Results were obtained using a computer with the following parameters: DualCore Intel Core i5 650 processor, 4GB of DDR3-1333 RAM, 64-bit Windows Server.

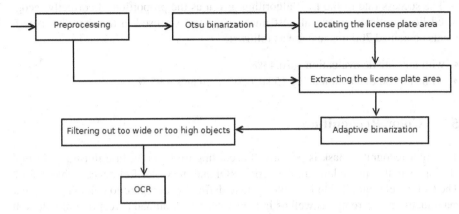

Fig. 8. Workflow of the LPR procedure

During the first preprocessing step, the license plate ROI taken from the GDE module is converted to a grayscale image, then blurred using the Gaussian filter and finally filtered by applying noise removal morphological operations. After that, a binarization using the Otsu method combined with dilation operation is applied. In the next step, the Canny Edge Detector, followed by the selected contour extraction method [9], were used to reject a frame surrounding the white license plate area as well as the elements outside this frame. This step allows extraction of an area limited only to the gray license plate numbers on the light background. To extract the numbers properly, the adaptive binarization procedure, with the binarization threshold determined according to the neighborhood of successive pixels, is used. Finally, filters based on factors computed according to contour properties of the extracted objects, are applied to remove elements which differ significantly from license plate numbers they are too wide or too tall.

Selected examples of license plate ROIs and results of the last step mentioned above are shown in Fig. 9.

TK 5807E	TK 5807E
TK 5807E	TK 580₁E
TK 5807E	T _5807E

Fig. 9. License plate ROIs (on the left) and results of their processing, respectively (on the right)

The results depicted in Fig. 9 show that the accuracy of the LPR algorithm strongly depends on the quality of the input ROI. However, statistical evaluation (taking into account a given number of successive frames with the same license plate), applied after the last OCR step, can significantly increase this accuracy.

The success rate of the LPR algorithm, given as the proportion of correctly recognized license plates among all test images (the test set used in the reported experiments contained 700 images) are as follows:

- with no statistic evaluation – 76,43%,
- with statistic evaluation using 15 successive images – 95 %.

5   Color Recognition

The color recognition task is performed according to the procedure illustrated in Fig. 10. Inputs to this procedure are the "grill" ROI and the Color Reference Table (CRT). The Color Reference Table is a color palette defined with regard to colors used by car manufacturers (currently as well as in the past) and the human perception of colors. It consists of eight colors described as ranges of RGB values and indexed as follows:

1. Pink – Red,
2. Brown – Orange – Beige,
3. Golden – Olive – Yellow,
4. Green – Lime,
5. Caesious – Blue Navy-blue,
6. Black,
7. White,
8. Gray.

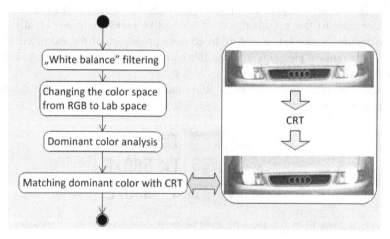

Fig. 10. Diagram of the CR algorithm

The color recognition algorithm begins with the "White balance" filtering step. The filter applied in this step uses the color of the road surface to modify the color curves, depending on the weather or lighting conditions. Surface images are registered (by the GDE module) every given period of time, when recognition modules are disabled (when no car is present in the camera FOV). The next step changes the color space from RGB to CIELAB according to the requirements of dominant color analysis which is carried out after that. Dominant color analysis is performed with regard to Dominant Color Descriptor (DCD) implementation based on MPEG-7 [17].

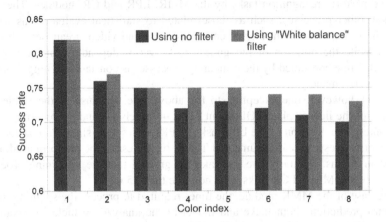

Fig. 11. Accuracy of the CR module

In the final step, the dominant color in the analyzed ROI is converted back from CIELAB to RGB space and referred to colors from CRT. The result of this reference is returned as the name of the predicted color.

Success rates relating to individual colors from the CRT table obtained with or without the use of the white balance filter are illustrated in Fig. 11.

Fig. 11 shows that the success rate of the CR module differs according to the color in the CRT table. The highest rate is obtained in the case of the Pink–Red color range, while the lowest is in Gray color range. Fig.11 also shows that results are slightly better when the white balance filter except in the case of the Pink–Red color range.

6   System Efficiency

As mentioned in Section 2, the effciency of the iCamera system depends mainly on the performance parameters of the applied CPU architecture. To analyze this dependency as well as to verify system assumptions and requirements, the following x86 platforms have been selected:

- Intel i5: CPU - Dual Core Intel Core i5 650, 3200 MHz, RAM - 4GB DDR3-1333 DDR3, system - Windows Server 2008 R2 Enterprise (64-bit),
- ATOM N270: CPU - ATOM N270, 1,6 GHz, RAM - 1GB DDR2 SDRAM 533.0 MHz, system - Linux Debian 3.2.0-4-686-pae,
- AMD Zacate: CPU - Dual-Core AMD Zacate E350/350D APU, 800 MHz, RAM - 4GB DDR3, system - Linux Ubuntu 13.04-desktop-amd64.

At the moment, the iCamera system implements serial computation. Taking this into account, the total processing time of a single frame is the sum of the times required to decode the video stream, create the frame object, detect and extract two types of ROIs and perform recognition tasks by the MMR, LPR and CR modules. There are, of course, other processes, such as those related to statistical evaluation as well as many others connected with internal communication and video stream servicing (see Fig. 4). While the duration of recognition tasks varies depending on the analyzed content, the time consumed by the remaining processes is constant and hinges only on hardware performance.

There is, however, one exception to the above rule. Because of the stable very small size of the license plate ROI (about 214 x 44 pixels)[9] and the recurrent nature of its content, the duration of the LPR task (TLPR) varies very slightly. In accordance with performed tests we can assume that TLPR, regardless of the platform used, is not larger than 20 ms. Similarly, we can take for granted that the remaining processes (TRP), except MMR and CR tasks, take no more than 15 ms.

In the case of the MMR module, the times required to process the single QI image and return prediction about make and model of the analyzed vehicles on examined platforms (TMMR) are illustrated in Fig. 12[2].

Relevant times needed to complete the task by the CR module (TCR) are portrayed in Fig 13.

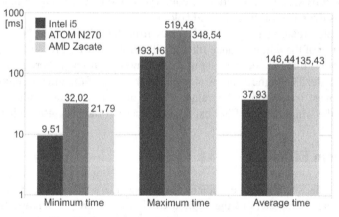

Fig. 12. Times required to complete the MMR task

Charts presented in Figs. 12 and 13 lead to the simple conclusion that the parameters of the Intel i5 architecture give better performance than other selected platforms. However, these charts also allow us to evaluate which frame rate of the IP camera would be most appropriate.

---

[2] Under the following set-up parameters: RI = 80, No. of clusters = 3000.

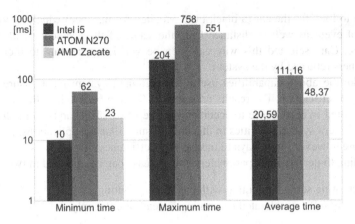

Fig. 13. Times needed to complete the CR task

Taking into consideration the times reported earlier in this section, the average duration of processing the single QI image in the iCamera system (T_{QI}) is as follows:

$$T_{QI} = T_{RP} + T_{MMR} + T_{LPR} + T_{CR} = 84 \text{ ms.} \qquad (2)$$

This means that the iCamera system is capable, when implemented on the Intel i5 platform or similar, to serially compute 11 frames of resolution 4CIF. Respectively, the frame rate of the IP camera can be 10 or 11 fps. This meets our assumptions about statistical evaluation, because to increase the accuracy of recognition tasks we need to predict by analyzing at least 10 frames. Otherwise, it is difficult to deduce when the distribution of subsequent predictions is flat.

7   Conclusions and Future Work

In summary, the main advantages of the current prototype implementation of the iCamera system presented in this paper are as follows:

1. the iCamera system is suitable for a wide range of traffic monitoring applications;
2. the current system parameters allow the system to efficiently identify license plate numbers in real time, recognize selected makes and models of cars, and classify real colors of cars into eight predefined categories;
3. statistical evaluation procedure built into the system allows it to increase the recognition rates in every category of analysis.

As shown in Section 2, assumptions made about camera settings were intended to monitor every individual traffic lane of city center streets, countryside roads, highways, parking lots, etc. The goal of traffic monitoring performed by the iCamera system is first of all to create opportunities for identifying offenders in traffic accidents, especially in cases where the offender has fled the scene. Relying on evidence given by witnesses of such accidents, authorized services (e.g. municipal ones) can use the material recorded by the multiple iCamera systems distributed over main crossroads in the city to look for the car (a black Ford Mondeo for instance) which, according to the time of event as well as distance from the scene of the accident, is likely to be responsible. Cars selected this way can then be verified according to their license plate numbers returned by the system.

To make the above capabilities useful, the iCamera system must ensure an adequate level of efficiency. The results presented in Section 6 as well as the success rate factors reported in accordance to accuracies of the MMR, LPR and CR modules confirm the iCamera system's utilities in this kind of surveillance applications.

There are however some ways to increase this efficiency.

According to performance parameters, the increase can be obtained in two ways:

- by substituting serial computing with parallel computing;
- by applying GPU-accelerated computing instead of CPU only.

Our experiments show that using a mixed CPU/GPU architecture combined with OpenCL (Open Computing Language) implementations can increase system performance by more than 5-fold. Moreover, it is reasonable to assume that parallel computing will also be able to accelerate the system at least twice.

According to the accuracies of the recognition modules, the system's efficiency can be improved first of all by increasing the number of frames taken into account by the statistical evaluation procedure. To achieve this, the iCamera system has to be able to process more than 10 fps as is the case at the moment. This aspect is however, strongly connected to performance parameters. We hope that proper implementation of both the technologies listed above will allow the frame rate of the applied cameras to be increased at least 25 fps, and in this way improve significantly the system's efficiency as a whole.

Acknowledgements. This work was supported by the European Regional Development Fund under the Innovative Economy Operational Programme, INSIGMA project no.POIG.01.01.02- 00-062/09. The numerical experiments reported in this paper were performed using computational equipment purchased as part of the framework of the EU Operational Programme Innovative Economy (POIG.02.02.00-26-023/09-00) and the EU Operational Programme Development of Eastern Poland (POPW.01.03.00-26-016/09-00).

References

1. Shi, Y., Lichman, S.: Smart Cameras: A Review. CCTV Focus (36), 34–43 & (37), 38–45 (2006)
2. IC Insights' 2013 O-S-D Report (2013), http://www.icinsights.com/services/osd-report/ (viewed February 10, 2014)
3. Status of the CMOS Image Sensors Industry, http://www.prnewswire.com/news-releases/status-of-the-cmos-image-sensors-industry-187871741.html (viewed February 10, 2014)
4. http://www.matrox.com/imaging/media/pdf/products/iris_gt_mil/iris_gt_mil.pdf (viewed February 10, 2014)

5. http://www.matrox.com/imaging/en/products/software/mil/
   (viewed February 10, 2014)
6. Stahlschmidt, C., Gavriilidis, A., Velten, J., Kummert, A.: People Detection and Tracking
   from a Top-View Position Using a Time-of-Flight Camera. In: Dziech, A., Czyżewski, A.
   (eds.) MCSS 2013. CCIS, vol. 368, pp. 213–223. Springer, Heidelberg (2013)
7. http://www.salsa-autonomik.de/ (viewed February 10, 2014)
8. Janowski, L., Kozłowski, P., Baran, R., Romaniak, P., Glowacz, A., Rusc, T.: Quality assessment for a visual and automatic license plate recognition. Multimedia Tools and Applications 68(1), 23–40 (2014)
9. Baran, R., Glowacz, A., Matiolanski, A.: The efficient real-and non-real-time make and
   model recognition of cars. Multimedia Tools and Applications (2013),
   doi:10.1007/s11042-013-1545-2.
10. Psyllos, A., Anagnostopoulos, C.N., Kayafas, E.: Vehicle model recognition from frontal
    view image measurements. Computer Standards & Interfaces 33(2), 142–151 (2011)
11. http://www.springsource.org (viewed February 10, 2014)
12. http://exif.org/specifications.html (viewed February 10, 2014)
13. Bay, H., Ess, A., Tuytelaars, T., Van Gool, L.: Speeded-up Robust Features (SURF).
    Computer Vision and Image Understanding 110(3), 346–359 (2008)
14. Cortes, C., Vapnik, V.: Support-vector networks. Machine Learning 20(3), 273–297
    (1995)
15. Witten, I.H., Frank, E.: Data Mining: Practical Machine Learning Tools and Techniques,
    2nd edn. Morgan Kaufmann, San Francisco (2005)
16. http://tesseract-ocr.repairfaq.org/ (viewed February 10, 2014)
17. ISO/IEC JTC1/SC29/WG11N6828, MPEG-7 Overview v10. MPEG, Palma de Mallorca
    (October 2004)

Public Transport Vehicle Detection Based on Visual Information

Mikołaj Leszczuk[1], Remigiusz Baran[2], Łukasz Skoczylas[1],
Mariusz Rychlik[3], and Przemysław Ślusarczyk[4]

[1] AGH University of Science and Technology, Department of Telecommunications,
al. Mickiewicza 30, 30-059 Krakow, Poland
leszczuk@agh.edu.pl, lskoczek@gmail.com
[2] Faculty of Electrical Engineering, Automatics and Computer Science,
Kielce University of Technology, al. 1000-lecia P.P. 7, 25-314 Kielce, Poland
r.baran@tu.kielce.pl
[3] University of Computer Engineering and Telecommunications,
ul. Toporowskiego 98, 25-553 Kielce, Poland
mr.mariusz.rychlik@gmail.com
[4] Institute of Physics, Jan Kochanowski University,
ul. Świetokrzyska 15, 25-406 Kielce, Poland
pslusarczyk@interbit.com.pl

Abstract. Freedom of movement is a major challenge for blind or visually impaired people. Movement in urban environment is for such people a big problem. Hence, the aim of the study presented in this paper is to develop an efficient method for identification of different public transport means. To simplify the solution as well as to avoid the need of infrastructure changes, recognition approaches based on visual information collected by smartphones have been assumed. According to the above, detectors based on Haar-like features as well as selected image processing algorithm have been prepared and analysed. Results obtained during performed tests have been reported and compared. Effectiveness of examined individual approaches has been discussed and concluded. Finally, an insight to possible future improvements has been also included.

Keywords: computer vision, object detection, Haar-like features, colour filter.

1 Introduction

Freedom of movement, especially in urban spaces, is a challenge for people with visual impairments. In areas with increased traffic flow, people with visual impairments have trouble overcoming barriers which pose no problems to able-bodied people. The specificity of this type of disability implies that in a task case, people affected by it are forced to be dependent on the help of others, resulting in significant reduction in quality of life and opportunities for adaptation to the surrounding reality.

A. Dziech and A. Czyżewski (Eds.): MCSS 2014, CCIS 429, pp. 16–28, 2014.

There should exist solutions to assist blind and visually impaired people in navigating in urban environments. The implementation as a mobile device application would be expected to present the blind or partially-sighted person with voice information about the means of transport due to arrive.

There are several ways of solving this problem. In developed areas, vehicle tracking based on the Global Positioning System (GPS) is common, enabling a phone application to inform the visually-impaired user of the vehicle's location. Unfortunately, in less developed areas, tracking is not available. The situation is even worse if transport involves using separate travel companies. Moreover, even if tracking is available, the data is commonly unavailable in standardized formats. As a result, GPS-based solutions usually require infrastructure modifications.

Instead, an image processing algorithm, based on photos of an oncoming vehicle, can be proposed. The simplest solution would be to use large Quick Response (QR) codes displayed on the vehicles; however, this brings us back to infrastructure changes. Hence, a solution is proposed that uses solely data available to able-bodied people, thus locating the vehicle and then generating information. It is assumed that a visually-impaired or blind person is standing at a bus or tram stop. On hearing the approaching vehicle, they aim their camera (built into a smartphone) in its direction. The application retrieves the images and converts them in order to identify the public transport vehicle.

The rest of the paper is organized as follows. Section 2 presents an overview of available solutions that help blind or sand-blind people. This section also includes a short presentation of image processing areas, related to the research reported. Section 4 contains a description of the problem of transport vehicles recognition. Section 3 is a description of the examined solutions. The individual subsections detail the matter closer. Finally, Section 6 is the summary of results and plans for further development.

2   Related Works

The problem of public transport vehicle location and identification combines issues of multiple CV (*Computer Vision*) solutions. These are elements of object detection. Examples are widely described in the literature as face detection [6,18]. This is closely related to the topic of real-time location of objects from images of urban scenes. These topics are covered in papers [4,5,16].

The authors of book [6] used an SVM (*Support Vector Machine*) classifier. The classifier training procedure requires the assembly of a large number of photos of examples. In the case of face detection [6,18] the task is facilitated by the availability of public databases of images that contain a large number of collected examples.

The proposed methods are universal. They make it possible for users to recognise any public transport vehicle (bus, tram, etc.), equipped with LED destination sign, both oncoming and waiting at the stop.

In conclusion, a large number of studies of image recognition in natural scenes show a great interest in this topic, and the need to create such systems. However, none of the related works fully solve the issue of detecting and recognizing public transport vehicles in the described scenario, aimed at people with visual impairments. Nevertheless, information collected in the accompanying literature has been of great use in our work.

3   Proposed Solutions

The following subsections briefly describe different approaches that have been prepared and tested to select the most successful solution for detecting and identifying various public transport means.

One of these approaches is based on a colour filter. It works by identifiing and locating LED destination sign areas of public transport vehicles.

Most public transport vehicles are equipped with modern destination signs in the form of LED displays. A characteristic feature is the orange colour of the LEDs[1]. Public transport vehicles have LED displays situated in two places. There are destination signs at the front upper part of the vehicle (Fig. 1), clearly visible when approaching the bus or tram stop[2].

Fig. 1. Front vehicle LED destination signs

---

[1] However, many vehicles do not use orange LED displays. In different cities, the colour of displays may also differ.

[2] There are visibility problems with the displays on sunny days, when a bright background causes reflections in the vicinity of the display.

Fig. 2. Side vehicle LED destination signs

LED displays are also arranged on the side of the vehicle, as shown in Fig. 2. They are seen easily when the bus or tram is at the stop.

The subsequent processing blocks of the colour filter approach that give a closer view of the characteristic elements of its individual modules are described in subsection 4.3. More details of this solution have been reported in [10].

The remaining approaches are Haar classifiers that have been individually trained for different purposes. They are described more precisely in 4.2. One of them, known as Cascade 1, aims to locate LED destination signs regardless of the type of vehicle, as in the case of the colour filter approach. The goals of the other three Haar classifiers are as follows:

- Cascade 2 - to identify fronts of public buses,
- Cascade 3 - to identify fronts of trams,
- Cascade 4 - to identify fronts of buses and trams concurrently.

Cascades listed above have been prepared and tested to verify their individual abilities to solve the problem as well as, after comparison with the results of colour filter approach, to find the most effective solution. In details, above comparison analysis, has been performed according to a testing scenario shown in Fig 3.

Testing scenario illustrated in Fig 3 assumes comparison between pairs of methods inside two different categories. Colour filter approach is to be compared with Cascade 1 inside the first, LED display detection category, while Cascade 4 is to be compared with Cascade 2 as well as Cascade 3 inside the second, fronts detection category.

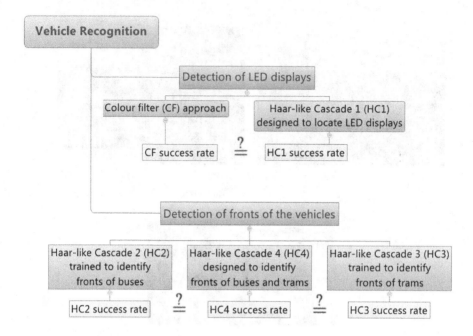

Fig. 3. Testing scenario

4   Applied Techniques and Technologies

This section presents the research methods and the tools and technologies used.

4.1   OpenCV Graphics Library

In the studies, an OpenCV (*Open Source Computer Vision*) library of image processing functions was used to solve the problem of locating and identifying public transport vehicles. In the case of Haar detectors, their different implementations have been trained with the *opencv_traincascade* application [1]. Multithreading and multitasking are the main advantages of this application. They are offered due to the TBB (Intel Threading Building Blocks) [2] library that *opencv_traincascade* includes.

OpenCV is released under a BSD license. The ongoing development of the library means it contains image processing functions corresponding to the current state of knowledge in this field [6,9]. It is a cross-platform tool.

4.2   Haar-Like Detectors

Automatic object detection has the advantage of being more efficient since object detectors are more robust towards scale and rotational changes, as well as being more sensitive to shapes of objects [7]. It is evident especially in the case of feature-based object detectors, such as those based on SIFT (Scale Invariant Feature Transform) [12], Harris-Affine [14] or shape context histogram [3] features. The Haar detectors/classifiers also belong to this category. The basis for Haar classifiers are the Haar-like features [17] that refer to contrast changes between neighbouring rectangular patches in an image.

Haar classifiers are cascade classifiers that consist of several stages formed by simpler classifiers, which, in turn, are built out of weak (basic) classifiers using boosting techniques (e.g. Gentle Adaboost, as in our research). These weak classifiers are decision-tree ones with at least two leaves. The previously mentioned Haar-like features [11] are a part of the analysis performed by the weak classifiers at every subsequent stage [15].

Training and Test Images. Our Haar classifier implementations have been trained using appropriate sets of relevant images. All training images used during our experiments have been collected in the field under various lighting conditions over a period of several months. According to the type of implementation, the training datasets contain different photos of fronts as well as sides of buses and trams. To take into account that public transport vehicles (including colour, appearance, make and model of the vehicles, etc.) vary depending on the city where they are used, the above datasets have been collected in Kraków and Kielce (excluding trams, which have been collected in Kraków only), home cities of the authors. Selected examples of training images - the positive samples - are shown in Fig. 4.

Fig. 4. Selected positive samples from the training dataset

Negative samples, in contrast to positive ones, have been collected by selecting natural scene images from private collections. The same set of negative samples, composed of 8199 images, has been used during our studies of all the prepared Haar detectors.

Alongside the training datasets, appropriate test datasets have also been prepared. Selected examples of test images are shown in Fig. 5.

Numbers of positive and negative samples within the training set, and the number of positive test images, vary according to the type of Haar cascade. The numbers are shown in Tab. 1. There is also a set of negative test images, containing 500 photos, which is common to all cascades.

Fig. 5. Selected test images

Table 1. Numbers of training and test images according to the type of cascade

	Cascade 1	Cascade 2	Cascade 3	Cascade 4
Training	3357	2416	1660	4075
Testing	400	201	365	566

4.3 Colour Filter Approach

The first step of the processing is to find an area which has the potential to contain an LED destination sign. A special feature of the LED destination sign is used to find an area of glowing orange LEDs, and therefore the colour filter is a major part of this approach.

The algorithm takes the following steps:

- loading an image file (allowed formats include jpeg, png),
- creating a copy of the source image and scaling it to a resolution of 640 × 480px, then working with the reduced image,
- creating Gaussian blur of the image,
- changing the colour space from RGB (*Red, Green, Blue*) to HSV (*Hue, Saturation, Value*),
- by applying thresholding, creating a binary mask image, where a value of 1 (white) corresponds to the presence of orange in the original image,
- applying of a morphological transformation in order to remove noise,
- extracting the contours of a binary mask,
- filtering the surface area, and eliminating very small and very large areas,
- describing the rectangles on the contours found,
- filtering rectangles that have the right proportions - they are wider than they are tall,
- scaling rectangular coordinates to the resolution of the source image,
- cutting the ROI within the full-resolution image.

In order to visualize the different algorithm steps and parameter selection, a filtering application was implemented.

Image Blurring. The resolution reduction and Gaussian blur are achieved using OpenCV library functions. Blur creates a stain on the average colour. A rectangle with width twice the height was selected experimentally (Fig. 6(a)).

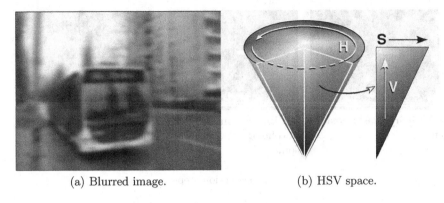

(a) Blurred image.   (b) HSV space.

Fig. 6. Location of the LED destination sign area

HSV Colour Space. Changing the colour space from RGB to HSVmakes it possible to specify a colour range of interest. The HSV colour space model (Fig. 6(b)) description is very well suited for filtering a specific colour in the image [9]. In OpenCV, HSV parameters (Fig. 6(b)) take values in the range: H: (0-180); S: (0-255); V: (0-255)

Fig. 7. Different layers of the HSV model. From left: Hue, Saturation, Value.

Binarization. A binary mask (binary image) is created, where white corresponds to pixels whose colour is in the specified range of thresholds for each HSV parameter. The empirically selected thresholds for the detection of the orange colour LEDs are: the lower threshold (5, 50, 100), the upper threshold (32, 255, 255).

To remove noise and individual pixels, as well as smoothing areas on the binary mask (Fig. 8(a)), a number of morphological transformations are used (Fig. 8(b)). Erosion creates image generalizations, as well as eliminating fine details. However, it also reduces the areas of objects. Dilation also causes image generalization frequently causing objects to fuse. Dilation increases the areas of objects, so that the same number of repeated dilation and erosion operations does not alter the surface of the objects.

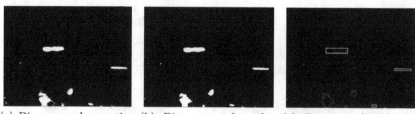

(a) Binary mask: creation effect.   (b) Binary mask: after morphological transformation.   (c) Contours (pink), potential signs (green).

Fig. 8. Detection steps

Contour Extraction and Describing Rectangle. The result of the algorithm is a cut-out rectangle which contains LED destination sign. For this purpose, a contour extraction is conducted on a prepared binary mask [8].

The contours whose field are very small and very large are then filtered out. Rectangles are placed on the other contours.

LED displays have a rectangular shape whose horizontal dimensions are greater than the vertical ones. Thus, all the rectangles that do not meet this target are filtered out (Fig. 8(c)).

Results. The coordinates of the rectangles are then scaled to the resolution of the source image and the ROI is cut. The cut out parts of the image are shown in Fig. 9. The first does not contain a proper table, although the colours found in these passages have been recognized by the classifier as matching the pattern.

Fig. 9. Effects. An LED display among the received images.

To sum up the effectiveness of the solution taken as a whole, as well as the impact of individual modules, the following summaries were prepared.

5   Summary of Obtained Results

True Positive (TP), False Negative (FN), False Positive (FP) and True Negative (TN) factors summing up the performance capabilities of individual Haar-like detectors are given in total in Tab. 2. In addition, the number of stages of individual detectors is given in the last column.

Table 2. Test results (and numbers of stages) for individual Haar-like detectors

	TP	FN	FP	TN	No. of stages
Cascade 1	186	214	163	491	24
Cascade 2	142	59	27	488	21
Cascade 3	120	245	5	496	25
Cascade 4	230	336	52	466	26

The results presented above let us calculate two important performance measures, known as Sensitivity or True Positive Rate (TPR) and False Discovery Rate (FDR) [13]. Sensitivity, defined as follows:

$$TPR = \frac{TP}{TP + FN}, \tag{1}$$

relates to the detector's ability to identify a given object correctly.

FDR shows the proportion of false positive values among all positive tests, as in the following equation:

$$FDR = \frac{FP}{TP + FP}. \tag{2}$$

It shows, for instance, the probability of detecting the front of a bus in a scene featuring no buses. In other words, the lower the FDR value, the greater the probability that the signal from the detector indicates the actual presence of the object of interest. For people with visual impairments such certainty is very important.

The itemised list below presents the effectiveness of the Colour Filter approach. It evaluates test images (from different dataset than the one used in the case of the Haar cascades analysis) containing visible destination signs (correctly recognized – success) and without destination signs (no result – success):

- number of test images: 1035,
- number of cases with correct final result: 463,
- overall detection effectiveness: 44.73%

Comparison. As it was mentioned in Section 3, the results given above have been compared according to the testing scenario illustrated in Fig. 3.

To compare methods of the first category - methods designed to detect LED destination signs - the results given for the Cascade 1 have to be recalculated. Knowing that a sum of TP and TN factors is equal to "success" cases given for the Colour Filter approach, the overall detection effectiveness (ODE) for the Cascade 1 can be evaluated as follows:

$$ODE = \frac{TP + TN}{N} * 100\%, \tag{3}$$

where: N is the number of test images.

Taking the above into account, the overall detection effectiveness for the Cascade 1 Haar-like detector is **75.22%**. Thus, it is nearly two times higher than in the case of the Colour Filter approach (**44.73%**)

In case of the second category methods, comparison can be carried out according to the TPR and FDR performance measures. Relevant TPR and FDR values are presented in Tab. 3.

Table 3. TPR and FDR values related to individual Haar-like detectors

	TPR	FDR
Cascade 2	0.71	0.16
Cascade 4	0.41	0.18
Cascade 3	0.33	0.04

Values given in Tab. 3 show as follows:

- in sense of TPR measure (alias Sensitivity) Cascade 2 is better than Cascade 4 as well as Cascade 4 is better than Cascade 3,
- according to FDR measure however, Cascade 2 is slightly better than Cascade 4, while the best results give Cascade 3.

6   Conclusions and Future Work

In conclusions to performed tests it can be emphasized that:

- Haar-like detectors are more accurate at detection of public transport means than methods based on colour analysis (as for instance Colour Filter approach),
- detector trained to identify LED destination signs is the most sensitive one within the category of Haar-like detectors (its accuracy is **75.22%**),
- detector trained to identify fronts of public buses is the most sensitive one within the second category of analysed methods,
- the Haar-like detector designed to identify fronts of trams ensures greater certainty that the others.

The obtained results as well as conclusions formulated above gave us an impulse to further research in the field of public transport vehicle detection methods aimed to assist people with visual impairments. To increase detection accuracy as well as to ensure as great level of certainty as possible, a combination of methods presented in this paper is assumed. It is planned for instance to verify whether the detection of fronts of vehicles, if combined with destination sign identification, can increase (and to what extent) the effectiveness of the solution. To carry out this verification, a testing scenario shown in Fig. 10 is to be performed.

Presented solutions were initially developed on a desktop platform, using Windows and/or Linux systems, for easy optimization of the algorithms and visualization of the individual process steps. However, mobile devices are assumed

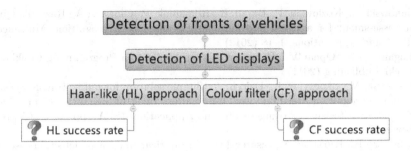

Fig. 10. Future testing scenario

as target ones for the final most effective solution (with the accuracy greater than at least 90%). According to technology accessibility, the Android system environment is the most suitable for such implementation. After that, field tests with blind and visually-impaired people are planned to be performed.

Acknowledgement. The research leading to these results has received funding from the Polish National Centre for Research and Development under Grant Agreement Number ROB02201/ID/22/3.

The numerical experiments reported in this paper have been performed using computational equipment purchased as part of the framework of the EU Operational Programme Innovative Economy (POIG.02.02.00-26-023/09-00) and the EU Operational Programme Development of Eastern Poland (POPW.01.03.00-26-016/09-00).

References

1. http://docs.opencv.org/doc/user_guide/ug_traincascade.html (viewed February 16, 2014)
2. https://www.threadingbuildingblocks.org/ (viewed February 16, 2014)
3. Belongie, S., Malik, J., Puzicha, J.: Shape matching and object recognition using shape contexts. IEEE Transactions on Pattern Analysis and Machine Intelligence 24(4), 509–522 (2002)
4. Chen, X., Yuille, A.: Detecting and reading text in natural scenes. In: Proceedings of the 2004 IEEE Computer Society Conference on Computer Vision and Pattern Recognition, CVPR (2004)
5. Chen, X., Yuille, A.L.: A time-efficient cascade for real-time object detection: With applications for the visually impaired. In: Proceedings of the 2005 IEEE Computer Society Conference on Computer Vision and Pattern Recognition, vol. 03 (2005)
6. Emami, S., Ievgen, K., Mahmood, N.: Mastering OpenCV with Practical Computer Vision Projects. Packt Publishing, Limited (2012)
7. Goh, K.M., Mokji, M.M., Abu-Bakar, S.A.R.: Surf based image matching from different angle of viewpoints using rectification and simplified orientation correction. World Academy of Science, Engineering and Technology 68, 1243–1247 (2012)

8. Janowski, L., Kozłowski, P., Baran, R., Romaniak, P., Glowacz, A., Rusc, T.: Quality assessment for a visual and automatic license plate recognition. Multimedia Tools and Applications, 1–18 (2012)
9. Laganière, R.: OpenCV 2 Computer Vision Application Programming Cookbook. Packt Publishing (2011)
10. Leszczuk, M., Skoczylas, L., Dziech, A.: Simple solution for public transport route number recognition based on visual information. In: 2013 Signal Processing: Algorithms, Architectures, Arrangements, and Applications (SPA), pp. 32–38 (September 2013)
11. Lienhart, R., Kuranov, A., Pisarevsky, V.: Empirical analysis of detection cascades of boosted classifiers for rapid object detection. In: Michaelis, B., Krell, G. (eds.) DAGM 2003. LNCS, vol. 2781, pp. 297–304. Springer, Heidelberg (2003)
12. Lowe, D.G.: Distinctive image features from scale-invariant keypoints. International Journal of Computer Vision 60(2), 91–110 (2004)
13. Macmillan, N.A., Creelman, C.D.: Detection Theory - A user's guide. Lawrence Erlbaum Associates, Mahwah (2005)
14. Mikolajczyk, K., Schmid, C.: Scale and Affine Invariant Interest Point Detectors. International Journal of Computer Vision 60(1), 63–86 (2004)
15. Reinius, S.: Object recognition using the opencv haar cascade-classifier on the ios platform (2013)
16. Sanketi, P., Shen, H., Coughlan, J.M.: Localizing blurry and low-resolution text in natural images. In: Proceedings of the 2011 IEEE Workshop on Applications of Computer Vision (WACV), WACV 2011, pp. 503–510. IEEE Computer Society, Washington, DC (2011)
17. Viola, P., Jones, M.: Rapid object detection using a boosted cascade of simple features, pp. 511–518
18. Viola, P., Jones, M.J.: Robust real-time face detection. International Journal Computer Vision (2004)

Four Years of Botnet Hunting: An Assessment

Gilles Berger-Sabbatel and Andrzej Duda

Grenoble Institute of Technology, CNRS Grenoble Informatics Laboratory UMR 5217
681, rue de la Passerelle, BP 72
38402 Saint Martin d'Hères Cedex, France
{Gilles.Berger-Sabbatel,Andrzej.Duda}@imag.fr

Abstract In this paper, we present a wrap up of the malware analysis done during the last four years. We have developed a platform that includes tools for capturing malware, running code in a controlled environment, and analyzing its interactions with external entities. The platform enables us to capture malware samples, classify them and observe their communication behavior in a protected environment in a way that the malware does not perform any harmful activity. We report on some statistics on the captured malware and provide an example of an analysis session with the MWNA tool.

1   Introduction

We have developed a platform for botnet-related malware analysis composed of a set of tools for capturing malware, running code in a controlled environment, and analyzing its interactions with external entities. The main tool is MWNA, a program that monitors network activity, acts as a programmable gateway to the Internet, and emulates the services such as DNS and SMTP required by the malware so that it executes as if it were on a victim machine. The platform supports automated analysis of malware activity in a way that the malware does not perform any harmful activity.

We have already described the details of the platform architecture in the previous papers [1][2][3][4]. In this paper, we present a wrap up of the malware analysis done on the platform during the last four years. In particular, we report on some statistics on the captured malware and provide an example of an analysis session with the MWNA tool.

2   Architecture of the Platform

As our platform constantly evolve time, we present below its main features and recently developed functionalities.

2.1   Malware Capture

The platform captures malware using a low interaction honeypot, i.e. a software that emulates the behavior of vulnerable services to capture malware samples.

A. Dziech and A. Czyżewski (Eds.): MCSS 2014, CCIS 429, pp. 29–42, 2014.

Malware samples are named with their MD5 sum to keep only samples different from the already captured ones.

Once captured, samples are automatically run in a sandboxed environment, allowing to monitor their network activities and determine the DNS addresses they query and the connections they attempt. Based on this information, we classify samples to identify new malware categories [3]. The test environment is composed of a virtual machine running Windows XP and MWNA, a program that monitors network activity. The disk of the virtual machine is emulated on a Linux logical volume (LVM) using snapshots, which has several advantages :

- The virtual disk can be mounted on the host to install malware binary so that it will be executed at start-up.
- The disk image can be restored to a clean state in a few seconds, whereas the copy of the whole disk takes 10 minutes for 3 Gbytes.
- The snapshot contains only modified parts of the file system and it is much smaller than the partition, so that more virtual machine images can be kept.

2.2   Malware Analysis

Malware programs identified as new are run again in a virtual machine connected to the Internet through MWNA that acts as a smart gateway allowing to monitor network activities, detect particular behavior, and prevent malicious activities.

The main component of MWNA is a *filter* that processes packets flowing through the gateway, and sends messages to a second component, the *reporter*, to signal interesting events.

The *reporter* is in charge of displaying messages to the operator, recording events in a data base, and recording traces in files. The reporter is a separate process executed with regular user privileges, so that it can use high level features for graphic display (*X11*), or data base processing (*sqlite*). It is not in the critical path of packet processing, so that the I/O operations do not delay packet processing. It can be executed at a lower priority or on a separate machine.

The *filter* processes packets exchanged between the virtual machine running the malware (the victim) and the Internet or the gateway itself. The processing comprises three stages:

- In the first stage, packets are analyzed. TCP connections and UDP flows are tracked. The processing can be performed up to the application level:
  - DNS-resolved IP addresses are recorded,
  - HTTP, IRC, STUN and SMTP protocols are analyzed to check if they are correctly used and extract information used in further processing (HTTP methods, URLs, IRC nickname and channel, etc.).
  - Other protocols, including HTTPS, NTP, IPP are checked, mainly to make sure that their ports are not used by another protocol.
  - Protocols such as IRC and HTTP can be detected even if they do not use their standard ports.

Packets are not modified in this stage. No decision is taken regarding the follow up of the processing, excepted packets sent to blacklisted ports which are dropped.
- In the second stage, higher level processing is performed by dynamically loaded plugins named *features*. Features can be activated and configured through a configuration file. They are sorted in lists according to the IP protocol (TCP, UDP, ...), connection status, and the application protocol (HTTP, IRC, DNS, ...). Features that match the current packet are tried until either every matching feature is processed, or a decision has been taken (usually dropping the packet). Features use the information gathered in the first stage to perform actions such as:

  - Detection of C&C (Command and Control service of the botmaster).
  - Detection and prevention of malicious activities.
  - Inspection of protocol payloads. In particular, it includes the detection of executable files in the HTTP payload independently of the file-name extension and the announced content-type.

  The plugins may modify packets, decide to drop them, or blacklist ports.
- In the last stage, a rule-based processing is applied. Rules are read from a configuration file and contain conditions that packets must match to apply the rule, and actions performed on matching packets.

  - Conditions may be based on the source or destination addresses, the protocol, the fact that the IP address has been DNS-resolved or not, etc.
  - Actions include dropping or accepting the packet, recording or displaying the packet, displaying a warning message to the operator.

TCP ports can be redirected to ports on the gateway, for example to redirect HTTP accesses to a proxy, or to redirect SMTP communications to a server able to record transmissions without actually sending mail. The redirection is performed by the Linux *Iptables* mechanism, but MWNA needs to keep a mapping of redirected ports for a consistent connection processing. Hence, the redirection is set by MWNA from directives read in its configuration file.

The main and primary use of MWNA is to process the flows of packets generated by malware during the analysis. However, it can also process flows recorded in the *pcap* format. As we cannot expect a deterministic and constant behavior from malware, this feature has been primarily implemented to ease testing of new features by running the program with a known network flow. However, it also allows forensic analysis of a recorded network incident as well as demonstrations of the software without requiring a connection to the Internet.

2.3   Analysis of Malicious Activities

The detection and monitoring of malicious activities are primary objectives of MWNA and we must carefully avoid that the analyzed malware causes any significant harm to third parties. On the other hand, this should interfere as less as possible with harmless activities of the malware such as communicating with their Command and Control service.

Scans and DoS Attacks. Basically, port scans and DoS attacks can be detected by controlling if the repetition of some kinds of events does not exceed configurable thresholds.

Port scans: For the detection of port scans, we consider the repetition of unanswered connection attempts to the same ports of different hosts whose address has not been DNS resolved. For the most frequently scanned ports, the detection is triggered after 5 connection attempts to 5 different hosts in a sliding time window of 2 seconds. We have never seen false positives.

TCP SYN DDoS: These attacks are based on the repetition of connection attempts to the same host. Actually, we have never seen such an attack during our tests. We do not check for reflection attacks based on the transmission of a request with a spoofed source address, but spoofed source addresses are detected, so that such attacks can be very easily detected and prevented.

Application-level DDoS: These attacks are harder to detect: we can detect HTTP flooding by detecting the repetition of queries for a same URL or simultaneous (unanswered) queries to the same host, but the thresholds are quite hard to determine : malware often performs HTTP accesses as a part of its regular operations and the access to a single WWW page may require dozens of downloads (HTML page, pictures, icons, style sheets, etc.). While our HTTP flood detector was triggered in some cases, we have no evidence that it was actually DDoS, so that our detector has never been confronted with a proven actual attack.

Practically, the only kind of DDoS attack that we have observed was against a DNS service and will be presented in more detail in Section 5. The attack has been recorded, which allowed us to implement and test several rules to detect such an attack:

- Queries sent to several external DNS servers: the gateway provides a DNS service to the victim, hence it should not query an external server unless it needs a "friendly" server. So querying multiple external servers is a good sign of an attack. A limit of five servers allowed for a fast detection.
- Repeated queries of the same host address: in regular operations, the timeout on DNS queries is quite long and queries should not be retransmitted very fast. We have conservatively fixed a limit of 15 queries in 10 seconds.
- Repeated queries of different hosts in the same domain: in the observed attack, all queries were for the same host, but the attack could be also efficient with different random host names. Hence, we have fixed a limit of 30 queries in the same domain in 10 seconds.
- High number of unanswered queries: this should be a sure sign of a DDoS attack, as an attacked server will be unlikely to respond fast to queries, and an attack sends numerous queries regardless of whether they are answered or not. We have fixed a limit of 50 queries in 10 seconds.

When a scan or a DDoS attack is detected, it is stopped either by blacklisting the port (for scans) or the destinations address (for TCP or HTTP DDoS). DNS attacks are stopped by dropping packets sent to external servers.

Command and Control Detection. Usually, the first activity of newly installed malware is to connect to its C&C channel to get instructions. Hence, the detection of C&C is another important feature of our tool. C&C could be contacted by any protocol, but it is most often contacted through a well known protocol (IRC, or HTTP), some textual proprietary protocol that is in fact a modified IRC, or some random binary protocol.

Practically, when a connection runs the IRC protocol or any unknown (textual of binary) protocol, it is very likely to be C&C. The problem is harder with HTTP, which is used very often by malware to get some information and to contact C&C.

This kind of problems is commonly solved by the use of Bayesian algorithms, but they require statistics of previously identified malware activities and we do not have such statistics. Even worse, the activities of malware may change very quickly, so that the statistics on previous activities will very likely be irrelevant.

Hence, we have used a scoring system to identify C&C from a small set of candidate connections (usually, one or two):

- Connections are candidates for C&C, if their protocol is HTTP, HTTPS, IRC, or an unknown textual or binary protocol.
- Candidate connections get an initial score depending on their protocol: lower for HTTP or HTTPS, higher for IRC and unknown protocols.
- Each connection gets a score bonus when the following conditions are met:
  - the connection is opened on a non standard port for this protocol. For example, a HTTP connection on a port other than 80, or an IRC connection on a port other than 194.
  - This is the first opened connection.
  - No malicious activity has been detected before.
  - The connection uses a port reserved for another protocol. For example, an IRC connection opened on port 80 usually used by HTTP. As this is one of the ports less likely to be blocked by firewalls, such "port hijacking" is commonly used by malware.
- A HTTP-based C&C query should include some information to identify and authenticate the client, so that we define a score bonus for every item that can carry such identification in HTTP transactions :
  - the request sent credentials for authentication,
  - the POST method was used,
  - the URL is unusually long,
  - the URL included a long chain of parameters.

Email Transmission. Emails can be used to send information to the botmaster, or to send spams. In any case, we must monitor mail transmission attempts (so that we should not reject connections to the SMTP port), to detect and stop spam transmission, and to prevent the transmission of emails.

- The SMTP protocol is analyzed and the information about the transmitted mails is extracted (origin, destination).

- Mail transmission can be prevented. However, dropping packets on an already opened connection would be unfriendly for the server. Hence, we forge a "*QUIT*" packet sent to the server, so that it cleanly and securely turns down its connection without wasting resources.
- The rules for spam detection have been deduced from the analysis of a spam sending session [4] : the malware tried to connect to several SMTP servers and sent mails through servers that accepted the connection. Hence, spam transmission is detected if one of the following conditions are met:
  - Connection attempts to some number of SMTP servers. In some cases, this could allow to detect spam transmission before any mail transmission is attempted.
  - Parallel use of connections with several SMTP servers. For normal mail transmission, a single server is used.
  - Attempt to transmit a given number of messages to different destinations.

The payload of spam transmission can also be analyzed by redirecting SMTP connections to a local fake email relay [4].

Other Activities. Other malicious activities could be processed by MWNA, but this is not implemented yet:

- Purchase on e-commerce sites : this is one way to get money from stolen credit card numbers, and botnets allows to perform anonymously many purchases. The detection would need to analyze an HTTP session to identify a related HTTPS activity used for the payment. A simple preventive measure can be to block HTTPS transmissions, but with the risk of missing interesting HTTPS transmissions used for C&C, for example.
- Click frauds: malware can emulate a user clicking on an pay-per-click commercial link, in order to increase either the revenue of the publisher, or the expenses of the advertiser. As far as we do not let the malware run for a long time, this would not cause a significant prejudice to the advertiser, but it would be anyway interesting to detect and prevent this kind of activity.
- Propagation of the malware: this is the main objective of scans and it is mostly prevented by the detection of scans. However, there is a very small risk that a connection succeeds before scan detection and even a smaller risk that it has the opportunity to exploit some vulnerability. It could be prevented through an analysis of protocols used for malware propagation.

3   Honeypot Activity

Our honeypot operated from April 2010 to August 2013 and it was finally stopped, as it captured almost no new malware at the end of the period.

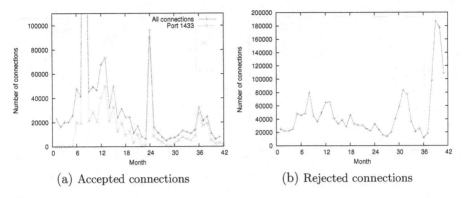

(a) Accepted connections   (b) Rejected connections

Fig. 1. Connections received by the honeypot

3.1 Accepted Connections

Figure 1 shows the number of connections accepted by the honeypot on all ports and on port 1433 (a) and rejected (b) during this period: every connection should be considered as an attempted attack against services emulated by the honeypot.

On average, 32000 connections were accepted per month, with a maximum of 318498 in November 2010. Most connections targeted one of five ports including port 1433 (cf. Figure 1a, lower plot) that supports the Ms-Sql service and gets a very high part of connections: attacks to this port are mainly due to malware exploiting newly discovered vulnerabilities in this service. They are the main cause of the peaks of November 2010 and March 2012. The honeypot does not actually support the Ms-Sql service, so that no vulnerabilities are exploited.

While attacks on the port 22 (ssh) are very common, the honeypot does not see them because the ssh service is used for the administration of the machine.

On average, 49524 connections were rejected per month, with a maximum of 186652 in June 2013. 8093 ports are targeted, with 80% of connections on 10 ports. The most targeted port is 139 (*netbios-ssn* service) with 34.2% of connection attempts. The second one is 39254 with 30% of attempted connections. This port is not assigned to any service. The third port is 8888 with 5% of connection attempts. Most remaining ports have no known official assignment.

Figure 2a plots the connections accepted by the honeypot on ports 135 and 445 that support Windows Smb services. Here, we can see a slow, but regular decrease of the number of connections since August 2011. The services are available on any Windows system and are targeted by most attacks on user systems. However, port 445 is the only one that leads to malware downloads on our honeypot.

Finally, Figure 2b plots connections to ports 80 and 3306 that support the Http and MySql services, respectively. The aspect of the curves is also chaotic, as attacks on these services are also related to the dissemination of malware exploiting new vulnerabilities. However, the number of attacks is relatively low.

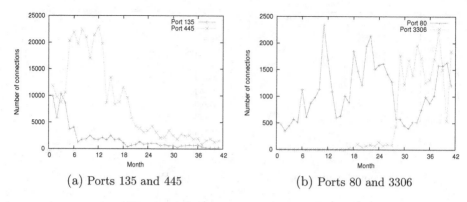

(a) Ports 135 and 445   (b) Ports 80 and 3306

Fig. 2. Connections to ports 135 and 445

3.2 Downloaded Malware Samples

The honeypot downloaded 82972 malware samples, 3984 of them are different. Hence, malware samples have been downloaded 20.8 times on average.

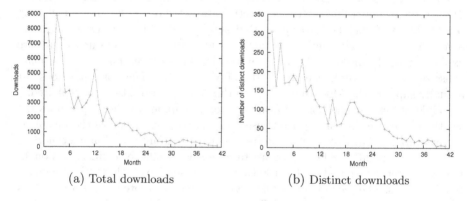

(a) Total downloads   (b) Distinct downloads

Fig. 3. Number of downloaded malware samples

Figure 3a presents the monthly evolution of the total number of downloads. As downloads are caused by exploits on a service running on the port 445, we could expect the plot to have a similar aspect as in Figure 2b. This is not the case, as there is not a 1:1 correspondence between connections and downloads: some attacks may fail and some attacks may require several connections. Anyway, we can see that, from September 2010, the number of downloads is decreasing with only a peak in March 2011.

Figure 3b presents the evolution of the monthly number of downloads of new malware samples (not already captured). The form of the curve is almost the same as the curve of the total downloads with substantially smaller values. However, as much malware tends to replicate itself with a small change in an attempt to escape detection by an anti-virus (polymorphism), the number of different samples is not significant for the number of different malware.

3.3 Discussion

By the end of August 2013, we noticed that the honeypot captured very few malware and most captured malware did not perform any network activity when tested. This is clearly related to the declining number of attacks. On the other hand, the Dionea honeypot did not release significant updates the last year.

It seems that the exploitation of network vulnerabilities is no longer the dominant way of malware propagation: this is very probably due to the fact that systems are more secure, through the use of firewalls, more secure implementation of network services, and Internet providers more concerned about security.

Unfortunately, there is no related decrease of malicious activities on the Internet! In fact, malware propagation now uses several different means such as emails, links to malicious Web sites [5], social networks [6], etc.

Emails, and more specifically spams, are one possible vector of infection. We have developed a script to scan spam received on various mailboxes. Very few suspicious contents were found in attachments. Such contents could be hidden inside documents to exploit vulnerabilities in their reader software, but we had not enough time to implement the analysis of these documents. We have collected the URLs inside emails, to look for URL pointing on malicious content. An URL is considered as suspicious if it is alone in a mail, or even more, if it is repeated several times in different links, so that the user is more likely to follow it. New suspicious URLs are submitted to Wepawet [7] for analysis and the result is stored in a database. During the past four months, 1911 URLs have been analyzed and Wepawet classified 333 of these as suspicious. However, this does not mean that browsing these URLs will lead to an infection, as it would depend on vulnerabilities found in the browser. Until now, we did not succeed to infect a system by browsing a suspicious URL, but we did not perform systematic tests that would require the use of several browsers and plugin versions.

Most attacks try to lead the user into following a bad link, so that the discovery of malware would need either an exhaustive search, which is time consuming, or some kind of artificial intelligence to find on which link a human user would tend to click. The same apply to social networks : finding malware would need to emulate the behavior of an average naïve user.

4   Malware Analysis

As stated in Section 3.2, 3984 unique malware samples have been downloaded by our honeypot. Other samples have been captured before April 2010 by a previous version of our honeypot.

After September 2013, we performed an automatic analysis of 6860 recent malware samples downloaded from MalShare and virusShare, two repositories collecting malware samples for the research community.

So, a total of 11166 samples have been automatically analyzed and classified in 980 classes. 531 malware samples have been manually analyzed. As we focused more on the development of tools and the manual analysis is time consuming, we only performed a preliminary analysis of malware.

Most of the analyzed malware captured by the honeypots appeared to be botnet-related, but only a small part of malware downloaded from repositories are: most of them only open a browser with some advertisement.

4.1 C&C Discovery

Almost all botnet-related malware captured by the honeypot get the address of their C&C server from one or several DNS names. Obviously, such botnets are now quite easily torn down with DNS sink-holing.

Twenty analyzed samples used *TXT* DNS queries (no DNS query other than *TXT* before connection to C&C). This is probably an attempt to escape detection and sink-holing.

Yet, a few botnets attempted connections without performing any DNS query, which means that they used hard-coded IP addresses: this resists to DNS sink-holing, but not to IP address filtering, nor to the seizure of the C&C address.

Until now, we have seen no botnets using alternatives techniques such as peer to peer [8], or fast flux [9][10]. In fact, a few malware sent a high number of DNS requests with apparently random names, but this appeared as a fallback method, as eventually the only request that did not fail was the same for each execution.

Table 1. C&C protocols

Protocol	Number
IRC	87
UTXT	46
UBIN	35
HTTP	96
HTTPS	1

4.2 C&C Protocols

Table 1 displays the number of the detected C&C protocols extracted from the database storing results of MWNA.

IRC is known to be a very popular protocol for botnet C&C [11]. It is only used by malware captured on the honeypot and is the most used protocol for these malware. All IRC C&C use a port different from the standard one.

Unidentified textual protocols (labeled UTXT in the table) have only been encountered in the malware captured on the honeypot. We encountered only one such protocol, a variant of IRC with changed keywords.

HTTP has been detected 5 times on malware captured by the honeypot. It is mostly detected in malware downloaded from repositories, but this includes a high number of false positives from non botnet-related malware. However, we have also found real botnets that use HTTP as the C&C protocol among these malware. HTTP is used on a non standard port in only 2 cases.

Unknown binary protocols have been encountered 35 times. We did not attempt to analyze these protocols. We have only one occurrence of HTTPS, which is probably a false positive.

4.3 Malicious Activities

Scans are the most frequently detected malicious activity. Malware captured from the honeypot usually scans port 445 (on which they have been captured, as said in Section 3.1): these scans are most probably attempts to find hosts on which the malware can replicate itself. A few malware also scan port 135. We also encountered scans using the ICMP protocol as well as scans on port 80 (HTTP). A few scans on port 25 (SMTP) are performed as a preparation of spam sending.

Five of analyzed malware performed spam transmission, which is commonly considered as the most popular use of botnets. We have already reported on a case of a spam sending malware [4].

We have no reliable count of DoS attacks: some TCP SYN detected DoS are the result of repeated connection attempts on a blacklisted port or unreachable host. The only actual Dos attack was against a DNS server. 6 HTTP floods have been detected, but without enough evidence.

For most analyses, there was no malicious activity at all, maybe due to the relatively short duration of most analyses (at most 15 minutes)

5   Case Study

Figure 4 shows a screen capture of the analysis of a malware downloaded in November 2013 from a malware repository.

The DNS area shows that the malware queried 6 Dns addresses.

The detected network activities are the following :

1. A connection is opened on an address that has not yet been resolved. There was no pevious activity, so that this address must be hardcoded in the malware code. The application activity area shows that this connection is only used for an HTTP GET. The answer is an empty HTML document with a cookie, presumably used to generate a credential in the sequel.
2. The malware gets the addresses of 3 hosts in the qvod.com domain (a Chinese video-on demand operator). Then, the malware uses the STUN protocol (Session Traversal Utilities for NAT) with one of these sites.

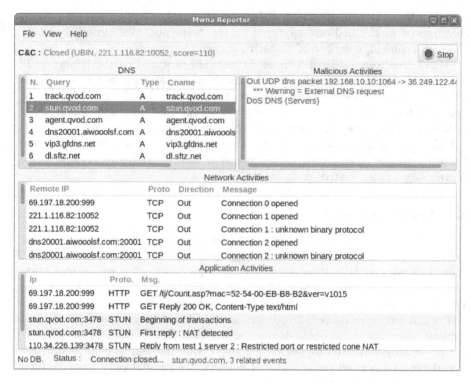

Fig. 4. Screen capture of the analysis

3. UDP packets are exchanged with a set of 35 non DNS-resolved IP addresses. 7 of them got no answer. Most of the exchanges are very short (6 packets for a total of 78 bytes), but a few are longer (up to 68 packets for a total of 16449 bytes). A closer exalination of some of these flows, using Wireshark, showed a variant of the BitTorrent protocol used by Qvod. So, we may be in presence of a malware abusing this service as a part of its C&C.

4. 24 ms after receiving the first of these longer replies, the malware opens a TCP connection. The address has not been DNS resolved, but it is contained in the previously received answer. A few packets are exchanged in an unidentified binary protocol, for a total of 5008 bytes. Meanwhile, the UDP exchanges continue for 1.5 more seconds.

5. A connection is opened to dns20001.auwooolsf.com, port 20001 with an unknown binary protocol. After an exchange of a few packets, the malware got the DNS name of a site, followed by 9 IP addresses in dotted decimal format.

6. Right after that, the malware begins to query for the address of the received DNS name using external DNS servers. The addresses of these servers are the addresses included in the previous exchange.

7. MWNA warns for the transmission of a DNS query to an external server. This message is displayed only once to avoid being flooded by the same

message. Then, the DoS is detected and MWNA starts to drop the external DNS queries.

5.1 Discussion

This piece of malware shows the difficulty of analyzing the malware network behavior with several unexpected features:

- The use of numerous UDP flows and STUN.
- The use of a P2P protocol, which we had never observed yet.
- The use of an HTTP request with an empty HTML reply and a cookie.
- A rather complex C&C, involving P2P, HTTP, and two connections on different hosts with a binary protocol. The first of these connections has been identified as C&C by MWNA, but only the second one is directly related to a malicious activity.
- A DNS DoS. This led us to implement a feature for the detection of this kind of attacks.

While MWNA has been useful to analyze this behavior, some features are still missing:

- More ways to determine relationships between the events, based on time, on order of events, etc...
- A real time trace of UDP flows—they are currently only listed at the end of execution. This raises the problem of avoiding to be flooded by the information when many flows are successively opened.

On the other hand, as MWNA needs to work in real time, we cannot overload it with complex functionalities, such as the unknown protocol analysis, or search of correlations between packets (such as finding the destination address of a connection in the previous packets). Such a task could be performed by forensic analysis of captured traffic, either by MWNA or by another tool.

6   Conclusions and Future Work

The paper has presented the use of our platform for botnet-related malware analysis. The platform supports automated analysis of malware activity in a harmless way. We have used the platform during last four years and this paper presents the main results of the malware analysis along with some statistics on the captured malware. We have also provided an example of an analysis session with the MWNA tool.

We continue the development of the platform features to follow ever changing behavior of malware. Nevertheless, the current state of the platform is sufficiently mature for providing the tools to the community of researchers in cybersecurity and forensic analysts. We plan to release an open source version that will contribute to the better understanding of malware and its confinement.

Acknowledgments. This work was partially supported by the EC FP7 project INDECT under contract 218086.

References

1. Berger-Sabbatel, G., Korczyński, M., Duda, A.: Architecture of a Platform for Malware Analysis and Confinement. In: Proceedings of the MCSS 2010: Multimedia Communications, Services and Security, Cracow, Poland (June 2010)
2. Berger-Sabbatel, G., Duda, A.: Analysis of Malware Network Activity. In: Dziech, A., Czyżewski, A. (eds.) MCSS 2011. CCIS, vol. 149, pp. 207–215. Springer, Heidelberg (2011)
3. Berger-Sabbatel, G., Duda, A.: Classification of Malware Network Activity. In: Dziech, A., Czyżewski, A. (eds.) MCSS 2012. CCIS, vol. 287, pp. 24–35. Springer, Heidelberg (2012)
4. Korczyński, M., Berger-Sabbatel, G., Duda, A.: Two Methods for Detecting Malware. In: Dziech, A., Czyżewski, A. (eds.) MCSS 2013. CCIS, vol. 368, pp. 95–106. Springer, Heidelberg (2013)
5. Provos, N., McNamee, D., Mavrommatis, P., Wang, K., Modadugu, N.: The ghost in the browser analysis of web-based malware. In: Proceedings of the First Conference on First Workshop on Hot Topics in Understanding Botnets, HotBots 2007, p. 4. USENIX Association, Berkeley (2007)
6. Yan, G., Chen, G., Eidenbenz, S., Li, N.: Malware propagation in online social networks: Nature, dynamics, and defense implications. In: Proceedings of the 6th ACM Symposium on Information, Computer and Communications Security, ASIACCS 2011, pp. 196–206. ACM, New York (2011)
7. Invernizzi, L., Benvenuti, S., Comparetti, P.M., Kruegel, C., Vigna, G.: EVILSEED: A Guided Approach to Finding Malicious Web Pages. In: Proceedings of the 33th IEEE Symposium on Security and Privacy (S&P), San Francisco, CA, USA (May 2012)
8. Steggink, M., Idziejczak, I.: Detection of peer-to-peer botnets. Research report for system and network engineering, University of Amsterdam, The Netherlands (2008), http://work6.delaat.net/rp/2007-2008/p22/report.pdf
9. Caglayan, A., Toothaker, M., Drapaeau, D., Burke, D., Eaton, G.: Behavioral analysis of fast flux service networks. In: Proceedings of the 5th Annual Workshop on Cyber Security and Information Intelligence Research: Cyber Security and Information Intelligence Challenges and Strategies, CSIIRW 2009, pp. 48:1–48:4. ACM, New York (2009)
10. Nazario, J., Holz, T.: As the net churns: Fast-flux botnet observations. In: 3rd International Conference on Malicious and Unwanted Software, pp. 24–31 (October 2008)
11. Zhuge, J., Holz, T., Han, X., Guo, J., Zou, W.: Characterizing the irc-based botnet phenomenon. Technical report, Department for Mathematics and Computer Science, University of Mannheim; TR-2007-010 (2007)

Challenges for Migration of Rule-Based Reasoning Engine to a Mobile Platform*

Szymon Bobek, Grzegorz J. Nalepa, and Mateusz Ślażyński

AGH University of Science and Technology
al. Mickiewicza 30, 30-059 Krakow, Poland
{szymon.bobek,gjn,mateusz.slazynski}@agh.edu.pl

Abstract. Research in the area of context-awareness has recently been revolutionized by the rapid development of mobile devices like smart phones and tablets, which became omnipresent in daily human life. Such devices are valuable sources of information about their user location, physical and social activity, profiles and habits, etc. However, the information that can be obtained is not limited to the hardware sensors that the device is equipped with, but can be extended to every sensor that is available in a communication range of a device. Although the concept of multiple sensors and devices, exchanging information and working together as one big pervasive system is not new, there is still a lot of research that has to be done to allow building such systems efficiently. In this paper the prototype of a rule-based inference engine for mobile devices is described and evaluated. The most important challenges connected with migration from desktop to mobile environment were defined, and a comparison of Prolog-based platforms, as a portable environments for mobile context-aware systems were presented. We consider implementation using a portable Prolog compiler on Android platform.

Keywords: context-awareness, mobile computing, GIS, knowledge management, STM, INDECT.

1   Introduction

One of the areas of the INDECT project concerns the development of user-driven distributed reporting and notification systems that improve citizen security, as well as their cooperation with authorities. Such systems have been becoming more common and widely adopted in recent years. Objectives of such systems include the increase of awareness and participation of citizens to provide a collaborative environment to gather and report information on different security threats in a given neighborhood or a wider location. On the other hand, such a system should provide instant notification for a number of possible threats relevant to a given user in a given context. These threats can be considered wrt

---

* The research presented in this paper is carried out within the EU FP7 INDECT Project: "Intelligent information system supporting observation, searching and detection for security of citizens in urban environment" (http://indect-project.eu).

A. Dziech and A. Czyżewski (Eds.): MCSS 2014, CCIS 429, pp. 43–57, 2014.

different categories, such as crime, natural disasters, accidents or traffic related events, and their taxonomy can be formally modeled.

The authors of the paper were involved in the development of a system called *Social Threat Monitor* (STM) [3] which serves purposes given above. STM is a GIS-based solution that assists citizens in reporting security threats together with their severity and location, using a flexible web-based interface. The possible threats are categorized using a general top-level ontology, with domain ontologies supporting the detailed specification of threats. The information about the threats is stored in a knowledge base which allows for lightweight reasoning about with the gathered facts. Information of the threats and results of user queries are visualized on a web-accessible map that can be analyzed by a group of users, e.g., police officials, regular citizens, etc.

The original version of the system was a typical web-based solution, composed of a server-side GIS-based service providing access to the knowledge base and a client in the form of a web-browser [3]. Another method for interfacing with the system on the application level was provided by a dedicated web API.A clear limitation of that system was related to the use of mobile devices on the client side. Currently the most common use case scenario for such systems includes the use of a mobile hand-held device e.g. a smartphone or a tablet. In our previous work we proposed and discussed a design of a prototype of a new interface for STM targeted at mobile devices [8]. It used the context-aware application paradigm that improves usability from the user perspective, and simplifies the use of multi sensor data available on the mobile devices.

The principal objective of this paper is the presentation of the new mobile inference service for STM (called Mobile Social Threat Monitor) that puts emphasis on portability. A lightweight, Prolog-based inference engine called tuHeaRT was used for the evaluation, that was performed on the Android operating system. Mobile STM uses data gathered by mobile device sensors and perform on-line reasoning about possible threats, based on the information provided by the main STM system.

The rest of the paper is organized as follows. In Section 2, related works in this area are discussed. This gives foundation for presenting the challenges for providing a truly mobile and distributed reasoning service for STM in Section 3. A comprehensive comparison of Prolog platforms for mobile devices need to provide such a solution is then discussed in Section 4. For this work a particular usecase based on the tuProlog solution was analyzed in Section 5. The evaluation of this solution was given in in Section 6. Finally, summary and directions for future work are given in Section 7.

2   Related Work and Motivation

In recent years, a lot of development was devoted to build applications that use mobile devices to monitor and analyze various user contexts.

The SocialCircuits platform [14] uses mobile phones to measure social ties between individuals, and uses long- and short-term surveys to measure the shifts in individual habits, opinions, health, and friendships influenced by these ties. Jung [23] focused on discovering social relationships between people. He proposed an interactive approach to build meaningful social networks by interacting with human experts, and applied the proposed system to discover the social networks between mobile users by collecting a dataset from about two millions of users. Given a certain social relation (e.g., isFatherOf), the system can evaluate a set of conditions (which are represented as propositional axioms) asserted from the human experts, and show them a social network resulted from data mining tools. Sociometric badge [28] has been designed to identify human activity patterns, analyze conversational prosody features and wirelessly communicate with radio base-stations and mobile phones. Sensor data from the badges has been used in various organizational contexts to automatically predict employee's self-assessment of job satisfaction and quality of interactions. Eagle and Pentland [18] used mobile phone Bluetooth transceivers, phone communication logs and cellular tower identifiers to identify the social network structure, recognize social patterns in daily user activity, infer relationships, identify socially significant locations and model organizational rhythms.

Besides research projects, there exist also a variety of application that are used for gathering information about context from mobile devices, like SDCF [5], AWARE [1], JCAF [7], SCOUT [33], ContextDriod [32], Gimbal [2]. These are mostly concerned with low-level context data acquisition from sensors, suitable fur further context identification. On the other hand, they do not provide support nor methodology for creating complex and customizable context-aware systems.

Although there are a lot of frameworks and middlewares developed for context-aware systems, they are usually limited to a specific domain and designed without taking into consideration mobile platforms. Examples include CoBrA [12] and SOUPA [13] for building smart meeting rooms, GAIA [29] for active spaces, Context Toolkit [15], etc.

There is still space for research in a field of lightweight context modeling and context reasoning targeted at mobile devices. Some attempts were made to develop such frameworks, like SOCAM [21], or Context Torrent [22]. However, these frameworks do not provide full support for all of the challenges that are crucial for mobile computing, with respect to the context modeling and context-based reasoning [26].

Taking all the above, a lightweight context-based reasoning approach was presented in [8]. It is based on the HeaRT [25] rule-based inference engine. However, HeaRT reasoning engine was initially developed as a desktop application and has not been designed to work properly in a mobile environment. This paper presents evaluation of the migration of the HeaRT reasoner to a mobile platform, for the purpose of mobile, context-aware interface for the Social Threat Monitor System (STM) [3]. The challenges connected with providing a mobile reasoning service for the STM are presented in the following Section.

---

[1] http://www.awareframework.com/

[2] https://www.gimbal.com/

3   Challenges for Delivering a Mobile Reasoning Service

The work presented in this paper is continuation of research on mobile context-based framework for monitoring threats in urban environment presented in [8].

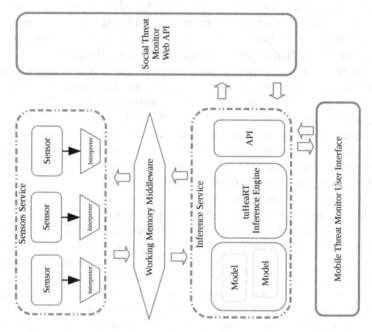

Fig. 1. Architecture of the mobile context aware framework [8]

The framework assumes architecture that is presented in Fig. 1. The architecture of the framework is divided into three layers:

1. Sensor Service – that is responsible for gathering contextual information and initial pre-processing of raw data
2. Working Memory Middleware – that is responsible for semantization of contextual data, to fit model requirements. This layer also assumes implementation of machine learning algorithms for learning user habits to optimize query time and minimize energy usage [9].
3. Inference Service – that is responsible for context-based reasoning.

In this paper, we have focused on the description of implementation and evaluation of the inference service layer. The challenges defined in our previous research [8] had to be revised and refined for this specific layer. The following requirements and challenges were identified as crucial in mobile environments:

– **Responsiveness (R1).** The inference layer has to work under soft real-time constraints. Mobile environment is highly dynamic, and the inference layer should follow rapid changes of context in such an environment.

- **Resource limitation (R2)**. It should consume as least resources as possible to work transparently in the background.
- **Privacy (R3)**. The reasoning service should not send any confidential data to the external servers, but perform all the reasoning locally.
- **Robustness (R4)**. It should work properly when the contextual data is incomplete or uncertain. This requirement is beyond of the scope of this article and is just briefly described in the following paragraphs.
- **Intelligibility (R5)**. It should be able to explain its decision to the user, and thus improve intelligibility of the system.
- **Portability (R6)**. The inference engine should be portable and as independent of the operating system as possible.

The core element of the inference layer is HeaRT inference engine. HeaRT is a lightweight rule-based inference engine that uses XTT2 [27] notation for knowledge representation [24]. It is written in Prolog and can be installed on mobile device together with tuProlog [3] interpreter, providing autonomous inference service. This guaranties that the context-based inference can be performed locally, and thus the requirement R3 is fulfilled. Although the requirements R1 and R2 are easily satisfiable for HeaRT in a desktop environment, they no longer hold on mobile platform. Issues concerning migration from desktop to mobile platforms and possible solutions are presented in the Section 4.

The requirement R4 is strictly connected with the nature of the mobile environment. Although the mobile devices are currently equipped with variety of sensors, the contextual data provided by them is not always complete nor certain. For instance the location provider will not work properly underground, where there is no access to the GPS or the Internet. Machine learning algorithms implemented to detect user activities may also be error prone and thus provide low quality data, or do not provide them at all. The lack of data, or low quality of data may cause the inference engine to work improperly, or not work at all. The possible solution to this problem is to include additional layer in the system architecture that would provide support for the inference engine in situations where the contextual information is incomplete or low quality. Such a layer could use incremental data mining algorithms [20] to detect dependencies between different context providers. Dependencies in a form of association rules could be used to predict contextual values of context provider that is not available. The automatically detected rules could be later verified by the user via mediation mechanisms [17]. Incorporating user into the inference process will allow to build better user-centric application. It may also change the idea of intelligent system to no longer be an autonomous, black-box system, but rather a social, conscious companion of a user, who understands and controls its actions.

HeaRT inference engine is a rule-based reasoner that have high capabilities of self-explaining its decisions. This allows almost immediate satisfaction of requirement R5, as the reasoning process performed by HeaRT can be retrieved and presented to the user in a form of explanation of the system decisions. This improves the intelligibility of the system, defined as an ability of the system to

---

[3] See http://alice.unibo.it/xwiki/bin/view/Main/.

being understood [16]. Example of such explanatory mechanism was presented in Section 5 in Figure 4.

The portability requirement (R6) is one of the most difficult to be satisfied in the area of mobile and embedded systems. Each of the existing operating systems for mobile devices use different native programming language. Thus, it is not possible to use one of the most popular programming languages like Java, Objective C or C#, as it will only be supported by fraction of mobile systems. This is why, we decided to use independent platform like Prolog, which can work as a virtual platform on the top of a native operating system. However, such a migration is not trivial, and requires a lot of effort to allow the rest of the requirements defined in this section hold. The following section describes details connected with this issue on the example of migrating Prolog implementation to Android-based platform.

4   Comparison of Prolog Platforms for Mobile Devices

One of the most challenging tasks, which have to be solved in order to use HeaRT inference engine on the mobile platforms, is to find a properly working environment capable of executing code written in Prolog language. Originally HeaRT was developed using SWI–Prolog, open source ISO-compliant Prolog implementation, written mainly in C and distributed under the LGPL license [31]. Despite the many advantages, good built-in debugger, threads and TCP support, this solution comes with the burden of technology created before the era of mobility. It should be ported to the new platforms or replaced with the modern mobile equivalent. Such equivalent should meet the certain requirements:

- It has to be fully ISO–compliant [1] and thus support Prolog meta-programming features, especially user–defined operators, broadly used in the current implementation of HeaRT.
- Preferably, could offer good integration with code written in Java, for the sake of the Android mobile platform.
- It should be fast and light enough to perform reasoning on low-memory and power consuming devices. This is a direct consequence of R1 and R2 requirements from the previous section.

Traditionally, Prolog used to be executed by a virtual machine, implemented in the low level programming languages [30], or even directly in the hardware [2]. The Warren Virtual Machine, created in the 1976 by David H. D. Warren, is the standard execution model in the majority of the modern Prolog environments [30,4]. Other, less popular, solutions include direct translation of the Prolog code into different programming language or implementation as Domain Specific Language, especially in the LISP family of languages. There exist early attempts to implement Prolog as a just-in-time compiler, but this subject needs more research in order to be production-ready [10].

Due to its small size and vast choice of execution environments, Prolog can be perceived as a layer of abstraction, which enables sharing of the one code base between diverse mobile platforms. At the present time we are focused however only on the solution for the Android operating system; other platforms will be possibly treated separately in the future works. During our research for the HeaRT Android execution environment we have distinguished three possible classes of solutions: (1) use of the existing Java implementation of Prolog; (2) porting the SWI–Prolog to the Android; (3) translation of the Prolog code into Java. All our attempts will be described and evaluated in the next paragraphs.

4.1   Existing Java Implementations

The most simple and elegant approach to execute Prolog programs on Android is use of the existing Java implementations of WAM (or other Prolog virtual machine). There exists a rather vast choice of free Java libraries, theoretically compliant with mobile environment. During research we have tested the four most promising:

(1) tuProlog [4] – a lightweight Prolog system released under the LGPL license; it is actively developed and supports both JVM and CLR virtual machines. During the tests we used the most recent version 2.7, but due to the bug in dynamic clauses support, we were forced to use the testing branch of the project. It should be noted that due to the CLR support tuProlog has the potential also to be used on mobile devices with Windows operating system.

(2) jekejeke Prolog [5] – Prolog interpreter already used in existing Android application; it seems to be actively developed but its real status is rather unclear. We have used the 0.9.11 version, released on the October 2013.

(3) GNU Prolog for Java [6] – free and open source attempt to implement ISO Prolog in Java. The last 0.2.6 release had been published in 2011. It is distributed under the terms of the LGPL3 license.

(4) jinniprolog [7] – designed and implemented by Paul Tarau; uses a special flavor of WAM virtual machine named Binary WAM [11]. Released in 2012 and distributed under the GPL3 license.

Unfortunately, despite the promising descriptions none of the mentioned environments was an ISO compliant Prolog implementation. All lacked definitions of many standard Prolog predicates, so we had to implement them by ourselves – fortunately we could reuse the definitions from the SWI–Prolog source code [8]. The more serious, common flaw for jekejeke, jinniprolog and GNU Prolog was the incomplete support for operator defining, which is crucial for input parsing in the HeaRT engine. Therefore only the tuProlog system could be tested without the significant changes in the HeaRT itself.

---

[4] http://apice.unibo.it/xwiki/bin/view/Tuprolog/
[5] http://www.jekejeke.ch/idatab/doclet/intr/en/docs/package.jsp
[6] http://www.gnu.org/software/gnuprologjava/
[7] http://code.google.com/p/jinniprolog/
[8] http://www.swi-prolog.org/git/pl.git

On the other hand, tuProlog had issues regarding the dynamic clauses. Thanks to the support of the project authors we were informed that they were already resolved in the testing version of the system. Moreover before we were able to run a HeaRT query, we had to make some further refinements in the HeaRT code – it had to be merged into a single file and some operators had to be enclosed by single quotation marks because of the parsing problems. Finally, we managed to obtain a working instance of HeaRT on the Android device, it had some two major flaws though. Firstly, tuProlog does not provide any debugging utility, which could be very helpful in the further development of the HeaRT engine. Secondly, the duration of even simple test query was unacceptably long, approximately ten times longer than the duration of the same query executed by the SWI–Prolog. These shortcomings motivated us to look after more robust and native execution environments.

4.2   Porting the SWI–Prolog

The Android system is an Unix–like operating system based on the Linux kernel, therefore it should execute programs (especially SWI–Prolog) working already on the other Linux based systems. Unfortunately, there exist four key reasons making this transition hard to achieve:

1. Mobile devices work mainly on the different processor architecture.
2. Android maintains its own toolkit for native development (namely NDK) and uses different standard library for C.
3. Many common libraries do not exist in the Android ecosystem.
4. Even native code must be executed under control of the Java virtual machine.

In the present state the SWI–Prolog does address only the first issue as its code can be compiled on the ARM architecture. Other problems can be easily bypassed by replacing Android with the other Linux distribution installed on the mobile device [9] – this approach however is not an acceptable solution for the common user. Technically it should be possible to build SWI–Prolog using the Android NDK, but there is none known successful attempt. We have identified three main causes of this situation. Firstly, there is a problem with the process and thread handling part of SWI–Prolog, because it uses mainly the GLibc standard library. Secondly there is a lack of some popular libraries (for example 'readline') required by SWI–Prolog executable. Finally, building of the SWI–Prolog libraries includes so called 'bootstraping' – it uses its own compiled executable to build other parts of itself.

There exists also other independent issue: even if we manage to build the environment, there is no certainty whether existing Java interface for SWI–Prolog [10]

---

[9] http://www.swi-prolog.org/build/linuxonandroid.html
[10] http://www.swi-prolog.org/packages/jpl/

will work with the Dalvik virtual machine. For these reasons we do not believe that SWI–Prolog can be currently used for our purposes.

4.3 Translation to Java

The last tested execution environment was Prolog Cafe [11] – a Prolog-to-Java translator system. Theoretically it could compile HeaRT into Java binary file, therefore eliminating the necessity of the Prolog Java implementation. Furthermore, its authors claim that the generated code is only three times slower (on average) than the SWI–Prolog solution [6]. The project, in spite of being not developed for nearly two years, offers many desirable features like good parallelism support, seamless mixing of Prolog and Java code and simple debugging tools. Unfortunately it seems to be incompatible with the current HeaRT code state, because it does not allow dynamic clauses to be used simultaneously like the normal static clauses (all dynamic facts have to be added to the knowledge base using the 'assert' predicate). However, Prolog Cafe, due to its comparatively small and easy to comprehend source code, seems to be a good candidate for further development into a mature tuProlog alternative. Furthermore, while Prolog Café uses a standard WAM machine, there may exist more efficient models for translation, especially in context of the optimizations performed by the Java Virtual Machine [19].

5 HeaRT on tuProlog: Use Case Scenario

The following use-case scenario is an implementation of a prototype described in [8]. It assumes that the tuProlog implementation of the HeaRT inference engine called tuHeaRT [12] is working on the mobile device as a reasoning service which delivers to the user a context-filtered notification about urban threats.

The system was designed as a mobile front end for a Social Threat Monitor system, that assists citizens in reporting and being informed about security threats together with their severity and location. Being in a given situation, and location (i.e., context) the user can be automatically notified by their mobile device about the threats relevant to him and the situation. Relevance to the person may be related to their role defined in the STM system, as well as the context, e.g. a person who walks should not be bothered by warnings relevant only to drivers in the same location.

The inference engine performs reasoning that is triggered by the appearance of a new contextual information, and the results are presented to the user in a form of filtered threats. For the evaluation of a reasoning service a tuProlog implementation was chosen. The tuProlog was the only Java implementation of Prolog which supported almost (at the time of writing) full Prolog ISO standard.

---

[11] https://code.google.com/p/prolog-cafe/
[12] https://bitbucket.org/sbobek/tuheart/wiki/Home

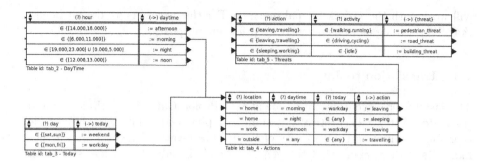

Fig. 2. Example of the model for a mobile threat monitor [8]

An exemplary XTT2 model (see Figure 2) presented in this section allows to alert users about threats in a context-aware way. The system takes into consideration spatial (localization of the user) and temporal (time of a day) contexts, as well as user activities. This allow the intelligent threats filtering. For instance, the model will prevent from warning a user who is driving a car about threats that are applicable to pedestrians only. This is achieved by selecting only these rules that are valid in current context.

Information about threats is fetched from Social Threat Monitor system via the WEB API (see [3] for details). Other contextual information such as location and user activity is delivered to the system by the AWARE framework layer [13]. A set of recognized user activity includes: walking, traveling in a vehicle, riding a bicycle and remaining still. The recognition is based on the Google API, that uses machine learning algorithms to detect the current user activity with the low energy cost [14].

Taking into consideration an example model from Figure 2, and assuming that it is Monday, 8 o'clock am, and the user is driving a car, the system will process following rules: (1) rule 1 from *DayTime* table, (2) rule 2 from *Today* table, (3) rule 4 from *Actions* table, (4) and rule 2 from *Threats* table. When the inference is finished, the information about specified threats are pulled via STMJava [15] API from web service and is display it to the user. The following section describes details about the implementation and evaluation of the use case scenario.

6   Implementation and Evaluation

For the evaluation a Samsung Galaxy Tab II (GT-P5100) was used, with Android 4.1.2 installed. The Aware framework in version 2 for context-management and Google play services library for activity recognition revision 14 was used. As a Prolog interpreter for tuHeaRT engine, tuProlog 2.8.0 was used, as the official

---

[13] http://awareframewok.com
[14] http://developer.android.com/training/location/activity-recognition.html
[15] https://bitbucket.org/mslazynski/stmjava

release, which at the time of writing is 2.7.2, has critical bug in retract predicate. The XTT model presented in Fig. 2 was used to provide context-based threats filtering. The tuHeaRT was implemented as a part of a service that works in a background. The reasoning is triggered by the new contextual information delivered by the Aware framework. The inference process is performed locally, to preserve requirement R3. The threats are fetched from STM via STMJava API and are presented to the user in a form of system notification (See Figure 4).

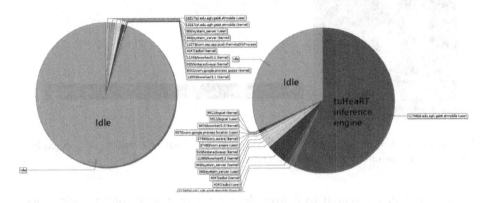

Fig. 3. CPU load without (left) and with inference engine working as a service (right). The biggest pies represent respectively idle and inference processes.

When the user decides to check details of the threat, a new activity is presented, where the full explanation of the decision made is presented to him or her. The explanation is made based on the trace of the inference process which is delivered to the application as s system sate. An example of such trace is presented below.

```
10 ?- xstat current: Value.
Value = [hour, 8] ;           Value = [day, mon] ;
Value = [location, home] ;    Value = [activity, walking] ;
Value = [daytime, morning] ;  Value = [today, workday] ;
Value = [action, leaving] ;   Value = [threat, [pedestrian_threat]] ;
```

The explanation based on the state trace from the listing above is presented in the Figure 4. This preserves the requirement R5, providing basic intelligibility feature to the system.

Responsiveness of the reasoning service was calculated as an average of time required to deliver the value of the *threat* attribute after invoking the inference process. The average time for the inference for the model presented in Figure 2 equals 1800 milliseconds. The results were surprisingly bad, even comparing to the desktop environment, where the average execution time was on the level of 600 milliseconds. The bad results were caused by the optimization issues in tuProlog implementation. This makes the requirement R1 not satisfied.

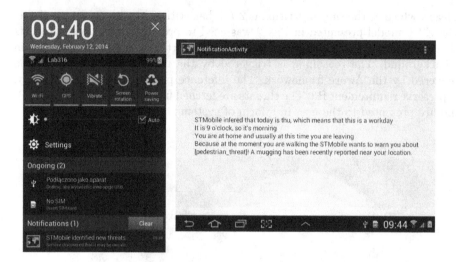

Fig. 4. Notification in a system trace (left) informing about new threat, and an explanation of the inference engine decision (right)

The CPU time required to deliver the answer by the reasoning engine was also investigated with Android Profiler tool. The difference in CPU usage of the system without and with inference service running is presented in fig. 3. The issue of very high CPU load is again connected with not optimal tuProlog implementation, that takes a lot of time to execute the Prolog queries. Thus, the requirement R2 for the tuHeaRT cannot hold.

Requirements R4 and R5 concerning robustness and portability of the system are beyond of the scope of this paper and are included in a future work.

7 Summary and Future Work

In this paper we presented an evaluation of an inference service implementation that is pat of the rule-based framework for mobile context-aware systems presented in [8]. The lightweight, Prolog-based inference engine called tuHeaRT was used for the evaluation. The implementation and evaluation was performed on the Android operating system.

We defined six issues that have to be solved by reasoning engine, designed to work in mobile environments. There are: responsiveness (R1), resource limitation (R2), privacy (R3), robustness (R4), intelligibility (R5), portability (R6). The comparison of existing Prolog interpreters implementations for mobile devices were presented, and major weaknesses of each was described.

The evaluation of the inference engine was performed on a Mobile Social Threat Monitor application, that uses data gathered by mobile device sensors and perform on-line reasoning about possible threats, based on the information provided by the Social Threat Monitor system. The evaluation revealed, that from the above six requirements, only two can be preserved in a current state of the Prolog implementations for mobile platforms. Resource limitation, and responsiveness appeared to be the major problems of currently available mobile Prolog interpreters.

These problems together with robustness and portability challenges are planned for a future work. To provide robustness of the inference engine, additional layer in the system architecture could be included that would provide support for the inference engine in situations where the contextual information is incomplete or low quality. Such a layer could use incremental data mining algorithms [20] to detect dependencies between different context providers. Such dependencies in a form of association rules could be used to predict contextual values of context provider that is not available.

References

1. ISO/IEC 13211: Information technology - Programming languages - Prolog, Geneva (1995)
2. Abe, S., Bandoh, T., Yamaguchi, S., Kurosawa, K., Kiriyama, K.: High performance integrated prolog processor ipp. In: Proceedings of the 14th Annual International Symposium on Computer Architecture, ISCA 1987, pp. 100–107. ACM, New York (1987), http://doi.acm.org/10.1145/30350.30362
3. Adrian, W.T., Ciężkowski, P., Kaczor, K., Ligęza, A., Nalepa, G.J.: Web-based knowledge acquisition and management system supporting collaboration for improving safety in urban environment. In: Dziech, A., Czyżewski, A. (eds.) MCSS 2012. CCIS, vol. 287, pp. 1–12. Springer, Heidelberg (2012), http://link.springer.com/book/10.1007/978-3-642-30721-8/page/1
4. Aït-Kaci, H.: Warren's Abstract Machine: A Tutorial Reconstruction. MIT Press, Gliwice (1999)
5. Atzmueller, M., Hilgenberg, K.: Towards capturing social interactions with sdcf: An extensible framework for mobile sensing and ubiquitous data collection. In: Proc. 4th International Workshop on Modeling Social Media. ACM Press (2013)
6. Banbara, M., Tamura, N., Inoue, K.: prolog cafe: A prolog to java translator system. In: Umeda, M., Wolf, A., Bartenstein, O., Geske, U., Seipel, D., Takata, O. (eds.) INAP 2005. LNCS (LNAI), vol. 4369, pp. 1–11. Springer, Heidelberg (2006), http://dx.doi.org/10.1007/11963578_1
7. Bardram, J.E.: The java context awareness framework (JCAF) – A service infrastructure and programming framework for context-aware applications. In: Gellersen, H.W., Want, R., Schmidt, A. (eds.) PERVASIVE 2005. LNCS, vol. 3468, pp. 98–115. Springer, Heidelberg (2005), http://dx.doi.org/10.1007/11428572_7
8. Bobek, S., Nalepa, G.J., Adrian, W.T.: Mobile context-based framework for monitoring threats in urban environment. In: Dziech, A., Czyżewski, A. (eds.) MCSS 2013. CCIS, vol. 368, pp. 25–35. Springer, Heidelberg (2013)
9. Bobek, S., Porzycki, K., Nalepa, G.J.: Learning sensors usage patterns in mobile context-aware systems. In: Proceedings of the FedCSIS 2013 Conference, Krakow, pp. 993–998. IEEE (September 2013)
10. Bolz, C.F., Leuschel, M., Schneider, D.: Towards a Jitting VM for Prolog Execution. In: PPDP 2010 - Proceedings of the 12th International ACM SIGPLAN Symposium on Principles and Practice of Declarative Programming. ACM, Hagenberg (2010)

11. Bruynooghe, M., Wirsing, M. (eds.): PLILP 1992. LNCS, vol. 631. Springer, Heidelberg (1992), http://dblp.uni-trier.de/db/conf/plilp/plilp92.html#Tarau92
12. Chen, H., Finin, T.W., Joshi, A.: Semantic web in the context broker architecture. In: PerCom, pp. 277–286. IEEE Computer Society (2004)
13. Chen, H., Perich, F., Finin, T.W., Joshi, A.: Soupa: Standard ontology for ubiquitous and pervasive applications. In: 1st Annual International Conference on Mobile and Ubiquitous Systems (MobiQuitous 2004), Networking and Services, Cambridge, MA, USA, August 22-25, pp. 258–267. IEEE Computer Society (2004)
14. Chronis, I., Madan, A., Pentland, A.S.: Socialcircuits: the art of using mobile phones for modeling personal interactions. In: Proceedings of the ICMI-MLMI 2009 Workshop on Multimodal Sensor-Based Systems and Mobile Phones for Social Computing, ICMI-MLMI 2009, pp. 1:1–1:4. ACM, New York (2009)
15. Dey, A.K.: Understanding and using context. Personal Ubiquitous Comput. 5(1), 4–7 (2001)
16. Dey, A.K.: Modeling and intelligibility in ambient environments. J. Ambient Intell. Smart Environ. 1(1), 57–62 (2009)
17. Dey, A.K., Mankoff, J.: Designing mediation for context-aware applications. ACM Trans. Comput.-Hum. Interact. 12(1), 53–80 (2005), http://doi.acm.org/10.1145/1057237.1057241
18. Eagle, N., (Sandy) Pentland, A.: Reality mining: sensing complex social systems. Personal Ubiquitous Comput 10(4), 255–268 (2006)
19. Eichberg, M.: Compiling Prolog to Idiomatic Java. In: Gallagher, J., Gelfond, M. (eds.) Technical Communications of the 27th International Conference on Logic Programming (ICLP 2011). Leibniz International Proceedings in Informatics (LIPIcs), vol. 11, pp. 84–94. Schloss Dagstuhl–Leibniz-Zentrum fuer Informatik, Dagstuhl (2011), http://drops.dagstuhl.de/opus/volltexte/2011/3176
20. Gharib, T.F., Nassar, H., Taha, M., Abraham, A.: An efficient algorithm for incremental mining of temporal association rules. Data Knowl. Eng. 69(8), 800–815 (2010), http://dx.doi.org/10.1016/j.datak.2010.03.002
21. Gu, T., Pung, H.K., Zhang, D.Q., Wang, X.H.: A middleware for building context-aware mobile services. In: Proceedings of IEEE Vehicular Technology Conference (VTC) (2004)
22. Hu, H.: ContextTorrent: A Context Provisioning Framewrok for Pervasive Applications. University of Hong Kong (2011)
23. Jung, J.J.: Contextualized mobile recommendation service based on interactive social network discovered from mobile users. Expert Syst. Appl. 36(9), 11950–11956 (2009), http://dx.doi.org/10.1016/j.eswa.2009.03.067
24. Ligęza, A., Nalepa, G.J.: A study of methodological issues in design and development of rule-based systems: proposal of a new approach. Wiley Interdisciplinary Reviews: Data Mining and Knowledge Discovery 1(2), 117–137 (2011)
25. Nalepa, G.J., Bobek, S., Ligęza, A., Kaczor, K.: Algorithms for rule inference in modularized rule bases. In: Bassiliades, N., Governatori, G., Paschke, A. (eds.) RuleML 2011 - Europe. LNCS, vol. 6826, pp. 305–312. Springer, Heidelberg (2011)
26. Nalepa, G.J., Bobek, S.: Rule-based solution for context-aware reasoning on mobile devices. Computer Science and Information Systems 11(1), 171–193 (2014)
27. Nalepa, G.J., Ligęza, A., Kaczor, K.: Formalization and modeling of rules using the XTT2 method. International Journal on Artificial Intelligence Tools 20(6), 1107–1125 (2011)

28. Olguin, D., Waber, B.N., Kim, T., Mohan, A., Ara, K., Pentland, A.: Sensible organizations: Technology and methodology for automatically measuring organizational behavior. IEEE Transactions on Systems, Man, and Cybernetics-Part B: Cybernetics, 43–55 (2009)
29. Ranganathan, A., McGrath, R.E., Campbell, R.H., Mickunas, M.D.: Use of ontologies in a pervasive computing environment. Knowl. Eng. Rev. 18(3), 209–220 (2003)
30. Roy, P.V.: 1983-1993: The Wonder Years of Sequential Prolog Implementation. J. Log. Program. 19/20, 385–441 (1994),
    http://dblp.uni-trier.de/db/journals/jlp/jlp19.html#Roy94
31. Wielemaker, J.: SWI Prolog Reference Manual 6.2.2. Books on Demand (2012),
    http://books.google.nl/books?id=q6R3Q3B-VC4C
32. van Wissen, B., Palmer, N., Kemp, R., Kielmann, T., Bal, H.: ContextDroid: an expression-based context framework for Android. In: Proceedings of PhoneSense 2010 (November 2010), http://sensorlab.cs.dartmouth.edu/
    phonesense/papers/Wissen-ContextDroid.pdf
33. Van Woensel, W., Casteleyn, S., De Troyer, O.: A Framework for Decentralized, Context-Aware Mobile Applications Using Semantic Web Technology. In: Meersman, R., Herrero, P., Dillon, T. (eds.) OTM 2009 Workshops. LNCS, vol. 5872, pp. 88–97. Springer, Heidelberg (2009)

Contribution of the INSIGMA Project to the Field of Intelligent Transportation Systems*

Wojciech Chmiel, Jacek Dańda, Andrzej Dziech, Sebastian Ernst,
Andrzej Głowacz, Piotr Kadluczka, Zbigniew Mikrut, Piotr Pawlik,
Piotr Szwed, and Igor Wojnicki

AGH University of Science and Technology
{wch,danda}@agh.edu.pl, adzie@tlen.pl,
{ernst,aglowacz,pkad,zibi,piotrus,pszwed,wojnicki}@agh.edu.pl

Abstract. With the growing number of vehicles traveling on public
roads, traffic congestion has become a serious problem, resulting in more
unpredictable travel times, increased fuel consumption and pollution.
Intelligent Transportation Systems (ITS), already being developed by
several countries, aim to improve safety, mobility and environmental performance. The goal of the INSIGMA project is to develop a system providing functionality of a typical ITS: real-time traffic monitoring, route
planning and traffic control. In this paper we discuss the concepts and
solutions developed within the project: dynamic map, sensors – videodetector and GPS tracker – as well as advanced route planning and traffic
control algorithms.

Keywords: Intelligent Transportation Systems, video detector, GPS,
architecture, route planning, traffic control.

1 Introduction

Recent years have seen significant development in the automotive sector and
increase in the total number of vehicles in the world. By some estimates [28], already in 2010, over a billion cars have been in use worldwide. The largest increase
can be observed in China and other developing countries with large numbers of
residents, including Brazil and Russia. In turn, the largest percentage of vehicles
per capita can be observed in well-developed countries, particularly in Europe,
USA, and Japan. In both groups, it is important important to maintain an
adequate road infrastructure that would meet the growing demands and expec-
tations of its users. The current capacity of roads is insufficient in many places,
especially in big cities, and intersections and access roads are the critical parts.

These problems are particularly noticeable during rush hours, where traffic
is the greatest. On one hand such situations result in tangible economic losses:

* Work has been co-financed by the European Regional Development Fund under the
Innovative Economy Operational Programme, INSIGMA project no. POIG.01.01.02-
00-062/09.

A. Dziech and A. Czyżewski (Eds.): MCSS 2014, CCIS 429, pp. 58–72, 2014.

time irretrievably lost in traffic jams and lost fuel [5]. An important factor is also the environmental aspect of the road traffic, because a standstill dramatically increases the emission of toxic compounds contained in exhaust gases from internal combustion engines. Another issue is related to the social effects associated with low comfort of transport for vehicle users. There are further transportation challenges including, among others: dangerous goods transportation [8], safety of critical infrastructure [22] or even risk assessment for transportation of hazardous materials in tunnels [19].

A prospective method to prevent traffic congestion lies in the next generation of Intelligent Transportation Systems (ITS) [2,3]. It is expected that dynamic traffic control and vehicle navigation will largely raise the constraints of road infrastructure development. Currently, such systems are mainly based on statistical data acquired from historical traffic statistics, which is insufficient, especially in a sudden increase in traffic related to accidents and road collisions and other unplanned events. Often, there is a narrow range of parameters in control programs that can be tuned. A similar situation occurs in car navigation systems. Statistical traffic data no longer allows for avoiding traffic jams and optimal solutions based on real-time data are necessary.

The INSIGMA system [1] includes advanced tools for traffic monitoring and detection of dangerous events. The first objective is to analyze traffic parameters using dynamic generated by means of developed system sensors. A dynamic map is a representation of the road transport infrastructure combined with information about existing traffic intensity and historical traffic data. Such a set of data includes map-related parameters stored in a database and their visualisation, which can be delivered to the end user via a dedicated mobile or web interface. The system includes algorithms for dynamic route optimisation, which operate on real data, as opposed to statistical data used by many existing road navigation applications.

Another problem is the limited area of the managed geographic region. Traffic detectors are mostly deployed in major highways, but their use in access roads is very sparse. Besides adding more sensors to the infrastructure, it is crucial to develop automatic methods of visual object observation and registration of their trajectory parameters using cameras and other sensors. These systems will provide low-level data from road junctions for generation of dynamic maps. In result, the INSIGMA system will enable interfaces to access optimal routes, information about dangerous events and other intelligent services.

The remainder of this paper is organised as follows. In Section 2, basic functions and services of ITS are discussed; in the following Section 3 the system architecture, basic types of sensors and control algorithms are presented. Conclusions are provided in Section 4.

2   ITS Functions and Services

Intelligent Transportation Systems (ITS) [4] integrate various underlying technologies: sensing, data interpretation, communications, information integration and control to build a large, efficient and real-time transportation systems. The main goals for development of ITS are safety, mobility and environmental performance [21]. ITS have been developed in various regions with a hope to significantly reduce the number of accidents, increase the throughput of road network, limit travel times and energy consumption, reduce pollution and amend travel comfort and driving conditions. Other expected benefits include lower costs of transport, logistics management and road infrastructure maintenance.

A taxonomy services of ITS [16] comprises more then thirty items grouped into families including:

1. Traveler information (route planning, on-trip information, weather and road condition information, route guidance)
2. Traffic management (transportation planning, traffic control, enforcing traffic regulations, infrastructure maintenance)
3. Emergency transportation operations (access to emergency services, enhanced information sharing, emergency management and operations, transportation operations during biohazard situations)
4. Vehicle services (vision enhancement, automated vehicle operation, collision avoidance, safety readiness)
5. Public transport (management, demand responsive transport management, shared transport)
6. Electronic tolling
7. Commercial vehicles (administrative process, on-board safety monitoring, fleet management)

The system developed within the INSIGMA project provides functions related to *Traveler information*, *Traffic management* and *Emergency transportation operations*.

3 INSIGMA System

The INSIGMA system is based on three main data-oriented components: the *Static Map*, the *Dynamic Map* and the *Dynamic Map Warehouse*, as presented in Figure 1. They handle slow-changing, fast-changing and historical data related to the transport infrastructure, respectively. The slow-changing data regards road infrastructure, including details like roads, junctions, lanes, traffic signs, and road accessibility. The accessibility parameter indicates whether particular roads are available for specific users, such as regular or emergency vehicles. An emergency vehicle, for instance, is allowed to use a sidewalk, while a regular vehicle is not. The fast-changing data regards dynamic parameters, so-called monitoring parameters, which represent the current or recent traffic conditions and events, including threat reporting or detection. The historical data regards aggregated fast-changing data with relationships to the slow-changing data objects. Separating it from the dynamic parameters provides means to conduct time-based analysis offloading the *Dynamic Map*.

Data gathered by these three data stores is accessible through web service-based interfaces: *IMS (INSIGMA-Map-Static) Interface*, *IMD (INSIGMA-Map-Dynamic) Interface*, and *IHD (INSIGMA-wareHouse-Dynamic) Interface*. Additionally, the *Dynamic Map Warehouse* provides an *OLAP Interface* allowing for ad-hoc multi-dimensional analysis. The system also has "raw" SQL-based interfaces for internal, high-performance communication. They are mainly used for data transfer from the maps into the warehouse during the ETL (Extraction, Transformation, Loading) process, performed by the *Dynamic Map ETL* component. They are also used by *Sensor Handlers* which read data from sensors and feed it into the *Dynamic Map*.

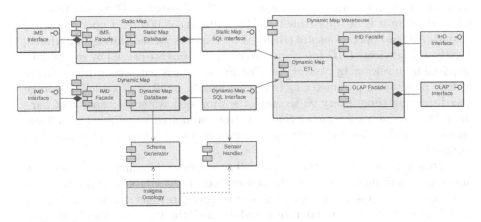

Fig. 1. Insigma base components

The data model is consistent across all three main components. It is based on a formal ontology (*INSIGMA Ontology*) describing the world under consideration [23]. While the ontology itself was used to design the main components, it can also be used to generate or validate data models and communications. One of such examples is the *Schema Generator*, which builds appropriate database schemas to store dynamically-changing monitoring parameter values. These values correspond to the ontological assertion components, called the ABox. At any time this data can be represented as a complete ontology consisting of both a TBox (a terminological component) and an ABox. Details of how the actual values are stored in the database and their relationship with the TBox is given in [29]. Another example is the *Sensor Handler* component which can verify if raw data coming from sensors meets formal criteria. It can be used to automatically detect sensor malfunctions.

Two main map-related components which are the *Static* and *Dynamic Maps* are designed and implemented using the *INSIGMA Ontology*, which has the following effects. It reinforces the system design process and makes data semantically available. Reinforcing the design process with ontology allows to precisely define data structures and data flows. In turn, it enables to establish clean interfaces between the system's components. Such an approach makes future alterations and extensions of the system easier. Semantic availability increases the integration capabilities of the system. Since all gathered data is available as ontological facts, they can be easily processed, analyzed, or transferred to third party applications. This way, Further semantic analysis of gathered knowledge is also possible.

Performance of the proposed architecture has been tested and verified. It mostly regards the *Dynamic Map* component, since it both serves and gathers dynamically-changing data. It has been verified that that a single *Dynamic Map* instance is capable of processing approximately 1,000 raw writes and 10,000 raw read operations per second. Retrieving or storing a single fact requires two raw reads or writes to sustain the database–ontology consistency. Thus, fact processing performance is at approximately 500 write and 5,000 read operations per second. All read operations are triggered by requests passed through interfaces, mostly web services (*IMD Interface*). Write operations are caused by sensor data acquired from sensors by *Sensor Handler*. Since a statistical sensor delivers a set of four monitoring parameter facts (queue length, number of vehicles, average speed, passing time) every 90 seconds, the proposed system is capable of handling 11,250 sensors. Assuming that a metropolitan area is equipped with 2,000 sensors it would allow to handle up to five such areas by a single *Dynamic Map* instance.

A *Dynamic Map* system running at full throughput, handling 5 metropolitan areas and acquiring data from 11,250 sensors, generates a data growth rate of 500 facts per second. Assuming approximately 100 bytes per fact, the data volume is 28GB per week. Such a growth rate would overload the *Dynamic Map* by slowing down or crippling its processing capabilities. To prevent that, historical facts are transferred into the *Dynamic Map Warehouse*. To decrease the amount of data at the warehouse side, the facts are aggregated. Furthermore, the warehouse's database is capable of flexible storage and processing introducing horizontal scaling. Having separate interfaces to access current and historical data, the *IMD Interface* and the *IHD Interface* respectively, enables the client application to choose the proper one, depending on its needs. For the current traffic situation *IMD Interface* should be used. To analyze traffic flow in time, e.g. to extrapolate traffic intensity, the *IHD Interface* is the more appropriate choice.

3.1   Sensors

An important requirement that guided the design of the Dynamic Map was the assumed ability to integrate various types of sensors delivering information about traffic conditions. They include street cameras, inductive loops, microphone arrays, meteo stations and vehicle tracking devices. In this section we will discuss two types of sensors that can be considered complementary: the video detector and the GPS tracker.

The INSIGMA Videodetector. A "video detector" is the traditional name for a device which performs computer analysis of video streams in order to determine traffic parameters. The video streams come from cameras observing the traffic. Each camera is handled by one video detector instance. In its configuration file the user must define the areas in which the analysis will be conducted. These include polygons restricting lanes on which the length of the queue is computed and virtual lines, used to count the vehicles and calculate their instantaneous velocity. Configuration of the two real scenes is shown in Figure 2.

Fig. 2. Scene configuration of the Northern and Eastern cameras. There are 5 queue areas (denoted K) and 4 virtual lines (ZV) defined in each scene.

Traffic parameters described above are determined by the following procedures:

— *Length of the vehicle queue.* For a given lane, the point corresponding to the end of the last car is determined. The distance from this point to the STOP line is the length of the queue – only if there is a stationary vehicle on or near the STOP line. Queue length is zero if there is no stopped vehicle near the STOP line,
— *Number of vehicles leaving the intersection.* A virtual line located across the given lane is analyzed. Situations are detected when vehicle comes into contact with the line and then leave it. When that occurs, the vehicle counter is increased.
— *Instantaneous speed of vehicles* is computed in a similar way as the vehicle counter: additionally, the position of the vehicle's center of gravity is recorded and used to determine the instantaneous velocity.

These parameters are averaged over a specified time horizon. It is usually a period of a full cycle of traffic lights. Averaged traffic parameters are passed to the database (the *Dynamic Map*) through an interface based on the gsoap package.

The optical flow method, which detects moving objects, was chosen as the basis for detection of vehicles. In the authors' opinion, the advantage of methods based on the calculation of the optical flow against the methods that use background generation [9,15,27] is that the vehicle detection performance is independent from weather conditions and that it is possible to detection vehicles with a color similar to the background. However, the use of optical flow forces requires development of algorithms to track the detected vehicle and remember its position – especially when they are stopped.

A discussion on methods of optical flow calculation has been presented in [11]. Among several tested methods, the Horn-Schunck algorithm was chosen, as it proved to be quite fast and sufficiently accurate. For segmentation, the optical flow modulus was used, which was binarized using a fixed threshold. The algorithm takes the following issues into account: dividing one object into several parts, joining several objects into one and memorizing the temporally stopped objects.

The video detector prototype is running on a computer with a dual-core AMD Athlon II X2 240 (2800 MHz) and 8GB of memory, under Debian GNU/Linux 6.0.5. It analyzes the images coming from two IP cameras (with resulutions of 704x576 and 640x400 pixels) at a speed of about 8 fps. Exemplary results of counting and calculating the velocity of vehicles are presented in Table 1.

Table 1. Results of counting/speed calculation [km/h] averaged over several cycles of traffic lights (about 4.7 [min])

Line	Ground truth	Video detector	error	error [%]
ZV-N	51/33,99	52/41,21	1/7,22	2/21,24
ZV-E	32/38,55	35/36,00	3/-2,55	9/-6,61
ZV-W	33/47,75	33/46,18	0/-1,57	0/-3,29
ZV-S	59/33,17	55/33,13	-4/-0,04	-6/-0,12

The analysis of the recorded movies shows that worse results when counting vehicles on the virtual lines ZV-E are due to the same vehicle being counted twice, which pertains to these being driven near the middle of two-lane road. Quite a big error in speed calculation on lines ZV-N is due to the small size of objects (vehicles), caused by the phenomenon of perspective – see the upper right corner of Figure 1a).

After minor modifications, the video detector can be used to detect accidents, vehicle breakdowns or parking in unauthorized areas.

GPS Tracker. For years, sensors delivering vehicle positioning information, mainly GPS receivers, were used to provide personal route planning services. A typical route planning device is equipped with maps stored in the memory and onboard software, which performs route calculation, tracks the vehicle position and provides instructions for the driver. On the other hand, the growing popularity of smartphones being capable of sending and receiving data over the cellular network has given rise to services in which route calculation is performed at the server side. Moreover, the constant flow of vehicle positioning information can be used for tracking and calculation of traffic parameters (average speed or travel time for individual road segments). Examples of systems which employ such approach are Nericell [18], Mobile Millenium [25], INRIX [13] and Google Maps [12].

All services based on vehicle positioning face the problem of *accuracy*. Sensor readings are affected by noise with gaussian distribution [26]. Hence, the actual vehicle position is expected to be within a circular or elliptical region around the obtained reading, whose diameter is about 10m for GPS sensors, and about 50m for location based on WiFi maps or cellular triangulation. GPS sensors are quite accurate in open areas, but may yield corrupted data in an urban environment due to poor satellite visibility, e.g. when moving in street canyons or under trees along the road [17].

Reliability services such as vehicle tracking or real-time traffic monitoring depends heavily on correct map-matching, i.e. on establishing a vehicle's location on a road segment based on uncertain positioning data. Map-matching algorithms decide which of several candidate road segments should be assumed as the vehicle's location, based on current sensor readings and/or the history containing past data for a given period. More than thirty map-matching algorithms are surveyed by Quddus et. al in [20], including geometric (e.g. point to segment matching), topological (taking into account road segment joins), probabilistic methods (based on confidence region), as well as application of the Kalman filter or fuzzy rules. Other approaches include particle filters or Hidden Markov Models (HMM) [24].

Within the INSIGMA project, we have developed a traffic monitoring subsystem based on vehicle positioning information, called the *GPS tracker*. Two alternative map-matching algorithms were used. The first [10] employs geometric matching of two consecutive sensor readings on map segments. The second algorithm is fairly more complex. It is comprised of three processing steps: data cleansing with a Kalman filter, interpolation to align the data with the map density and, finally, proper map matching by building a sequence of HMM models. The actual vehicle trajectory is represented as the most probable path in a lattice of HMM states. Unlike the algorithm described in [24], our algorithm is incremental, i.e. it may return a certain part of a trajectory on arrival of new data.

The GPS tracker subsystem stores determined vehicle trajectories and analyzes them to calculate such traffic parameters as average speed or travel time for a road segment. Fig. 3 presents the results of speed parameter calculation overlaid on a map of Kraków, Poland. As a limited number of input traces were processed during the test, the results obviously do not cover the entire city area.

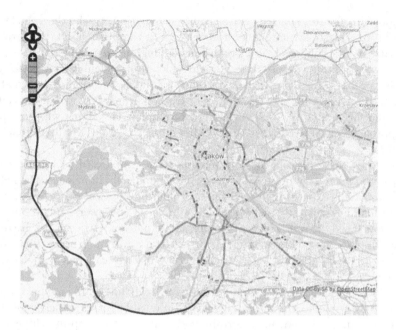

Fig. 3. The map with marked average speed values. Legend: red [0,20); yellow [20,50); green [50,90); blue: [90,∞]. Assumed units: km/h.

3.2 Privacy

In the INSIGMA system, privacy is related to both video and GPS/GLONASS tracking. Each digital image from the camera can contain sensitive data, taking into account the privacy of registered persons or vehicles. Special attention is paid to the protection of images of faces, license plates and other information that can be used to identify identity. On the other hand, the stream of images from video monitoring system should be available for advanced tools, such as automatic traffic analysis, threat detection, and possibly to the authorized operator in an emergency service.

Digital watermarking is a technique that allows for embedding information in digital images. The most common use of these solutions includes the protection of rights to protected material by adding a visible item, such as a logo, in a selected image region. A more sophisticated approach is to modify small, unobtrusive parts of an image, such as a selected set of points scattered throughout the image and visible only in the form of a gentle noise, that encode the required information. That way data within a digital image can be protected.

The INSIGMA system allows for securing access to selected data, as well as some protection against image forgery. It is possible to place a copy of the entire image or its fragments in reduced quality in the watermark. At this point, a distinction between the quality of processing different parts of the image should be made. An important observation is that, in practice, a substantial part of the image containing the sensitive contents (e.g. faces, plates, etc.) is generally contained in a small area of the image. This part requires high-quality reconstruction. In contrast, most of the image is the background that can be encoded with low quality. In the particular case of the INSIGMA system, background can be unencoded at all, while protecting sensitive subject content that is pixelized in the protected image [7]. As a result, third parties do not obtain access to identifiable private data.

In another INSIGMA use case [6], placing a copy of the image in a digital watermark enables its protection against counterfeiting. Unauthorized modification is automatically detected and the original content can be restored.

Another important aspect is privacy of mobile users using devices with GPS/ GLONASS receivers. For this purpose, the information stored in the system does not include user identification data or record its activity. The collection of data is statistical in nature and limited in location, with particular attention given to intersections. Also, the security of communication between the devices and the system is ensured.

With the above assumptions, the INSIGMA system supports the privacy of its users and bystanders.

3.3 Route Planning Services

In the INSIGMA project, several optimization algorithms were proposed, which allow to improve the city traffic using the information from the Dynamic Map. On one hand, it is achieved by route optimization for individual drivers and, on the other hand, by improving the global throughput of a road network. Route optimization in the city is a very difficult problem due to a high variation of travel times. The reason for this is irregularity of vehicle streams moving along the city streets. An unexpected traffic fluctuation can affect significant areas of the road network. It makes the optimal route planning problem very difficult to solve. The problem of vehicles stream control in the city using traffic lights is also a big challenge. Its difficulty arises not only from the computational complexity, but also from the specificity of the subject of control.

Within the INSIGMA project, several approximation algorithms were developed, with a particular emphasis on population algorithms like GA (genetic algorithms) and PSO (Particle Swarm Optimization). Due to the design of these algorithms, they can simultaneously determine a set of alternative routes, in case of an unexpected traffic fluctuation.

Modeling of Uncertainty. It can be assumed that the exact travel times are not known, which closely resembles real-life situations. The unknown (or more precisely, uncertain) travel times are modeled using different approaches, including stochastic modeling, interval arithmetics and the fuzzy set theory. Several algorithms for route planning based on uncertain information were proposed and developed. The efficiency of the proposed algorithms was verified using the real traffic network in the city of Kraków. The experimental research was also conducted using the SUMO space-continuous traffic simulator [14].

Route Planning under Uncertainty. The usefulness of any model largely depends on the accuracy and reliability of its output. Because precise input data is sometimes hard to obtain (e.g. in real-world production planning and scheduling), output values may be subject to imprecision. The main issue in that case is to select a proper representation of uncertain input data and then appropriately propagate those uncertainties throughout computations. When solving many practical problems, fuzzy or interval numbers are often used to model uncertainty, as these methods are simple yes powerful. The interval number represents the level of uncertainty of the travel time on a certain route. If we find a route not affected by travel time changes, we will make a special assumption about the it route. In the discussed approach, a representation of interval number x in the form of the scalar $\breve{x} = f(x, \alpha)$ was proposed. Parameter α describes the confidence level of the average value which well describes the real travel time. Representation of the interval number as a scalar allows us to use the simple and fast *Dijkstra* or A^* search algorithms. For example, if $\alpha = 1$, we do not take the interval width of x under consideration and assume that the average value well describes the real travel time. Otherwise, if $\alpha = 0$, we consider only the interval width of x. In this case, using *Dijkstra* or A^* algorithms leads to finding the path characterized by the minimal range of travel time changes. The main problem is to define the α value. It can be assumed that this value depends on route network properties, day time, size of vehicle streams and some other factors. The value of α can be determined on the basis of simulation tests using a real road network model simulator and information collected by the Dynamic Map. For example (see Fig. 4), for Kraków, the best value of α is between 0.7 and 0.8 (this value depends on the time of day).

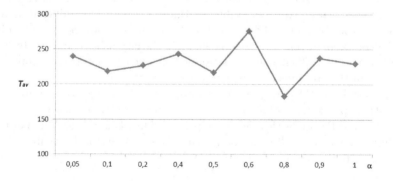

Fig. 4. Dependence the average travel time (T_{av}) and α for 1,000 different paths (repeated 100 times at different time points) in Kraków.

Global Traffic Management under Uncertainty. Thanks to the information from Dynamic Map, the *Route Planning Subsystem* (*RPS*) provides routes for users on the basis of current road network situation. For this purpose, the information (e.g. road travel time, queue length) from many detectors is analysed.

However, parameters originate from various types of detectors, which operate in various conditions. This is the reason for which the supplied parameters are characterized by limited accuracy, resulting from measurement noise.

Developed within the INSIGMA project, the centralized navigation system has an ability to react to the current road situation. In case of the traffic conditions change in a way which affects the previously computed route, a new route based on the current parameter values acquired from the Dynamic Map is calculated and sent to the mobile application installed in vehicles connected to the system.

Due to the constant fluctuation of traffic parameter values (acquired from the sensors, which are characterized measurement errors), it is crucial decide when a new route should be calculated (due to travel time changes) and sent to the user. In case of the RPS, which has been designed to handle several thousands of customers, it is important to implement the methods, which give a fast response to this question. During research, a theory enabling to resolve this problem was developed.

3.4 Traffic Lights Control Solutions

Several approximation and construction algorithms for controlling streams of vehicles using traffic lights were designed, tested and developed. A number of methods for traffic lights control were examined, including cyclic, acyclic, triggered strategies as well as one based on the number of stopped vehicles. The goal of the traffic control subsystem is to determine values of control parameters for changing traffic conditions. The system reacts to the current traffic situation by actions such as changing length of the traffic lights phases or changing the applied optimization algorithm. The decision to recalculate parameters or to change the algorithm is made when the quality of control decreases (i.e., the difference between the predicted and the observed traffic state is increased). In case of significant changes of traffic conditions, the optimization algorithm may

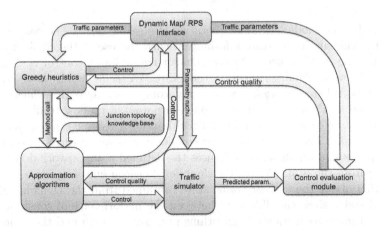

Fig. 5. Traffic control system architecture

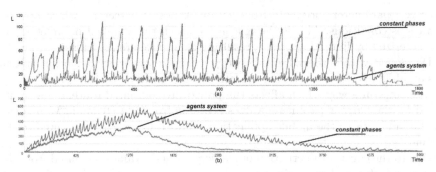

Fig. 6. Summary length of the vehicle queues waiting to pass the junction (L) in the subsequent intervals of time for the constant phases (red line) and the agents system (blue line); (a) – medium traffic, (b) – intense traffic

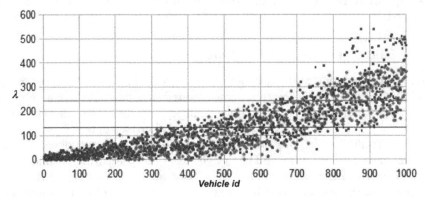

Fig. 7. The relation of drive and stop time for 1000 vehicles (λ) for the constant phases of the traffic lights (black points) and the phases calculated by SA algorithm (gray points)

be changed. Such mode of system operation is possible due to the constant access to the current traffic state information with the use of the efficient traffic simulator. The architecture of the system for traffic lights control is shown in Figure 5. Below, the main elements of the INSIGMA traffic lights control system are presented, where *Greedy heuristics* – low-complexity heuristics which enable dynamic and local control of traffic lights – are used in the low traffic case and *Approximation algorithms* are a set of algorithms designed and developed for use in intense traffic. The *Traffic simulator* enables evaluation of the solution found by the approximation algorithms. It uses the detailed road network description (obtained from the Static Map), the *Junction topology knowledge base* and the information about the current traffic state (obtained from the Dynamic Map). Figures 6 and 7 show the difference between the performance of constant light phases and more sophisticated algorithms (an agent system and the simulated annealing algorithm SA) used to control 30 junctions.

4 Conclusions

From a variety of functions which can be provided by an ITS (c.f. Section 2), the system developed within the INSIGMA project supports: *traveler information*, including route planning, on-trip traffic information and route guidance, as well as *traffic management* (transportation planning and traffic control). The key concept within the system is the Dynamic Map, which integrates the description of a road network with dynamically-changing traffic information. Traffic parameters are currently delivered by two types of sensors: video detector and GPS tracker. However, the design of the system is flexible enough to integrate almost any type of sensor. One important issue related to data collection is privacy protection and security. This aspect was addressed during the system design. Within the project, advanced algorithms for dynamic route planning and traffic control have been developed. It is expected that their application in real life will significantly improve mobility and environmental performance.

References

1. INSIGMA project, `http://insigma.kt.agh.edu.pl` (last accessed: March 2014)
2. Intelligent transport system,
   `http://ec.europa.eu/transport/themes/its/index_en.htm`   (last   accessed:
   March 2014)
3. RITA intelligent transportation systems. `http://www.its.dot.gov` (last accessed:
   March 2014)
4. An, S.H., Lee, B.H., Shin, D.R.: A survey of intelligent transportation systems. In:
   2011 Third International Conference on Computational Intelligence, Communication Systems and Networks (CICSyN), pp. 332–337. IEEE (2011)
5. Deloitte Research: Combating gridlock: how pricing road use can easy congestion
   (2003)
6. Dziech, A., Bialas, J., Glowacz, A., Leszczuk, M., Matiolanski, A., Baran, R.:
   Overview of recent advances in CCTV processing chain in the INDECT and INSIGMA projects. In: Proceedings of the International Conference on Availability, Reliability and Security, pp. 836–843. IEEE CPS, Regensburg (2013)
7. Dziech, A., Glowacz, A., Korus, P., Szmuc, W.: Method and system for restricting
   access to sensitive contents of digital images (2012), Patent App. 13/524,609
8. Fabiano, B., Curro, F., Reverberi, A.P., Pastorino, R.: Dangerous good transportation by road: from risk analysis to emergency planning. Journal of Loss Prevention
   in the Process Industries 18, 403–413 (2005)
9. Gaborski, R.S., Paskali, J.: A cognitively motivated video detection system. Journal
   of Applied Science and Engineering Technology 1(1), 51–57 (2007)
10. Gleba, K., Caban, P., Wiacek, H., Kantyka, G.: The concept of gpstracker for
    intelligent system for global monitoring detection and identification of threats (insigma). In: Military Communications and Information Systems Conference (MCC),
    pp. 1–6 (October 2013)
11. Głowacz, A., Mikrut, Z., Pawlik, P.: Video detection algorithm using an optical
    flow calculation method. In: Dziech, A., Czyżewski, A. (eds.) MCSS 2012. CCIS,
    vol. 287, pp. 118–129. Springer, Heidelberg (2012)

12. Google Official Blog: The bright side of sitting in traffic: Crowdsourcing road congestion data, http://googleblog.blogspot.com/2009/08/bright-side-of-sitting-in-traffic.html (online: last accessed: December 2013)
13. INRIX: Inrix home page, http://www.inrix.com/default.asp (online: last accessed: December 2013)
14. Krajzewicz, D., Erdmann, J., Behrisch, M., Bieker, L.: Recent development and applications of SUMO - Simulation of Urban MObility. International Journal on Advances in Systems and Measurements 5(3&4), 128–138 (2012)
15. Li, Q., Dang, H., Zhang, Y., Wu, D.: Video vehicle detection and tracking system. In: Zhou, M., Tan, H. (eds.) CSE 2011, Part II. CCIS, vol. 202, pp. 24–31. Springer, Heidelberg (2011)
16. McQueen, B., McQueen, J.: Intelligent transportation systems architectures. Artech House Publishers, Norwood (1999)
17. Modsching, M., Kramer, R., ten Hagen, K.: Field trial on GPS accuracy in a medium size city: The influence of built-up. In: 3rd Workshop on Positioning, Navigation and Communication, pp. 209–218 (2006)
18. Mohan, P., Padmanabhan, V.N., Ramjee, R.: Nericell: rich monitoring of road and traffic conditions using mobile smartphones. In: Proceedings of the 6th ACM Conference on Embedded Network Sensor Systems, pp. 323–336. ACM (2008)
19. Nathanail, E.G., Zaharis, S., Vagiokas, N., Prevedouros, P.D.: Risk assessment for transportation of hazardous materials through tunnels. Transportation Research Record 2162, 98–106 (2010)
20. Quddus, M.A., Ochieng, W.Y., Noland, R.B.: Current map-matching algorithms for transport applications: State-of-the art and future research directions. Transportation Research Part C: Emerging Technologies 15(5), 312–328 (2007)
21. Research and Innovative Technology Administration (RITA) : Intelligent transportation systems (ITS). http://www.its.dot.gov/ (online: last accessed: February 2014)
22. Ronchia, E., Colonnaa, P., Capoteb, J., Alvearb, D., Berlocoa, N., Cuestab, A.: The evaluation of different evacuation models for assessing road tunnel safety analysis. Tunnelling and Underground Space Technology 30, 74–84 (2012)
23. Szwed, P., Kadluczka, P., Chmiel, W., Glowacz, A., Sliwa, J.: Ontology based integration and decision support in the insigma route planning subsystem. In: Ganzha, M., Maciaszek, L.A., Paprzycki, M. (eds.) FedCSIS, pp. 141–148 (2012)
24. Thiagarajan, A., Ravindranath, L., LaCurts, K., Madden, S., Balakrishnan, H., Toledo, S., Eriksson, J.: Vtrack: accurate, energy-aware road traffic delay estimation using mobile phones. In: Proceedings of the 7th ACM Conference on Embedded Networked Sensor Systems, pp. 85–98. ACM (2009)
25. University of California, Berkeley: Mobile millenium project, http://traffic.berkeley.edu/ (online: last accessed: December 2013)
26. Van Diggelen, F.: GNSS accuracy: Lies, damn lies, and statistics. GPS World 0107, 26–32 (January 2007)
27. Wang, Y., Zou, Y., Shi, H., Zhao, H.: Video image vehicle detection system for signaled traffic intersection. In: HIS - Ninth International Conference on Hybrid Intelligent Systems, pp. 222–227. IEEE CS Press (2009)
28. Ward's Automotive Group: Vehicles in operation by country (2010)
29. Wojnicki, I., Szwed, P., Chmiel, W., Ernst, S.: Ontology oriented storage, retrieval and interpretation for a dynamic map system. In: Dziech, A., Czyżewski, A. (eds.) MCSS 2012. CCIS, vol. 287, pp. 380–391. Springer, Heidelberg (2012)

Practical Application of Near Duplicate Detection for Image Database

Adi Eshkol[1], Michał Grega[2], Mikołaj Leszczuk[2], and Ofer Weintraub[1]

[1] Orca Interactive, 22 Zarhin Street, Ra'anana 43662, Israel
[2] AGH University of Science and Technology, al. Mickiewicza 30, PL-30059 Krakow, Poland
grega@kt.agh.edu.pl

Abstract. Traditional program guides, TV applications, and online portals alone are no longer sufficient to expose all content, let alone offer the content that consumers want, at the times they are most likely to want it. DEEP, (Data Enrichment and Engagement Platform) by Orca Interactive, a comprehensive new content discovery solution, combines search, recommendation, and second-screen devices into a single immersive experience which invites exploration. The automated generation (using internet sources) of digital magazines for movies, TV shows, cast members and topics is a key value of DEEP. Unfortunately, using the internet as a source for pictures can result in the acquisition of so-called "Near Duplicate" (ND) images – similar images from a specific display context - for example, multiple red carpet images showing an actor from very similar angles or degrees of zoom on him/her. Therefore, in this paper we present a practical application of ND detection for image databases. The algorithm used is based on the MPEG-7 Colour Structure descriptor. For images that were provided by the developers of the DEEP software the algorithm performs very well, and the results are almost identical to those obtained during the training phase.

Keywords: Image Descriptors, Scalable Colour, Near Duplicates, Query by Example, QbE, MPEG-7.

1 Introduction

Traditional program guides, TV applications, and on-line portals alone are no longer sufficient to expose all content, let alone offer the content that consumers want, at the times when they are most likely to want it [18].

DEEP (Data Enrichment and Engagement Platform), by Orca Interactive, a comprehensive new content discovery solution, combines search, recommendation and second-screen devices into a single immersive experience which invites exploration. Using a combination of sophisticated discovery and recommendation technologies and an innovative digital magazine format, it presents consumers with an endless variety of personalized TV and Web content. This modular Orca Interactive solution also creates exciting new kinds of revenue opportunities for content service providers. The automated generation of digital magazines for movies, TV shows, cast members and topics is a key value of DEEP. Orca Interactive recently proved this capability as part of a trial of DEEP with a large broadcast network in the U.S. In the course of this trial, Orca

A. Dziech and A. Czyżewski (Eds.): MCSS 2014, CCIS 429, pp. 73–82, 2014.
© Springer International Publishing Switzerland 2014

Interactive received around 100 movies and TV shows with basic metadata as part of a certain broadcast channel. Within 24 hours, DEEP had generated a thousand different magazines for TV shows, movies, actors, article topics, and more, all completely automatically. Search and recommendation can be made more valuable by using sources beyond the traditional structured forms of metadata used by providers today. The internet is host to a wealth of unstructured information which can also be evaluated, all the way from movie reviews and the opinions of other consumers, to information about a movie setting as a tourist destination, to red carpet pictures of public figures and celebrities [18]. Unfortunately, using the Internet as a source of pictures can result in the acquisition of so-called "Near Duplicate"1 (ND) images – similar pictures from a specific display context, for example multiple red carpet images which show an actor from very similar angles or degrees of zoom on him/her (see Fig. 1).

Fig. 1. ND images

In this paper, we present a practical application of ND detection for image databases. We focus on a specific type of images – so called red carpet photos. Such images are taken usually during public events, when the celebrities enter or exit the event. Such type of photos was used according to the requirements of the industrial partner.

The remainder of this paper is structured as follows. Section 2 presents the state of the art for ND detection of images and discusses how much our work differs from that of others. Section 3 ddescribes the algorithm and the results. The paper is concluded and future work is drafted in Section 4.

2   State of the Art for Near Duplicate Detection of Images

ND detection applications can be divided into those for general use and those dedicated to specific content and/or context. Those for general purpose are usually not as accurate as those for specific purposes, which again rarely check outside a dedicated range of applicability. Table 1 shows the most commonly used contents/contexts, applications and databases used for training and testing.

Table 1. Overview of existing ND detection applications (based on: [10])

Content/Context	Application	Database
Frames of news videos	[1,2,5,19,23,25,27]	"TRECVID" [17]
Frames of various videos	[24,26]	"MUSCLE VCD" [8]
Images of various objects and people	[3,4,11,21]	"Google Image"s
Personal holiday photos	[22,26]	"INRIA Copydays" [9]
Images of landmarks	[11,22]	"Oxford buildings" [15]
Brand logos	[12]	"Internet partial-duplicate" [20]
Images of various objects	[22]	"UKbench" [14]
Various images	[3,5]	"Corel Photo CD"

Because we did not find a dedicated solution for red carpet pictures, we decided to create our own.

3   The Algorithm and the Results

In this section, we provide a description of test sets used in the experiment. We describe the algorithm and its training phase. We also provide and discuss the results of algorithm verification on two distinctive test sets.

3.1   The Test Sets

We tested the proposed algorithm on three test sets. The first consisted of 38 photographs. These photographs were accepted by the user as good examples of content to be processed by the system. This test set was used to train the algorithm. The second test set was hand-picked by the user. It consisted of 42 photographs. This set was used for verification of the algorithm. For both test sets, we manually created a ground truth. For each pair of photographs, we made a decision whether it was similar to any other image or not. This ground truth was stored in a correlation matrix. Such a matrix contains binary values which denote whether the images are similar (binary 1) or not similar (binary 0) to each other.

If we denote $A = a_{ij}$ as a correlation matrix than a_{ij} denotes similarity between ith and jth image. $a_{ij} = 0$ means, that the images i and j are not similar and $a_{ij} = 1$ means, that the images i and j are similar. Correlation matrices have always 1 on the main diagonal (as each image is similar to itself) and are symmetric as $a_{ij} = a_{ji}$.

As an additional test, we used the CaliforniaND database [10], which provides both 701 images and correlation matrices. All three test sets are presented in Figure 2.

What distinguishes the first two sets from the third is that we observed that the duplicate images our algorithm would work with were either very similar images coming from the same photographic session, or close-ups (crops) of images. By comparison, the duplicate images in the CaliforniaND test set are commonly less visually and more contextually similar.

Fig. 2. Databases used for training and testing the algorithm

3.2 The Algorithm

The algorithm used is based on the MPEG-7 Colour Structure descriptor [13]. During the algorithm training phase we considered two descriptors — Edge Histogram and Colour Structure. We have decided to test those descriptors as our previous research has proven, that these provide the best results for all of the visual descriptors in the MPEG-7 set for Near Duplicate detection [6]. We have also applied them for other multimedia services and obtained satisfactory results [7].

The algorithm is straightforward. We calculate the values p and q of the descriptor for a pair of images. We use a 256-value descriptor length ($n = 256$). Then we compare the obtained descriptors using the L_1 distance (Equation 1) (also referred to as the Manhattan distance [16]) and obtain the d_1 distance value. We use this specific metric as it is recommended in literature by the standards' authors [13]. Finally, we compare the distance value with a threshold t. The value of t was obtained during the training phase of the algorithm. If $d_1 > t$ we consider the images to be different. Otherwise we consider them to be similar.

$$d_1(\mathbf{p}, \mathbf{q}) = \|\mathbf{p} - \mathbf{q}\|_1 = \sum_{i=1}^{n} |p_i - q_i| \tag{1}$$

3.3 Algorithm Training

To train the algorithm, we performed experiments for two descriptors (Colour Structure, CSD and Edge Histogram, EH). For these descriptors we tested a set of hypothetical t values ranging from 1 to 5000 (for CSD) and 1 to 400 (for EHD).

We also tested three approaches for image comparison. In the first approach, we compared full images. In the second, we compared the full first image to selected areas of the second image. The method of dividing the image is presented in Figure 3. In this approach we have obtained five distances ($d_{1A} \ldots d_{1E}$). In the third approach we compared only the middle part of an image (denoted ans E in Figure 3) to a whole image. We expected the latter two approaches to capture crops of images.

The results for the algorithm training are presented in Table 2. TP denotes the number of True Positives (similar images recognised as similar), FP denotes the number of False Positives (similar images recognised as not similar), TN denotes the number of true negatives (not similar images recognised as not similar) and FN denotes the number of False Negatives (not similar images recognised as similar). Precision, Sensitivity, Specificity and F-measure are calculated using the standard formulas for binary classification problems.

Table 2. Experiment results for algorithm training

	TP	FP	TN	FN	Precision	Sensitivity	Specificity	F-measure
Experiment 1	42	7	671	2	0.85	0.95	0.98	0.90
Experiment 2	38	11	666	7	0.77	0.84	0.98	0.80
Experiment 3	254	285	7316	85	0.47	0.74	0.96	0.58
Experiment 4	117	442	7089	314	0.22	0.27	0.94	0.24
Experiment 5	89	58	2011	8	0.60	0.92	0.97	0.73
Experiment 6	54	93	1974	45	0.37	0.54	0.95	0.44

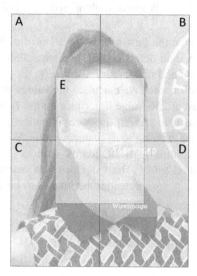

Fig. 3. Method of image division

Experiment 1 provided the best result (meaning the best-performing hypothesis for t) for comparing whole images using the CSD descriptor. Experiment 2 provided the best result (meaning the best-performing hypothesis for t) for comparing whole images using the EHD descriptor. Experiment 3 provided the best result for comparing divided images using the CSD descriptor. The overall number of samples is larger, as each image was divided into five parts. Experiment 4 provided the best result for comparing divided images using the EHD descriptor. As in the previous case, the overall number of samples is larger, as each image was divided into five parts. Experiment 5 provided the best result for comparing part E of the image with a whole image using the CSD descriptor. Experiment 6 provided the best result for comparing part E of the image with a whole image using the EHD descriptor.

As we can see, Experiment 1 obtained the best results overall, and its methodology and value of t was chosen for further verification and implementation.

3.4 Verification

For verification, we used a verification test set consisting of 42 photographs. Photographs in this test set were hand-picked by the developers of the DEEP software and represent the type of photographs which will be processed by the system. We used the descriptor and the value of t as selected from Experiment 1 of the training phase. Results of the verification using this test set are presented in Table 3.

We also validated the algorithm on the CaliforniaND test set, which consists of 701 natural images. Results for the CaliforniaND test set are presented in Table 4.

The CaliforniaND test set provides 10 different correlation matrices, one for each of the test subjects who assessed the similarity of images [10]. Table 4 pprovides the results for each of the matrices and the test subjects, as well as the average and median for the experiment.

Table 3. Results for verification using DEEP images

	TP	FP	TN	FN	Precision	Sensitivity	Specificity	F-measure
Value	53	8	836	6	0.87	0.90	0.99	0.88

Table 4. Results for the CaliforniaND test set

	TP	FP	TN	FN	Precision	Sensitivity	Specificity	F-measure
subject 0	2689	1942	240637	783	0.58	0.77	0.99	0.66
subject 1	2828	1803	240499	921	0.61	0.75	0.99	0.67
subject 2	2192	2439	241091	329	0.47	0.87	0.99	0.61
subject 3	1869	2762	241089	331	0.40	0.85	0.99	0.55
subject 4	2616	2015	240920	500	0.56	0.84	0.99	0.68
subject 5	2648	1983	240830	590	0.57	0.82	0.99	0.67
subject 6	2269	2362	240875	545	0.49	0.81	0.99	0.61
subject 7	2337	2294	241004	416	0.50	0.85	0.99	0.63
subject 8	2713	1918	240692	728	0.59	0.79	0.99	0.67
subject 9	3049	1582	239528	1892	0.66	0.62	0.99	0.64
Average	2521	2110	240717	704	0.54	0.80	0.99	0.64
Median	2616	2015	240830	590	0.56	0.81	0.99	0.64

3.5 Experiment Summary

In the first part of the experiment, we tested several approaches to the problem of near duplicate removal. We selected the best-performing, the Colour Structure descriptor, for comparing whole images. We also chose a value of t.

In the second part of the experiment, we, tested the algorithm. For images which were provided by the developers of the DEEP software, the algorithm performs very well, and the results are almost identical to those obtained during the training phase.

For the test performed on the external test set the results are much worse. The chosen value of t has made the algorithm over specific for this kind of content. What has to be noted, is that there is no formal definition of near duplicate images.

For the test performed on the external test set, the results are much worse. The chosen value of t has made the algorithm over–specific for this kind of content. It should be noted is that there is no formal definition of near duplicate images.

When comes to performance assessment, we did not take exact measurements. This is for two reasons. Firstly, at the time of experiments we did not have access to the production environment of the industrial partner. Secondly, the ND detection algorithm is not expected to be a time critical application nor to work in real time. From the authors' experience the time of analysis of a single image is proportional to the resolution in pixels and takes up to a second for full-HD images.

Two general conclusions may be drawn from our research. First, images which are processed for the DEEP software have to be very visually similar in order to be considered as near duplicates. This is unlike the near duplicates in the CaliforniaND test set, where contextual similarity is enough to consider a pair of images similar. The second general conclusion is that each near duplicate removal algorithm has to be trained in the context of the specific task it has to perform.

4   Conclusions and Future Work

In this paper, we present a practical application of ND detection for image databases. For images which were provided by the developers of the DEEP software, the algorithm performs very well and the results are almost identical to those obtained during the training phase. Nevertheless, the ND removal algorithm has to be trained in the context of the specific task it has to perform.

In future, we want to further investigate the approach in which we compare a full first image to selected areas of the second image, as we expect this approach to better capture crops of images. We also plan to investigate possibility of taking into account multiple MPEG-7 features.

Acknowledgements. The work was co-financed by The Polish National Centre for Research and Development (NCBR), as a part of the EUREKA Project IMCOP no. E! II/PL-IL/10/01A/2012.

References

1. Chum, O., Philbin, J., Zisserman, A.: Near duplicate image detection: min-hash and tf-idf weighting. In: British Machine Vision Conference (2008)
2. Chum, O., Philbin, J., Isard, M., Zisserman, A.: Scalable near identical image and shot detection. In: Proceedings of the 6th ACM International Conference on Image and Video Retrieval, CIVR 2007, pp. 549–556. ACM, New York (2007), http://doi.acm.org/10.1145/1282280.1282359
3. Foo, J.J., et al.: Clustering near-duplicate images in large collections (2007)
4. Foo, J.J., Sinha, R., Zobel, J.: Sico: A system for detection of near-duplicate images during search. In: 2007 IEEE International Conference on Multimedia and Expo, pp. 595–598 (July 2007)
5. Foo, J.J., Sinha, R.: Using redundant bit vectors for near-duplicate image detection. In: Kotagiri, R., Radha Krishna, P., Mohania, M., Nantajeewarawat, E. (eds.) DASFAA 2007. LNCS, vol. 4443, pp. 472–484. Springer, Heidelberg (2007), http://dx.doi.org/10.1007/978-3-540-71703-4_41
6. Fraczek, R., Grega, M., Liebau, N., Leszczuk, M., Luedtke, A., Janowski, L., Papir, Z.: Ground-truth-less comparison of selected content-based image retrieval measures. In: Daras, P., Ibarra, O.M. (eds.) UCMedia 2009. LNICST, vol. 40, pp. 101–108. Springer, Heidelberg (2010), http://dblp.uni-trier.de/db/conf/ucmedia/ucmedia2009.html#FraczekGLLLJP09
7. Grega, M., Łach, S.: Urban photograph localization using the instreet application – accuracy and performance analysis. Multimedia Tools and Applications pp. 1–12 (2013), http://dx.doi.org/10.1007/s11042-013-1538-1
8. INRIA: Video copy detection evaluation showcase (2007), https://www.rocq.inria.fr/imedia/civr-bench/data.html

9. Jegou, H., Douze, M., Schmid, C.: Hamming embedding and weak geometric consistency for large scale image search. In: Forsyth, D., Torr, P., Zisserman, A. (eds.) ECCV 2008, Part I. LNCS, vol. 5302, pp. 304–317. Springer, Heidelberg (2008), http://dx.doi.org/10.1007/978-3-540-88682-2_24

10. Jinda-Apiraksa, A., Vonikakis, V., Winkler, S.: California-nd: An annotated dataset for near-duplicate detection in personal photo collections. In: Burnett, I.S. (ed.) QoMEX, pp. 142–147. IEEE (2013)

11. Lee, D.C., Ke, Q., Isard, M.: Partition min-hash for partial duplicate image discovery. In: Daniilidis, K., Maragos, P., Paragios, N. (eds.) ECCV 2010, Part I. LNCS, vol. 6311, pp. 648–662. Springer, Heidelberg (2010), http://dl.acm.org/citation.cfm?id=1886063.1886113

12. Li, L., Wu, Z., Zha, Z.J., Jiang, S., Huang, Q.: Matching content-based saliency regions for partial-duplicate image retrieval. In: 2011 IEEE International Conference on Multimedia and Expo (ICME), pp. 1–6 (July 2011)

13. Manjunath, B., Salembier, P., Sikora, T.: Introduction to MPEG-7: multimedia content description interface. John Wiley & Sons Inc. (2002)

14. Nister, D., Stewenius, H.: Scalable recognition with a vocabulary tree. In: Proceedings of the 2006 IEEE Computer Society Conference on Computer Vision and Pattern Recognition, CVPR 2006, vol. 2, pp. 2161–2168. IEEE Computer Society, Washington, DC (2006), http://dx.doi.org/10.1109/CVPR.2006.264

15. Philbin, J., Chum, O., Isard, M., Sivic, J., Zisserman, A.: Object retrieval with large vocabularies and fast spatial matching. In: Proceedings of the IEEE Conference on Computer Vision and Pattern Recognition (2007)

16. Reinhardt, C.: Taxi cab geometry: History and applications

17. Smeaton, A.F., Kraaij, W., Over, P.: The TREC VIDeo retrieval evaluation (TRECVID): A case study and status report. In: Proceedings of RIAO 2004 (2004)

18. Viaccess-Orca: Going deep into discovery. Tech. rep., Viaccess-Orca (2013), http://www.viaccess-orca.com/resource-center/white-papers/462-going-deep-into-discovery.html

19. Wang, Y., Hou, Z., Leman, K.: Keypoint-based near-duplicate images detection using affine invariant feature and color matching. In: 2011 IEEE International Conference on Acoustics, Speech and Signal Processing (ICASSP), pp. 1209–1212 (May 2011)

20. Wu, Z., Xu, Q., Jiang, S., Huang, Q., Cui, P., Li, L.: Adding affine invariant geometric constraint for partial-duplicate image retrieval. In: 2010 20th International Conference on Pattern Recognition (ICPR), pp. 842–845 (August 2010)

21. Wu, Z., Ke, Q., Isard, M., Sun, J.: Bundling features for large scale partial-duplicate web image search. In: IEEE Conference on Computer Vision and Pattern Recognition, CVPR 2009, pp. 25–32 (June 2009)

22. Xie, H., Gao, K., Zhang, Y., Tang, S., Li, J., Liu, Y.: Efficient feature detection and effective post-verification for large scale near-duplicate image search. IEEE Transactions on Multimedia 13(6), 1319–1332 (2011)

23. Xu, D., Cham, T.J., Yan, S., Duan, L., Chang, S.F.: Near duplicate identification with spatially aligned pyramid matching. IEEE Transactions on Circuits and Systems for Video Technology 20(8), 1068–1079 (2010)

24. Yang, X., Zhu, Q., Cheng, K.T.: Near-duplicate detection for images and videos. In: Proceedings of the First ACM Workshop on Large-scale Multimedia Retrieval and Mining, LS-MMRM 2009, pp. 73–80. ACM, New York (2009), http://doi.acm.org/10.1145/1631058.1631073

25. Zhang, D.Q., Chang, S.F.: Detecting image near-duplicate by stochastic attributed relational graph matching with learning. In: Proceedings of the 12th Annual ACM International Conference on Multimedia, MULTIMEDIA 2004, pp. 877–884. ACM, New York (2004), http://doi.acm.org/10.1145/1027527.1027730
26. Zheng, L., Qiu, G., Huang, J., Fu, H.: Salient covariance for near-duplicate image and video detection. In: 2011 18th IEEE International Conference on Image Processing (ICIP), pp. 2537–2540 (September 2011)
27. Zhu, J., Hoi, S.C.H., Lyu, M.R., Yan, S.: Near-duplicate keyframe retrieval by semi-supervised learning and nonrigid image matching. ACM Trans. Multimedia Comput. Commun. Appl. 7(1), 4:1–4:24 (2011), http://doi.acm.org/10.1145/1870121.1870125

RSSI-Based Real-Time Indoor Positioning Using ZigBee Technology for Security Applications

Anna Heinemann, Alexandros Gavriilidis, Thomas Sablik,
Carsten Stahlschmidt, Jörg Velten, and Anton Kummert

Bergische Universität Wuppertal
42097 Wuppertal, Germany
{heinemann,gavriilidis,sablik,stahlschmidt,
velten,kummert}@uni-wuppertal.de

Abstract. Localization in indoor environments is an important aspect with regard to mobile security applications. Because here, the global positioning system (GPS) is not available or very imprecise, other positioning systems are required. For that matter wireless sensor networks provide two common approaches based on received signal strength indicators (RSSI). The first one uses fingerprints and the second is based on trilateration. Because fingerprinting needs a lot of training and (re-)calibration, this paper presents a new indoor positioning system based on RSSIs and trilateration using ZigBee technology. Since RSSI measurements are very susceptible to noise, the gathered RSSIs have to be preprocessed before they can be used for position calculations. For this reason, the RSSIs were averaged using time-dependent weights and smoothed over time so that outliers and old RSSIs can be eliminated. The presented indoor positioning system was verified by experiments.

Keywords: Indoor Positioning, ZigBee, RSSI based Position Estimation, Trilateration.

1 Introduction

Localization is an important aspect regarding mobile security applications. It enables to determine the location of the security guards at a public building, an airport, a mall or a large industrial plant and to coordinate their operation. Also, it could allow to determine the position of a missing person and therefore, it would be possible to search more efficiently. This could make operations of security forces or firefighters less dangerous and could allow victims/missing persons to get help faster.

For almost all outdoor positioning applications, the Global Positioning System (GPS) can be used for localization. Within a building, however, GPS is usually not available or very imprecise. Therefore, other positioning systems have to be used.

In this paper the focus is on an indoor positioning system (IPS) based on received signal strength indicators (RSSIs) using ZigBee technology. Stationary

A. Dziech and A. Czyżewski (Eds.): MCSS 2014, CCIS 429, pp. 83–95, 2014.

receiver nodes (called: anchors) are deployed at known positions inside a room. Mobile transmitter nodes (called: tag) do not know their current two-dimensional position, but are able to send a signal to the anchors. Using RSSIs at at least three anchors, it is possible to calculate the two-dimensional position of a tag, wherein the influence of the third dimension (height) is omitted. Some related or other procedures are briefly introduced in the next subsection.

1.1   Related Work

Range-based IPSs in wireless sensor networks (WSNs) can use four different kinds of measurements to calculate the position of a mobile node [5,10,11,17,21]. If a strict time synchronization is possible, then the time-of-arrival (TOA) or the time-difference-of-arrival (TDOA) can be used to calculate the position of a tag. However, time synchronization between each and every node (stationary and mobile) is difficult to implement and cost intensive. Another technique uses the angle-of-arrival (AOA). In order to measure the AOA each receiver needs additional hardware. In contrast, measuring RSSIs does not need additional hardware and is less cost intensive than time synchronization. Therefore, the focus of this paper is on RSSI-based IPSs.

There are two techniques that can be used to realize a RSSI-based IPS. First, so called fingerprints can be used to estimate the position of a tag. A fingerprint is a vector or set of RSSIs that belongs to a specific location [15, 19]. Comparing eleven different area- and point-based fingerprinting algorithms, [15] gives a brief overview about several fingerprinting techniques. The nearest neighbor method or nearest neighborhood estimation model (NN) represents another localization algorithm based on fingerprinting not mentioned in [15], but presented in [16,17]. [18] describes a learning algorithm based on expectation-maximization, which enables the IPS to be aware of changes in the environment. In [19] another algorithm is presented, which is aware of environmental changes, but using interval trees and signal strength clustering. [20] introduces a method called *received signal strength distribution modeling using the mirror-image method* (RDMMI), which considers reflective waves. Second technique using RSSIs enables to calculate the distance between a transmitter and a receive. Because fingerprinting needs a lot of training and recalibration, this paper focuses on the second technique. There have been several researches on this type of RSSI-based IPSs. In [10] adaptive filters are used to improve localization results, whereas in [11] an approach with tags that are able to adjust their transmission power was presented. The usage of two transmitting antennas per tag to improve position calculation was presented in [12]. In [13] and [14] calibration free methods were introduced. In [21] the indoor positioning algorithm is improved by means of neural networks.

All RSSI-based positioning algorithms can be used in any wireless network as long as the environmental effects on the signal propagation are comparable [15].

1.2   Organization of the Paper

The Paper has eight sections and is organized as follows. Section 2 describes different effects the environment has on the signal propagation. Section 3 introduces the path loss model used in this paper. Section 4 presents the used averaging and smoothing algorithms. Section 5 describes the technique of trilateration. Section 6 discusses the developed IPS. Section 7 shows the experimental setup as well as the results obtained during the experiments. The last Section 8 concludes the paper.

2   Influences on RSSI

Developing a RSSI-based (indoor) positioning system, it is challenging to find a precise relation between the measured RSSI and the distance between an anchor and a tag [18]. The reason is that the relation between distance and RSSI is non-linear, but is subject to path loss, multipath (or small-scale) fading and shadowing [9]. A signal propagating in space loses power on its way from its tag to an anchor, this is due to effects of the propagation channel and dissipation of the tag's radiated power. This effect is known as path loss. Multipath or small-scale fading occurs when a signal gets reflected multiple times and diffused into many directions by an obstacle [23]. Each reflected or diffused signal undergoes further attenuation, delay, phase shift or distortion, which results in an altered RSSI. Obstacles attenuate a signal not only by scattering, but also by absorption, reflection and diffraction. Which effects the RSSI of a signal as well as path loss and fading. In [23] Karl and Willig also mention Doppler fading as another phenomenon that may distort signals. Doppler fading describes the shift in frequency if tag and anchor move relative to each other.

In [8] a fixed breakpoint b, which subdivides the area of propagation into near and far regions each with their own path loss exponent (PLE), is introduced. This model is a so called two-slope model. b is defined as

$$b = \frac{2\pi h_b h_m}{\lambda}, \tag{1}$$

where λ is the wavelength, h_b represents the height of the anchor and h_m represents the height of the tag. Using ZigBee hardware with frequency $f = 2.4GHz$ and assuming h_b and h_m to be $h_b = h_m = 1.25m$, b results into $b = 78.6m$. If it is ensured that at least three anchors are placed within a quadrangular area with a diagonal length of b, the one-slope model is sufficient for describing the PLE. the distances between anchors are smaller than b the one-slope model is sufficient to describe the PLE.

Besides the distinction between near and far field it must also be considered that walls and floors have influence on the power level of each signal passing through. In [5–7] the wall attenuation factor (WAF) is used in the propagation models. To simplify the propagation models, the floor attenuation factor (FAF) was excluded. Both factors can be calculated by summing up the attenuation factors of each wall (for WAF) or floor (for FAF) the signal passes through. For the indoor positioning system presented in this paper it is assumed that the loss due to walls is big enough to result in very small RSSIs if a signal from a tag in one room reaches an anchor in another room or at another floor. Furthermore it is assumed that at least three anchors in the same room as the tag will receive higher RSSIs as an anchor anywhere outside the room.

3   Log-Distance Path Loss Model

The mathematical link between the measured RSSI R_{ij} at an anchor j and the distance d_{ij} between this anchor j and the respective tag i of the signal is given by [1] with

$$R_{ij} = R_{ij}^0 - 10\eta_{ij} \log_{10}(d_{ij}) \tag{2}$$

where R_{ij}^0 represents the RSSI at an 1m obstacle free distance from tag i on line of sight (LOS) to a possible anchor j and η_{ij} represents the PLE between tag i and anchor j, with $i \neq j$. (2) is known as *log-distance path loss model*.

According to Shou et al [2] (2) is due to

$$R_R = \frac{R_T}{d^\eta} \tag{3}$$

where R_R is the received and R_T the transmitted power level. Note that in [2] and some other sources (due to definition) R_{ij}^0 has a negative sign.

Rearranging (2) gives two significant equations

$$\eta_{ij} = \frac{R_{ij} - R_{ij}^0}{-10\log_{10}(d_{ij})}, \tag{4}$$

$$d_{ij} = 10^{\frac{R_{ij} - R_{ij}^0}{-10\eta_{ij}}}. \tag{5}$$

(4) enables to calculate η_{ij}, if d_{ij} and R_{ij}^0 are known. Experiments suggest that this parameter is likely to change a lot in dependence of the position within a given room. Therefore, it should be calculated between each pair of anchors.

(5) enables to calculate the distance d_{ij} between a tag i and an anchor j on bases of η_{ij} and R_{ij}.

4   Averaging and Smoothing of RSSIs

Since the RSSI measurement is very susceptible to noise, it is useful to average and to smooth gathered RSSIs before further processing. Zhang et al present both aspects in [4]. This idea was adopted and adapted to fit the requirements of this paper. For calculating the average of the last RSSIs the weighted coefficients method is used. Zhang et al imposed the conditions that for all w_k

$$w_1 + w_2 + \cdots + w_n = 1 \text{ and} \tag{6}$$

$$w_1 < w_2 < \cdots < w_n < 1, \tag{7}$$

where n represents the number of RSSIs which have to be averaged. Therefore, the actual elapsed time since the reception is used. Using this change the average RSSI $\overline{R}_{ij}$ may be calculated to

$$\lambda = \sum_{l=0}^{n} e^{-t_l}, \; l = \{0, 1, \ldots, n\}, \tag{8}$$

$$w_k = \frac{e^{-t_k}}{\lambda}, \tag{9}$$

$$\overline{R}_{ij} = \sum_{l=0}^{n} R_{ij,l} \cdot w_l. \tag{10}$$

In contrast to [4] it is assumed that it is unnecessary to divide the sum of the weighted RSSIs in (10) by n, as the weights w_i are already normalized (6). Figure 1 shows the weights w_i for $n = 11$ with $t_i = \{0, 1, \ldots, 10\}$ (gray circles) and for $n = 3$ with $t_i = \{0, 1, 2\}$ (black squares).

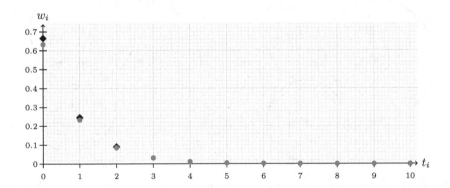

Fig. 1. This figure shows the w_i for $n = 11$ and $t_i = \{0, 1, \ldots, 10\}$ (gray circles) and for $n = 3$ and $t_i = \{0, 1, 2\}$ (black squares)

After the averaged RSSIs have been calculated they still need to be smoothed. Zhang et al [4] did a simple filtering with fixed coefficients. Since this type of smoothing does not take the age of a $\overline{R}_{ij}$ into account, it has been adapted so that older $\overline{R}_{ij}$ get a lower smoothing factor than younger $\overline{R}_{ij}$. Thus results for the smoothed RSSIs $\tilde{R}_{ij}$

$$\tilde{R}_{ij}(t_n) = (1 - (\alpha(1-\alpha)^{\Delta t}))\overline{R}_{ij}(t_n) + \alpha(1-\alpha)^{\Delta t}\tilde{R}_{ij}(t_{n-1}), \tag{11}$$

where $\alpha \in]0,1]$, $\tilde{R}_{ij}(t_n)$ represents a smoothed $\overline{R}_{ij}$ at time t_n and Δt is the time that has elapsed between t_{n-1} and t_n. For $\Delta t = 0$ both summands in (11) should have the same weight, so $\alpha = 0.5$ is suggested as a natured choice here.

5   Trilateration

Knowing the distances between a tag and at least three anchors with defined positions, it is possible to calculate the position of the tag using trilateration. If the distances are correct, the three circles resulting from the position of the anchor and the distance between anchor and tag intersect in one point (see left figure in fig. 2), indicating the position of the tag. Unfortunately, due to inaccuracies during the RSSI measurements the distance between an anchor and a tag usually can not be calculated that way. Possibly, instead of one intersection for all three circles an area is spanned where the tag is likely to be (see right figure in fig. 2). In this case the position of the tag is assumed to be represented by the mean of three intersections lying next to each other and each belonging to another pair of circles. If only two or none of the circles intersect, then the three distance values are increased until each pair of circles has at least one intersection. Trilateration is also used and described in [2, 5, 12, 13, 21, 22].

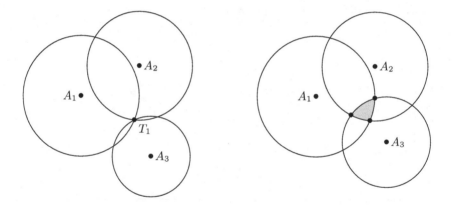

Fig. 2. This figure shows two possible cases that can occur in trilateration. The one on the left side represents the ideal case. There is one intersection for all three circles, which indicates the position of the tag. The second case on the right side represents the case that an area is spanned where the tag is likely to be.

6   Indoor Positioning Algorithm

The IPS consists of two phases. The first phase is called offline-phase. During this phase PLE η_{ij} between to anchors i and j are calculated for each pair of anchors with $i \neq j$. Phase number two is called the online-phase, which represents the actual IPS. Figure 3 gives a brief overview about the processes of the IPS.

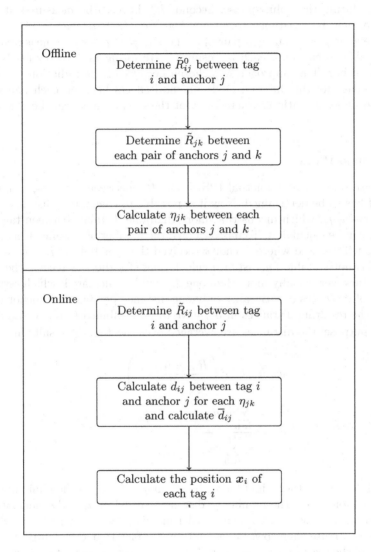

Fig. 3. This figure shows the two phases and the flow in each phase of the IPS.

6.1 Offline-Phase

As mentioned before, PLEs are calculated during this phase. First of all each anchor has to be placed at its final position, which should be very accurately known. Inaccurately known positions of anchors will lead to false position calculations during the online-phase. Second, $\tilde{R}_{ij}^0$ have to be measured at a one meter obstacle free distance to anchor i and on LOS to each anchor j with $i \neq j$. Next, $\tilde{R}_{ij}$ between each pair of anchors $(i \neq j)$ has to be measured. Now it is possible to calculate each η_{ij} using (4), resulting in a vector of PLEs $\boldsymbol{\eta}_i$ for each anchor. This approach was chosen because of the radiation pattern of the antennas and the different environmental effects between each pair of anchors. So at least static characteristics of the environment can be taken into account.

6.2 Online-Phase

This phase represents the actual IPS. First, $\tilde{R}_{ij}$ between each tag i and each anchor j has to be determined. Now it is possible to calculate a distance d_{ij} for each entry in $\boldsymbol{\eta}_j$, which means that more than one distance between tag i and anchor j can be calculated. To narrow down the number of distance values, only those η_{jk} will be used where anchor k received the signal of tag i. It is assumed that η_{jk} is not suitable for distance calculations if k did not receive the signal of tag i. However, usually more than one d_{ij} will be calculated, which results in a vector of distances $\boldsymbol{d}_{ij}$. Because only one distance per tag and anchor pair is needed, the resulting distances in $\boldsymbol{d}_{ij}$ have to be combined to one distance $\overline{d}_{ij}$. For this purpose, the distances are averaged over the $\tilde{R}_{ik}$. $\overline{d}_{ij}$ results in

$$w_k = floor\left(\frac{\tilde{R}_{ik} - \tilde{R}_{i,min}}{3}\right) + 1, \tag{12}$$

$$\overline{d}_{ij} = \frac{\sum\limits_{l=0}^{m} w_l d_{ij,l}}{\sum\limits_{l=0}^{m} w_l} \tag{13}$$

where w_k represents the weight for d_{ij} based on η_{jk}, $\tilde{R}_{i,min}$ is the minimum RSSI determined for i, m is the number of distances stored in $\boldsymbol{d}_{ij}$. The calculation of w_k based on the assumption, made earlier in this paper, that higher RSSIs are less prone to noise than lower ones and on the fact that every 3dB there is a doubling of the received signal power. Adding '1' makes sure that each $w_k \neq 0$. If the distances between the tag and three anchors have been calculated, a triplet

$$\overline{\boldsymbol{d}}_i = \begin{pmatrix} \overline{d}_{ij} \\ \overline{d}_{ik} \\ \overline{d}_{il} \end{pmatrix} \tag{14}$$

remains, which can be used to calculate the position x_i of tag i using trilateration. As described in section 5 it might be necessary to increase the remaining distances to get one intersection for all three anchors or at least an area where tag i is positioned. First, the error between each pair of distances in $\overline{d}_i$ and the distance between their anchors has to be calculated

$$
\begin{aligned}
e_{jk} &= d_{jk} - \overline{d}_{ij} - \overline{d}_{ik}, \\
e_{jl} &= d_{jl} - \overline{d}_{ij} - \overline{d}_{il}, \\
e_{kl} &= d_{kl} - \overline{d}_{ik} - \overline{d}_{il}.
\end{aligned}
\tag{15}
$$

Note that the distances d_{jk}, d_{jl} and d_{kl} between the anchors are known by definition. Ideally there would be no or a negative error. If at least one error has positive sign, then the distances have to be increased. Therefore, the maximum error e_{max} has to be determined. Next, the new distances have to be adapted

$$
\begin{aligned}
\overline{d}_{ij}^{e} &= \overline{d}_{ij} + \frac{e_{max}}{2} + \epsilon, \\
\overline{d}_{ik}^{e} &= \overline{d}_{ik} + \frac{e_{max}}{2} + \epsilon, \\
\overline{d}_{il}^{e} &= \overline{d}_{il} + \frac{e_{max}}{2} + \epsilon.
\end{aligned}
\tag{16}
$$

Due to rounding errors ϵ gets additionally added to avoid *NaN* errors during the position calculations. The adapted distance values can now be used to calculate the position of tag i using trilateration.

7   Experiments and Results

For a total of three experiments, a room of 5.8m × 6.3m has been selected. Three anchors have been deployed at coordinates (2.0|2.0|1.0), (3.7|2.0|1.0) and (2.86|4.8|1.0). Only one tag with a new position during each measurement series was used. It was tuned so that it sent a signal every second. The position of the tag was recalculated every three seconds.

In the first experiment the tag was positioned at (3.0|3.53|1.0). During this measurement series a maximum accuracy of 3.41cm was achieved. The minimum accuracy was 30.03cm with a 95th percentile of 30cm.

Deploying the tag at (2.17|3.0|1.0), in the second experiment the maximum accuracy was 22.83cm and the minimum accuracy was 42.31cm. In this experiment 30cm was about the 80th percentile.

A maximum accuracy of 11.43cm and a minimum accuracy of 24.36cm was achieved in the third and last experiment. During this experiment the tag's position was (3.0|2.99|1.0).

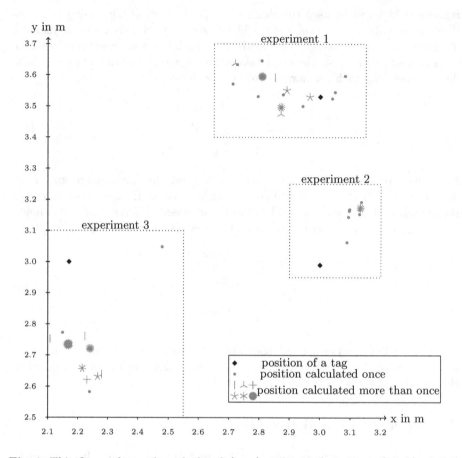

Fig. 4. This figure shows the calculated (gray) and actual positions (black) of the tag during each of the three experiments. Positions marked with dots have only been calculated once during the experiment. A position that has been calculated more than once is marked with a n-pointed star, where n is the number of times a position has been calculated. The dotted lines mark the results of the different experiments.

Figure 4 shows the calculated and actual positions of the tag during each experiment. Each rectangle marked with dotted lines belongs to one of the three experiments.

Figure 5 shows a cumulative frequency curve for each experiment and one for the combination of all three experiments. As can be seen, during each experiment the accuracy of the calculated positions is over 42.31cm and a 90th percentile of 30cm. During experiment one, the 10th percentile was around 5cm with a minimal error of 3.41cm.

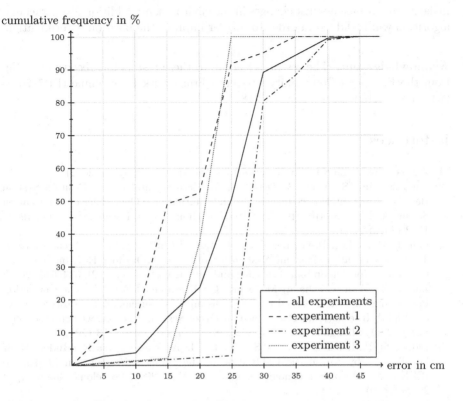

cumulative frequency in %

Fig. 5. Cumulative frequency curve of the results of the three experiments

8 Conclusion and Outlook

In this paper a RSSI-based IPS was presented. Because RSSI measurements are very susceptible to noise, the gathered RSSIs have been preprocessed before they were used for position calculations. Time-dependent weights were used to average gathered RSSIs, so RSSIs with increasing age find less consideration. After averaging gathered RSSIs they were smoothed over time, so again RSSIs with increasing age find less consideration. Time-based averaging and smoothing was chosen because it is assumed that tags will move and thus can change their position within a few seconds about a few meters.

The experiments made in a closed room resulted that the presented IPS enables to calculate the position of a tag with an accuracy of at least 42.31cm and a 90th percentile of 30cm.

In a next step the IPS-algorithm will be expanded so that changes in the environment can be taken into account. Therefore, the path loss exponent has to be determined not just in the offline-phase of the algorithm, but repeatedly during the online-phase. This should improve the accuracy of the positioning and make it more robust against changes in the environment. Additionally a tracking-algorithm will be added in order to further improve the position determination.

Acknowledgment. The research leading to these results has received funding from the European Community's Seventh Framework Programme (FP7/2007-2013) under grant agreement no. 218086.

References

1. ZigBee Cluster Library Specification, ZigBee Alliance (May 31, 2012)
2. Shuo, S., Hao, S., Yang, S.: Design of An Experimental Indoor Position System Based on RSSI. In: Proceedings of the 2nd International Conference on Information Science and Engineering, ICISE 2010, Hangzhou, China, December 4-6, pp. 1989–1992 (2010)
3. Lau, E.-E.-L., Lee, B.-G., Lee, S.-C.: Enhanced RSSI-based High Accuracy Real-Time User Location Tracking System for Indoor and Outdoor Environments. International Journal on Smart Sensing and Intelligent Systems 1(2), 534–548 (2008)
4. Zhang, Z., Wan, G., Jiang, M., Yang, G.: Research of An Adjacent Correction Positioning Algorithm Based on RSSI-Distance Measurement. In: Proceedings of the Eighth International Conference on Fuzzy Systems and Knowledge Discovery, FSKD 2011, Shanghai, China, July 26-28, vol. 4, pp. 2319–2323 (2011)
5. Barsocchi, P., Lenzi, S., Chessa, S., Giunta, G.: A Novel Approach to Indoor RSSI Localization by Automatic Calibration of the Wireless Propagation Model. In: IEEE 69th Vehicular Technology Conference, VTC 2009, Barcelona, Spain, April 26-29 (2009)
6. Barsocchi, P., Lenzi, S., Chessa, S., Giunta, G.: Virtual Calibration for RSSI-based Indoor Localization with IEEE 802.15.4. In: IEEE International Conference on Communications, ICC 2009, Dresden, Germany, June 14-18 (2009)
7. Borrelli, A., Monti, C., Vari, M., Mazzenga, F.: Channel Models for IEEE 802.11b Indoor System Design. In: Proceedings of the IEEE International Conference on Communications, ICC 2004, Paris, France, June 20-24, vol. 6, pp. 3701–3705 (2004)
8. Green, E., Hata, M.: Microcellular Propagation Measurements in An Urban Environment. In: Proceedings of the IEEE International Symposium on Personal, Indoor and Mobile Radio Communications, PIMRC 1991, pp. 324–328 (1991)
9. Ren, Z., Huang, Y., Chen, Q., Li, H.: Modeling and Simulation of Fading, Pathloss, and Shadowing in Wireless Networks. In: Proceedings of the IEEE International Conference on Communications Technology and Application, ICCTA 2009, Alexandria, Egypt, October 17-19, pp. 335–343 (2009)
10. Mehra, R., Singh, A.: Real TIme RSSI Error Reduction in Distance Estimation Using RLS Algorithm. In: Proceedings of the IEEE 3rd International Advance Computing Conference, IACC 2013, Ghaziabad, India, February 22-23, pp. 661–665 (2013)
11. Wang, J.-Y., Chen, C.-P., Lin, T.-S., Chuang, C.-L., Lai, T.-Y., Jiang, J.-A.: High-Precision RSSI-based Indoor Localization Using A Transmission Power Adjustment Strategy for Wireless Sensor Networks. In: Proceedings of the IEEE 14th International Conference on High Performance Computing and Communication & IEEE 9th International Conference on Embedded Software and Systems, HPCC-ICESS 2012, Liverpool, United Kingdom, June 25-27, pp. 1634–1638 (2012)

12. Goldoni, E., Savioli, A., Risi, M., Gamba, P.: Experimental Analysis of RSSI-based Indoor Localization with IEEE 802.15.4. In: Proceedings of the European Wireless Conference, EW 2010, Lucca, Italy, April 12-15, pp. 71–77 (2010)

13. El-Osery, A.I., Abd-Almageed, W., Youssef, M.: Calibration-Free RF-based Localization Algorithm for Sensor Actuator Networks Using Particle Filters. IEEE Antennas and Propagation Magazine 48(4), 166–173 (2006)

14. Patwari, N., Hero, A.O., Perkins, M., Correal, N.S., O'Dea, R.J.: Relative Location Estimation in Wireless Sensor Networks. Transactions on Signal Processing 51(8), 2137–2148 (2003)

15. Elnahrawy, E., Li, X., Martin, R.P.: The Limits of Localization Using Signal Strength: A Comparative Study. In: Proceedings of the First Annual IEEE Communications Society Conference on Sensor ans Ad Hoc Communications and Networks, SECON 2004, Santa Clara, California, USA, October 4-7, pp. 406–414 (2004)

16. Kao, K.-F., Liao, I.-E., Lyu, J.-S.: An Indoor Location-Based Service Using Access Points as Signal Strength Data Collectors. In: International Conference on Indoor Positioning and Indoor Navigation, IPIN 2010, Zurich, Switzerland, September 15-17 (2010)

17. Laoudias, C., Michaelides, M.P., Panayiotou, C.G.: Fault Detection and Mitigation in WLAN RSS Fingerprint-based Positioning. In: International Conference on Indoor Positioning and Indoor Navigation, IPIN 2011, Guimaraes, Portugal, September 21-23 (2011)

18. Wang, H.: Bayesian Radio Map Learning for Robust Indoor Positioning. In: International Conference on Indoor Positioning and Indoor Navigation, IPIN 2011, Guimaraes, Portugal, September 21-23 (2011)

19. Hansen, R., Wind, R., Jensen, C.S., Thomsen, B.: Algorithmic Strategies for Adapting to Environmental Changes in 802.11 Location Fingerprinting. In: International Conference on Indoor Positioning and Indoor Navigation, IPIN 2010, Zurich, Switzerland, September 15-17 (2010)

20. Teramoto, Y., Asahara, A.: Wireless LAN based Indoor Positioning using Radio-Signal Strength Distribution Modeling. In: International Conference on Indoor Positioning and Indoor Navigation, IPIN 2012, Sydney, Australia, November 13-15 (2012)

21. Luoh, L.: ZigBee-based Intelligent Indoor Positioning System Soft Computing. Soft Computing, 1–14 (2013)

22. Awad, A., Frunzke, T., Dressler, F.: Adaptive Distance Estimation and Localization in WSN using RSSI Measures. In: Proceedings of the 10th Euromicro Conference on Digital System Design Architectures, Methods and Tools, DSD 2007, Lübeck, Germany, August 29-31, pp. 471–478 (2007)

23. Karl, H., Willig, A.: Protocols and Architectures for Wireless Sensor Networks. Wiley, West Sussex (2005)

Evaluation of Sound Event Detection, Classification and Localization in the Presence of Background Noise for Acoustic Surveillance of Hazardous Situations

Kuba Łopatka, Józef Kotus, and Andrzej Czyżewski

Gdańsk University of Technology, Faculty of Electronics,
Telecommunications and Informatics, Multimedia Systems Department, Gdańsk, Poland
{klopatka,joseph,andcz}@multimed.org

Abstract. Evaluation of sound event detection, classification and localization of hazardous acoustic events in the presence of background noise of different types and changing intensities is presented. The methods for separating foreground events from the acoustic background are introduced. The classifier, based on a Support Vector Machine algorithm, is described. The set of features and samples used for the training of the classifier are introduced. The sound source localization algorithm based on the analysis of multichannel signals from the Acoustic Vector Sensor is presented. The methods are evaluated in an experiment conducted in the anechoic chamber, in which the representative events are played together with noise of differing intensity. The results of detection, classification and localization accuracy with respect to the Signal to Noise Ratio are discussed. The algorithms presented are part of an audio-visual surveillance system.

Keywords: sound detection, sound source localization, audio surveillance.

1   Introduction

Recognition and localization of acoustic events is a relatively recent practical application of audio signal processing, especially in the domain of acoustic surveillance. In this case the goal is to recognize the acoustic events that may inform us of possible threats to the safety of people or property. An additional influence is the acoustic direction of arrival, which can be used to determine the position of the sound source, i.e. the place in which the event occurred. The recognized classes of sound relate to dangerous events. Typically, such events include gunshots, explosions or screams [1,2]. The majority of sound recognition algorithms described in the literature are based on the extraction of acoustic features and statistical pattern recognition [3]. Ntalampiras et al.[1] and Valenzise et al.[2] employed a set of perceptual and temporal features containing Mel-Frequency Cepstral Coefficients, Zero Crossing Rate, Linear Prediction Coefficients and a Gaussian Mixture Model (GMM) classifier. The latter work also presents sound localization techniques with a microphone array based on the calculation of the Time Difference of Arrivals (TDOA). Lu et al.[4] used a

A. Dziech and A. Czyżewski (Eds.): MCSS 2014, CCIS 429, pp. 96–110, 2014.

combination of temporal and spectral shape descriptors fed into a hybrid structure classifier, which is also based on GMM. Rabaoui et al. [5], Dat and Li [6] as well as Temko and Nadeau [7] proposed the utilization of Support Vector Machine classifiers (SVM) to achieve this task. A comprehensive comparison of techniques for sound recognition (including Dynamic Time Warping, Hidden Markov Models or Artificial Neural Networks) was presented by Cowling and Sitte [8]. Some commercial systems also exist for the recognition of threatening events (especially gunshots). These systems, such as Boomerang [9], ShotSpotter [10] or SENTRI [11], incorporate acoustic event detection and localization to provide information about the location of the shooter. They utilize an array of acoustic pressure sensors as the data source and recurrent neural networks for classification.

We propose an approach using a multichannel sound intensity probe rather than an array of microphones for acoustic event localization and a threshold-based methodology for separating acoustic events from the background. A SVM classifier is used for discerning between classes of threatening events. Our system is meant to be a universal and adaptive solution which can work in low- and high noise conditions, both indoors and outdoors. It is employed in the acoustic monitoring of hazardous events in an audio-visual surveillance system. The information about detected events and their type can be used to inform the operator of the surveillance system of potential threats. In a multimodal application the calculated direction of arrival of the detected acoustic event is used to control the PTZ (Pan-Tilt-Zoom) camera [12,13]. Thus, the camera is automatically directed toward the localized sound source. The system operates in real time, both in indoor and outdoor conditions. Therefore, the changing acoustic background is a significant problem. Consequently, the impact of added noise on the performance of the algorithms employed needs to be examined in order for our research to progress.

The paper is organized as follows. In Section 2 we present our algorithms and methods for detection, classification and localization of acoustic events. In Section 3 we introduce the setup of the experiment, specifying the conditions under which the measurements were performed and the equipment used. In Section 4 we discuss the measurement results, leading to the conclusions presented in Section 5.

2   Methods

Commonly, the term Acoustic Event Detection (AED) refers to the whole process of the identification of acoustic events. We divide this process into three phases: detection, classification and localization. The general concept of sound recognition and localization system is presented in Fig. 1. The purpose of detection is to separate the foreground events from the acoustic background, without determining whether an event is threatening or not. Some researchers use foreground/background or silence/non-silence classifiers to achieve this task [2,7]. We employ dedicated detection algorithms which do not require training and are adaptive to changing conditions. The detection of a foreground event triggers classification and localization, after buffering the samples of the detected event. This architecture allows us to maintain a low rate of false alerts, owing to the robust detection algorithms, which we explain in more detail in the following subsections. The classification task is the proper assignment of the detected events to one of the predefined classes. In addition, the localization of the acoustic event is computed by analyzing the multichannel output of the Acoustic Vector Sensor (AVS). The employment of AVS and incorporation of the localization procedure in the acoustic surveillance system provide an addition to the state of the art in sound recognition technology. Stemming from acoustic principles, beamforming arrays have limitations in low frequencies and require line (or plane) symmetry. Data from all measurement points have to be collected and processed in order to obtain the correct results. The acoustic vector sensor approach is broadbanded, works in 3D acoustical space, and has good mathematical robustness [14]. The ability of a single AVS to rapidly determine the bearing of a wideband acoustic source is essential for numerous passive monitoring systems. The algorithms operate on acoustic data, sampled at the rate of 48000 samples per second with a bit resolution equal to 24 bits per sample.

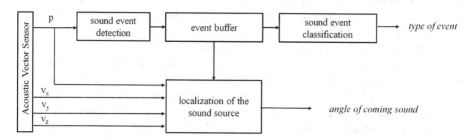

Fig. 1. Concept diagram of a sound detection, classification and localization system

2.1   Sound Event Detection

Initially the detector is in learning mode. After the learning phase is completed, the detection parameter is compared to the threshold value. This operation yields detection or no detection. The threshold (or acoustic background profile) is constantly updated to adapt to changing conditions. We assume that a distinct acoustic event has to manifest itself by a dissimilarity of its features from the features of the acoustic background. The choice of features to be taken into consideration depends on the type of event we intend to detect. This yields four detection techniques:

– based on the short-time level of the signal – applied to detecting sudden, loud impulsive sounds – named *Impulse Detector;*
– based on the harmonicity of the signal – applied to detecting speech and scream-like sounds – named *Speech Detector;*
– based on changes in the signal features over time – applied to detecting sudden narrow-band changes in the analyzed signal – named: *Variance Detector;*

  – based on the overall dissimilarity in the spectra of the event and background – applied to detecting any abnormal sounds – named *Histogram Detector* (since it employs a histogram of sound level in 1/3-octave frequency bands to model the spectrum of the acoustic background).

In general, all detectors rely on comparing the detection parameter P with the threshold T. Hence, the detection function D can be defined as follows:

$$D(i) = \begin{cases} 1 & P(i) > T(i) \\ 0 & P(i) \leq T(i) \end{cases} \tag{1}$$

where i is the index of the current frame. The threshold T is automatically updated to the changes in the acoustic background by exponential averaging according to the formula:

$$T(0) = P(0) + m$$
$$T(i > 0) = (1 - \alpha) \cdot T(i - 1) + \alpha \cdot (P(i) + m) \tag{2}$$

where m is the margin added to the value of the detection parameter, which serves as a *sensitivity parameter* of the detector. If the detection parameter changes exponentially, m can be a multiplier. The constant α is related to the detector's adaptation time. The adaptation time T_{adapt} is the period after which the previous values of the detection parameter are no longer important. It is related to the constant α according to the equation

$$T_{adapt}[s] = \frac{N}{SR \cdot \alpha} \tag{3}$$

where N is the number of samples in the frame and SR is the sampling rate. The different detection algorithms employed differ in the definition of the detection parameter and the frame sizes employed. The *Impulse Detector* is based on the level of the signal in short frames (10 ms) calculated as

$$L = 20 \cdot \log \left(\sqrt{\frac{1}{N} \sum_{n=1}^{N} (x[n] \cdot L_{norm})^2} \right) \tag{4}$$

where $x[n]$ are the signal samples and L_{norm} is the normalization factor equal to the level of the maximum sample value measured with a calibration device. *Speech Detector* is based on the *Peak-Valley-Difference* (PVD) parameter. The feature used is a modification of the parameter proposed by Yoo and Yook [15] and often used in *Voice Activity Detection* (VAD) algorithms. For typical signals, the spacing of spectral peaks depends on the fundamental frequency of the signal. Since this detection parameter is dedicated to the detection of vocal activity (e.g. screams) the PVD is calculated iteratively over a range of assumed peak spacing corresponding to the frequency range of human voice. Subsequently the maximum value is taken into consideration. The PVD is calculated as follows:

$$PVD = \frac{\sum_{k=1}^{N/2} X(k) \cdot P(k)}{\sum_{k=1}^{N/2} P(k)} - \frac{\sum_{k=1}^{N/2} X(k) \cdot (1-P(k))}{\sum_{k=1}^{N/2} (1-P(k))} \tag{5}$$

where $X(k)$ is the power spectrum of the signal's frame, $N = 4096$ is the length of the Fourier Transform (equal to the length of the detector's frame) and $P(k)$ is a function which equals 1 if k is the position of the spectral peak, 0 otherwise.

In turn, the *Variance Detector* is based on the variance of signal's features calculated over time. The feature variance vector $Var_f = \begin{bmatrix} V_{f1} & V_{f2} & \dots & V_{fN} \end{bmatrix}$ comprises the variances of a total of N signal features. For the n-th feature f_n the feature variance is calculated according to the formula:

$$V_{fn} = \frac{1}{I} \sum_{i=1}^{I} \left(f_n(i) - \overline{f_n} \right)^2 \tag{6}$$

where I is the number of frames used for calculating the variance, i.e. the length of the *variance buffer*. V_{fn} is then used as a detection parameter. The decision is made independently for each feature and the final decision is a logical sum of each feature's detection result. The variance detector is suitable for detecting narrow-band events, since it reacts to changes in single features, some of which reflect the narrow-band characteristics of the signal.

The final detection algorithm is based on a histogram model of acoustic background. The spectral magnitudes are calculated in 1/3-octave bands to model the noise background. 30 bands are used, and for every band a histogram of sound levels is constructed. The detection parameter d_{hist} is then calculated as a dissimilarity measure between the spectrum of the current frame X and the background model:

$$d_{hist}(X) = \sum_{k=1}^{30} h_k(X_k) \tag{7}$$

where $h_k(X_k)$ is the value of the histogram of spectral magnitude in the k-th band. The signals whose spectrum matches the noise profile yield high values of d_{hist}. The histogram-based detection algorithm is designed to deal best with wide-band acoustic events, whose spectral dissimilarity from the acoustic background is the greatest. The algorithm is similar to the GMM detection algorithm, only does not assume Gaussian distribution of sound levels.

2.2   Classification

The classification algorithm is based on the Support Vector Machine (SVM) classifier. The principles of SVM and its application in numerous fields has been widely described in the literature, namely in text classification [16], face detection [16] or acoustic event detection [7, 17]. It was proven in previous work that the Support Vector Machine can be an efficient tool for the classification of signals in an audio-based surveillance system, as it robustly discerns threatening from non-threatening events [18]. The difficulty pertaining to the employment of SVMs for acoustic event recognition is that SVM, being a non-recurrent structure, is fed a representation of the acoustic event in the form of a static feature vector. Since the length of environmental audio events can vary from less than 1 second to even more than 10 seconds, a correct approach is to divide the signal into frames, classify each frame separately and subsequently make the decision. Such an approach was proposed by Temko and Nadeau [7]. In our work a frame of 200 ms in length is used and the overlap factor equals 50%. The SVM model employed enables multi-class classification via the *1-vs-all* technique with the use of LIBSVM library written in C++ [19]. A polynomial kernel function was used. The output of the classifier, representing the certainty of the classified event's membership in respective classes, can be understood as a probability estimate:

$$P_i(x_n) = SVM\{F(x_n), i\} \qquad (8)$$

where P_i is the probability of the analyzed frame x_n belonging to class i. F denotes the feature calculation function. The final decision points to the class that maximizes the classifier's output. In the following subsections the calculation of signal features and the training of the classifier are described.

The elements of the feature vector were chosen on the basis of statistical analysis. Firstly, a large vector of 124 features is extracted from the training set. This large feature vector comprises MPEG-7 descriptors [20], spectral shape and temporal features [4, 21], as well as other parameters related to the energy of the signal, which were developed in prior work [22]. Secondly, a feature selection technique suited to SVM classification is employed to rank the features. This task is performed using the WEKA data mining tool [23]. The top 50 features in the ranking are chosen to form the final feature vector. The length of the feature vector was chosen by minimizing the error in the cross-validation check. The contents of the feature vector are presented in Tab. 1.

Table 1. Elements of the feature vector

symbol	feature	number of features
	MPEG-7 spectral features	
ASC	Audio Spectrum Centroid	1
ASS	Audio Spectrum Spread	1
ASE	Audio Spectrum Envelope	20
SFM	Spectral Flatness Measure	17
	temporal features	
ZCD	Zero Crossing Density	2
TC	Temporal Centroid	1
	other features	
SE	Spectral Energy	4
CEP	Cepstral Energy	1
PVD	Peak-Valley Difference	1
TR	Transient Features	2

The system recognizes 4 classes of threatening events and 1 non-threatening event class. The event samples were recorded with the Bruel & Kjaer PULSE system type 7540 in natural conditions, although with a low level of additive noise. Hence they will hereafter be recognized as *clean* sound events. The files are stored in 48000 Hz 24-bit floating point WAVE files. The training procedure comprises the calculation of features from all signals in the event database and solving the Support Vector problem, which is performed by employing the Sequential Minimal Optimization algorithm (SMO) [24]. Finally, a cross-validation check is performed, with 3 folds, to assess the assumed model and evaluate the training of the classifier.

2.3   Sound Source Localization

The single acoustic vector sensor measures the acoustic particle velocity instead of the acoustic pressure, which is measured by conventional microphones[25]. Each particle velocity sensor is sensitive only in one direction, so three orthogonally placed particle velocity sensors have to be used. In combination with a pressure microphone, the sound field in a single point is fully characterized and the acoustic intensity vector, which is the product of pressure and particle velocity, can also be determined [26]. This intensity vector indicates the acoustic energy flow. With a compact probe, the full three-dimensional sound intensity vector can be determined within the full audible frequency range of 20 Hz up to 20 kHz.

The intensity in a certain direction is the product of sound pressure (scalar) $p(t)$ and the particle velocity (vector) component in that direction $u(t)$. The time averaged intensity I in a single direction is given by Eq. 9 [27].

$$I = \frac{1}{T} \int_T p(t)u(t)dt \qquad (9)$$

In the algorithm presented the time average T was equal to 4096 samples (sampling rate was equal to 48000 S/s) [28]. It means that the direction of the sound source was updated more than 10 times per second. It is important to emphasize that using the 3D AVS presented, the particular sound intensity components can be simply obtained solely based on Eq. 21. The sound intensity vector in three dimensions is composed of the acoustic intensities in the three orthogonal directions (x,y,z) and is given in Eq. 10 [27]. When the particular components of the whole sound intensity vector produced by the sound source are known, the acoustic direction of arrival can be determined. The angle of the incoming sound in reference to the acoustic vector sensor position is the main information about the sound source position.

$$\vec{I} = I_x \vec{e}_x + I_y \vec{e}_y + I_z \vec{e}_z \qquad (10)$$

For the proper determination of the sound source position the proper buffering of the acoustic data and precise detection of the acoustic event are needed. Such a process enables the proper selection of the part of the sound stream which includes the data generated by the sound source. Only such samples are taking into account during the computation of the sound intensity components. Acoustic events used in the experiment executed had a different length. For that reason the buffered sound samples of the detected acoustic event were additionally divided into frames of 4096 samples in length. For each frame the sound intensity components and angle of the incoming sound were calculated. The final result was determined as a median of all particular angle values computed for the considered acoustic event

3   Experiment

Most reported results on the recognition of hazardous situations are obtained via experiments on a database of sound recordings, in most cases isolated from noise. Cowling and Sitte used a set of sounds recorded in quiet conditions [8]. Such methodology, however insightful into the characteristics of the algorithms employed, lacks addressing the common problems which appear when the acoustic surveillance system is set up in a real environment. The presence of noise causes the features of sound to change, often deteriorating the performance of the statistical pattern recognition techniques used to distinguish between the classes of sounds. Some attempts to evaluate the results of sound recognition and localization in noisy conditions have been made by Valenzise et al. [2] and Ntalampiras et al. [29]. However, to our knowledge no comprehensive study on the effect of different types and levels of noise on the accuracy of sound detection, classification and localization has yet been presented. Therefore an evaluation of recognition efficiency in the presence of noise is needed to assess the performance of the algorithms in less than ideal conditions.

In the experiment we make an attempt to evaluate the efficiency of detection, classification and localization of acoustic events in relation to the type and level of noise accompanying the event. These are: traffic noise, railway noise, cocktail-party noise and typical noise inside buildings. The key parameter is the *Signal-To-Noise Ratio* (SNR). We decide to perform the experiments in laboratory conditions, in an anechoic chamber. This environment, however far from being realistic, gives us the possibility to precisely control the conditions and to measure the levels of sound events and noise, which is substantial in this experiment. The drawback of this approach is that the signals reproduced by speakers are used, instead of real signals, which has its impact both on the recognition and localization of events.

3.1   Setup and Equipment

The setup of the measurement equipment employed in the experiment is presented in Fig. 2. In an anechoic chamber, 8 REVEAL 601p speakers, an USP probe and a type 4189 measurement microphone by Bruel & Kjaer (B&K) were installed.

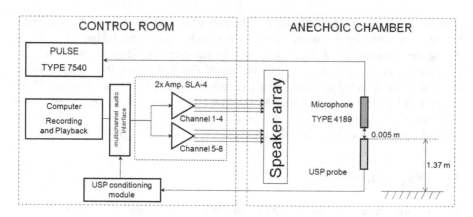

Fig. 2. Experiment setup

The USP probe is fixed 1.37 meters above the floor. The measurement microphone is placed 5 mm above the USP probe. In the control room a PC computer with Marc 8 Multichannel audio interface is used to generate the test signals and record the signals from the USP probe. Two SLA-4 type 4-channel amplifiers are employed to power the speakers. In addition, PULSE system type 7540 by B&K is used to record the acoustic signals. The PULSE measuring system is calibrated before the measurements using a type 4231 B&K acoustic calibrator.

3.2   Test Signals

Audio events were combined into a test signal consisting of 100 events, randomly placed in time. The average length of each event equals 1 second, and there is a 10 second space between the start and end of adjacent events. The length of the test signals equals 18 min 20 s. Four disturbing signals were prepared, each with a different type of noise:

- traffic noise, recorded in a busy street in Gdansk;
- cocktail-party noise, recorded in a university canteen;
- railway noise, recorded in Gdansk railway station;
- indoor noise, recorded in the main hall of Gdansk University of Technology.

All noise signals were recorded using a B&K PULSE system and were written to 24-bit WAVE files sampled at 48000 samples per second. The differences in the energy distribution for used signals were determined on the basis of energy normalized spectrums analysis. The indoor noise has the energy concentrated in the middle part of the spectrum (200 Hz–2000 Hz). The very high level of tonal components for railway noise was produced by the brakes.

3.3   Methodology

In the test signals the events were randomly assigned to one of four channels: 1,3,5,7. The order of the events with the numbers of channels they are emitted from and classes they belong to is stored in the *Ground Truth* (GT) reference list. At the same time, the other channels (2,4,6,8) are used to emit noise. Each noise channel is shifted in time to avoid correlation between channels. The gain of the noise channels is kept constant, while the gain of events is set to one of four values: 0dB, -10dB, -20dB and -30dB. This yields 16 recordings of events with added noise (4 types of noise x 4 gain levels). In addition, the signals of four types of noise without events and 4 signals of events without noise with different gain levels are recorded. These events are used to measure the instantaneous SNR. On the whole 23 signals have been gathered (indoor noise at -30dB gain was later excluded). The total length of the recordings equals 7 h 02 min.

3.4   Detection and Classification Rates

The experiment recordings are analyzed with the engineered automatic sound event detection and localization algorithms. The measures of detection accuracy are the *True Positive* (TP), and *False Positive* (FP) rates. The TP rate equals the number of detected events which match the events in the GT list divided by the total number of events in the GT list. The matching of event is understood as the difference between detection time and GT time of the event being not greater than 1 second. A FP result is considered when an event is detected which is not listed in the GT reference and is classified as one of the four types of event that are considered alarming (classes 1–4).

4   Results

4.1   Detection Results

The results of sound event detection are presented in Fig. 3. The TP rates of each of the detection algorithms vs. SNR are plotted. The combination of all detection algorithms yields high detection rates. The TP rate decreases significantly with the decrease of SNR. The algorithm which yields the highest detection rates in good conditions (SNR >10dB) is the Impulse Detector. It outperforms the other algorithms, which are more suited to specific types of signal. However, the Impulse Detector is most affected by added noise, since it only reacts to the level of the signal.

Other algorithms, namely Speech Detector and Variance Detector, maintain their detection rates at a similar level while SNR decreases. It is a good feature, which allows the detection of events even if they are below the background level (note the TP rate of 0.37 for SNRs smaller than -5dB). It is also evident that the combination of all detectors performs better than any of them alone, which proves that the engineered detection algorithms react to different features of the signal and are complementary. The Histogram Detector is disappointing, since its initial TP rate is the lowest of all detectors and falls to nearly 0 at 5dB SNR. The total number of detected events equals 1055 out of 1500 (for all SNRs combined) which yields an average TP rate of 0.7.

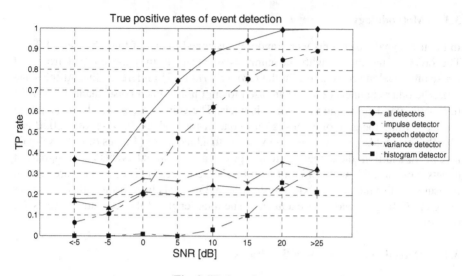

Fig. 3. TP detection rates

4.2   Classification Results

The adopted measures of classification accuracy, i.e. precision and recall rates, were calculated with respect to SNR. The results are presented in Fig. 4.

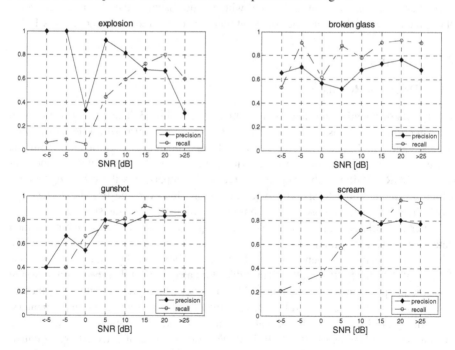

Fig. 4. Precision and recall rates of sound events in relation to SNR

The general trend observed is that the recall rate descends with the decrease in SNR. It can be seen, as far as explosion and broken glass are concerned, that the precision rate ascends with the decrease in SNR. In very noisy conditions these classes are recognized with greater certainty. The class of event which is least affected by noise is broken glass. The recall rate remains high (ca. 0.8 or more) for SNRs greater than or equal to 5dB. The low overall recall rate of explosions is caused by the fact that the events were reproduced through loudspeakers, which significantly changes the characteristics of the sound. It is apparent that when the noise level is high, the threatening events are often confused with other, non-threatening events. The errors between the classes of hazardous events are less frequent. It can also be seen that at 20dB SNR there are frequent false alarms, especially falsely detected explosions (in 10 cases) and screams (8 cases). In audio surveillance, however, such false alarms should always be verified by the human personnel, therefore such error is not as grave as classifying a hazardous event as non-threatening (false rejection).

4.3   Localization Results

In this analysis the results obtained are grouped in relation to particular sound sources (i.e. loudspeakers) and presented in Fig. 5 and Fig. 6. The true position of the loudspeaker and the localization results are shown in the Cartesian coordinate system. SNR values were indicated by different types of marker and the length of the radius. Distinctions due to the type of event and disturbance noise are not shown it this case. The main purpose of this presentation is the visualization of the distribution of localization error in relation to the SNR level. It is important to emphasize that the loudspeakers employed are not an ideal point source of sound.

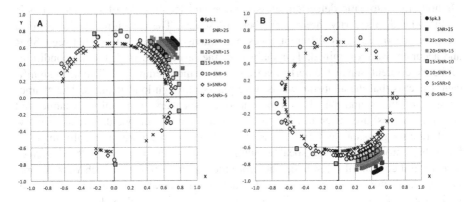

Fig. 5. Sound event detection and localization results: sound events presented from speaker 1 (plot A) and 3 (plot B). Different colored dots indicate the estimated positions for particular SNR values. The black dots (for the greatest radius) indicate the true position of the sound source

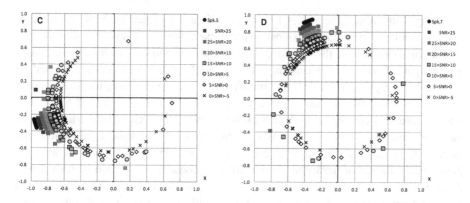

Fig. 6. Sound event detection and localization results, sound events presented from speaker 5 (plot C) and 7 (plot D). Different colored dots indicate the estimated positions for particular SNR values. The black dots (for the greatest radius) indicate the real position of the sound source

Every loudspeaker has its own linear dimensions and directivity. Those parameters should have an influence on the localization results obtained, especially for broadband acoustic events like gunshots, explosions or broken glass. For that reason, in practical situations when the real sound source rapidly emits the high level of acoustic energy its localization can be even more precisely determined than in the prepared experiments.

5   Conclusions

Methods for automatic detection, classification and localization of selected acoustic events related to security threats have been presented. The algorithms were tested in the presence of noise of different types and intensity. The relations between SNR and accuracy were examined. The analysis of the results shows that some conditions of the experiment impair the performance of the methods employed. The most significant aspect is that the acoustic events were played through loudspeakers. The characteristics of the sound which is reproduced by speakers (especially dynamic and spectral features) are different from those of real sounds. This yields a relatively low recall rate for gunshots and explosions. These types of event are practically impossible to be reproduced through speakers with enough fidelity to preserve the dynamics and spectral content of the sound. Therefore the training samples, which were recordings of real events, in some cases do not match the signals analyzed in this experiment in the space of acoustic features. The effect is that gunshots and explosions are either confused with non-threatening events, or confused with each other. The Signal to Noise Ratios of real gunshots and explosions will also be much greater than the SNRs achieved in this experiment, unless the events are heard from a great distance. In the future research attempts will be made to analyze the efficiency of sound event detection, classification and localization by employing real signals. However, in such cases it is very difficult to measure and control the SNR, which was the key aspect of this work.

For the localization technique considered, the accuracy was strongly connected with the SNR value. Its accuracy was high for SNR greater than 15 dB for impulsive sounds events and for SNR greater than 5 dB for screams. The research has proved that the engineered methods for recognizing and localizing acoustic events are capable of operating in noisy conditions with moderate noise levels with an adequate accuracy. It allows them to be implemented in an environmental audio surveillance system, working in both indoor and outdoor conditions. The proposed novel detection algorithms are able to robustly detect events even with negative SNRs. The classification of acoustic events is more prone to errors in the presence of noise. However, some events (especially broken glass) are still accurately recognized at low SNRs.

Acknowledgements. Research is subsidized by the European Commission within FP7 project "INDECT" (Grant Agreement No. 218086). The presented work has been also co-financed by the European Regional Development Fund under the Innovative Economy Operational Programme, INSIGMA project no. POIG.01.01.02-00-062/09.

References

1. Ntalampiras, S., Potamtis, I., Fakotakis, N.: An adaptive framework for acoustic monitoring of potential hazards. EURASIP J. Audio Speech Music Process. 2009, 594103, 1–15 (2009)
2. Valenzise, G., Gerosa, L., Tagliasacchi, M., Antonacci, F., Sarti, A.: Scream and gunshot detection and localization for audio-surveillance systems. In: Proc. IEEE Conf. on Advanced Video and Signal Based Surveillance, London, pp. 21–26 (2007)
3. Zhuang, X., Zhou, X., Hasegawa-Johnson, M., Huang, T.: Real-world acoustic event detection. Pattern Recognition Letters 31, 1543–1551 (2010)
4. Lu, L., Zhang, H., Jiang, H.: Content analysis for audio classification and segmentation. IEEE Trans. Speech Audio Process. 10(7), 504–516 (2002)
5. Rabaoui, A., Kadri, H., Lachiri, Z., Ellouze, N.: Using robust features with multi-class SVMs to classify noisy sounds. In: 3rd Int. Symp. on Communications, Control and Sig. Process., Malta, pp. 594–599 (2008)
6. Dat, T., Li, H.: Sound event recognition with probabilistic distance SVMs. IEEE Trans. Audio Speech Language Process. 19(6), 1556–1568 (2010)
7. Temko, A., Nadeu, C.: Acoustic event detection in meeting room environments. Pattern Recogn. Lett. 30, 1281–1288 (2009)
8. Cowling, M., Sitte, R.: Comparison of techniques for environmental sound recognition. Pattern Recogn. Lett. 24, 2895–2907 (2003)
9. Raytheon BBN Technologies, "Boomerang", http://www.bbn.com/boomerang
10. SST Inc., "ShotSpotter", http://www.shotspotter.com
11. Safety Dynamics Systems, "SENTRI", http://www.safetydynamics.net
12. Kotus, J., Łopatka, K., Kopaczewski, K., Czyżewski, A.: Automatic audio-visual threat detection. In: IEEE Int. Conf. on Multimedia Communications, Services and Security (MCSS 2010), Krakow, pp. 140–144 (2010)

13. Kotus, J., Łopatka, K., Cżyzewski, A.: Detection and localization of selected acoustic events in 3D acoustic field for smart surveillance applications. In: Dziech, A., Czyżewski, A. (eds.) MCSS 2011. CCIS, vol. 149, pp. 55–63. Springer, Heidelberg (2011)

14. Hawkes, M., Nehorai, A.: Wideband source localization using a distributed acoustic vector-sensor array. IEEE Trans. Sig. Process. 51, 1479–1491 (2003)

15. Yoo, I., Yook, D.: Robust voice activity detection using the spectral peaks of vowel sounds. J. of the Electronics and Telecommunication Research Institute 31, 451–453 (2009)

16. Hearst, M.A.: Support vector machines. IEEE Intelligent Systems & Their Applications 13(4), 18–28 (1998)

17. Rabaoui, A., Davy, M., Rossignol, S., Ellouze, N.: Using one-class SVMs and wavelets for audio surveillance. IEEE Trans. on Information Forensics and Security 3(4), 763–775 (2008)

18. Łopatka, K., Żwan, P., Czyżewski, A.: Dangerous sound event recognition using support vector machine classifiers. Advances in Intelligent and Soft Computing 80, 49–57 (2010)

19. Chang, C.C., Lin, C.J.: LIBSVM: A library for support vector machines. ACM Trans. on Intelligent Systems and Technology (TIST) 2(3), article 27 (2011)

20. Kim, H.-G., Moreau, N., Sikora, T.: Audio classification based on MPEG-7 spectral basis representations. IEEE Trans. on Circuits and Systems for Video Technology 14(5), 716–725 (2004)

21. Peeters, G.: A large set of audio features for sound description (similarity and classification) in the CUIDADO project (2004), http://www.ircam.fr/anasyn/peeters/ARTICLES/Peeters_2003_cuidadoaudiofeatures.pdf

22. Żwan, P., Czyżewski, A.: Verification of the parameterization methods in the context of automatic recognition of sounds related to danger. J. of Digital Forensic Practice 3(1), 33–45 (2010)

23. Machine Learning Group at University of Waikato, "Waikato Environment for Knowledge Analysis" (2012), http://www.cs.waikato.ac.nz/ml/weka

24. Platt, J.C.: Sequential minimal optimization: A fast algorithm for training support vector machines. Adv. in Kernel Methods, Support Vector Learning 208(14), 1–21 (1998)

25. Jacobsen, F., de Bree, H.E.: A comparison of two different sound intensity measurement principles. Journal of the Acoustical Society of America 118(3), 1510–1517 (2005)

26. Tijs, E., de Bree, H.-E., Steltenpool, S.: Scan & Paint: a novel sound visualization technique. In: Inter-Noise 2010, Lisbon (2010)

27. Basten, T., de Bree, H.-E., Tijs, E.: Localization and tracking of aircraft with ground based 3D sound probes. In: 33rd European Rotorcraft Forum, Kazan (2007)

28. Kotus, J.: Application of passive acoustic radar to automatic localization, tracking and classification of sound sources. Information Technologies 18, 111–116 (2010)

29. Ntalampiras, S., Potamtis, I., Fakotakis, N.: Probabilistic novelty detection for acoustic surveillance under real-world conditions. IEEE Trans. on Multimedia 13(4), 713–719 (2011)

Examining Quality of Hand Segmentation
Based on Gaussian Mixture Models

Michal Lech, Piotr Dalka, Grzegorz Szwoch, and Andrzej Czyżewski

Multimedia Systems Department
Gdansk Univ. of Technology, Faculty of Electronics, Telecommunications and Informatics
Gdansk, Poland
ksm@sound.eti.pg.gda.pl

Abstract. Results of examination of various implementations of Gaussian mixture models are presented in the paper. Two of the implementations belonged to the Intel's OpenCV 2.4.3 library and utilized Background Subtractor MOG and Background Subtractor MOG2 classes. The third implementation presented in the paper was created by the authors and extended Background Subtractor MOG2 with the possibility of operating on the scaled version of the original video frame and additional image post-processing phase. The algorithms have been evaluated for various conditions related to stability of background. The quality of hand segmentation when a whole user's body is visible in the video frame and when only a hand is present has been assessed. Three measures, based on false negative and false positive errors, were calculated for the assessment of segmentation quality, i.e. precision, recall and accuracy factors.

Keywords: Gaussian mixture models, hand segmentation.

1   Introduction

Hand segmentation is a crucial issue in computer vision systems realizing hand gesture recognition. The quality of segmentation can highly affect the performance of the overall recognition of both shape and motion. In typical gesture recognition systems in which an RGB camera is faced at a user, the complexity of the segmentation is related to varying background behind a user and user movements [1, 2]. In such cases a typical hand segmentation based on subtracting an image with a hand representation from an initial image containing only the background do not lead to satisfying results. Some computer vision systems realize gesture recognition in an RGB video stream in which a user is not visible. An example of such systems can be the Virtual Whiteboard application [3] or the virtual sound mixing console controlled by hand gestures [4]. The system bases on comparing a frame captured from a webcam with an image displayed by the multimedia projector. Although problems related to variability of a background and presence of a user do not exist in this solution, the distortions introduced by camera lens, projector lens, and lighting conditions also make the hand segmentation not trivial.

A. Dziech and A. Czyżewski (Eds.): MCSS 2014, CCIS 429, pp. 111–121, 2014.

The above mentioned problems have been addressed in advanced object segmentation methods based on the background modeling. An example of such methods is the Gaussian Mixture Models (GMM). The method have been assessed for three various implementations among which two originate from OpenCV library [5] and one was the own implementation of the authors. The algorithm basis for this algorithm has been presented in the following section.

2   Algorithm Basis

Gaussian mixture model (GMM) proposed first by Friedman and Russel [6] is a probabilistic method used for background modeling. Its improvements and modifications are extensively utilized in the image processing area due to the offered accuracy bearing in mind the algorithm complexity. GMM approach is based on the assumption that upon the observations made to an image point, the associated background representation can be chosen as the most frequent appearing value. As this esteem can fluctuate, even under strictly controlled conditions, e.g. due to image noise, the model of background for each pixel is described separately by a mixture of K Gaussian distributions. The probability that a pixel has value x_t at time t is given as:

$$p(x_t) = \sum_{i=1}^{K} w_t^i \eta\left(x_t, \mu_t^i, \Sigma_t^i\right) \tag{1}$$

where $p(x_t)$ is a probability that a pixel has value x_t at time t, w_t^i denotes weight, μ_t^i and Σ_t^i are the mean vector and covariance matrix of the i-th distribution at time t, and η is the normal probability density function defined as:

$$\eta(x, \mu, \sigma) = \frac{1}{(2\pi)^{0.5D} |\Sigma|^{0.5}} e^{-0.5\left[(x-\mu)^T \Sigma^{-1}(x-\mu)\right]} \tag{2}$$

where $D = 3$ for RGB color space.

The parameter K is usually a small number between 3 and 5 and is limited by the available computational power. For simplicity and in order to reduce memory consumption it is also assumed that RGB color components are independent, but their variances are not constrained to be identical as in method proposed by Stauffer [7]. In this way the covariance matrix Σ_i of the i-th distribution is a diagonal matrix with variances σ_{Ri}^2, σ_{Gi}^2 and σ_{Bi}^2 of RGB components on its main diagonal.

The parameters w, μ and Σ of distributions are constantly updated based on every new pixel value. Instead of the expectation maximization method, in which implementation would be very costly, as it requires an access to the past data, the on-line K-means approximation is used to update the mixture models. In the first step, distributions are ordered based on the value of r coefficient given by:

$$r = \frac{w}{\sqrt{|\Sigma|}} \tag{3}$$

where $|\Sigma|$ is the determinant of the covariance matrix. A particular color of the scene background is usually more often repeated in the observed data than any color of foreground objects and as such is characterized by a low variance. Hence, a distribution with higher r value represents the background color, more accurately.

Every new pixel x_t is checked against existing distributions, starting from the distribution with the highest r value, until the first match is found. The new pixel value matches a distribution provided every color component value lies within $\Delta = 2.5$ corresponding standard deviations of the distribution. If there is no match, a distribution with the lowest r value is replaced with the new one with the current pixel representing its mean value, an initially low weight and high variance.

The weights of distributions are updated according to the equation [8]:

$$w_t = (1 - \alpha)w_{t-1} + \alpha M_t \tag{4}$$

where α is a learning rate of the model and M_t is equal 1 for the first matching distribution and 0 for other distributions. After the adjustment, the weights are normalized.

If there is a matching distribution, its mean and variance values for every RGB component are adjusted as follows [8]:

$$\mu_t = (1 - \rho)\mu_{t-1} + \rho \cdot x_t \tag{5}$$

$$\sigma_t^2 = (1 - \rho)\sigma_{t-1}^2 + \rho(x_t - \mu_t)^2 \tag{6}$$

The ρ coefficient (usually equal to the parameter α used for weight adjusting) is used instead of a coefficient depending on the current probability density function value, as proposed by Stauffer [7]. The introduced inclusion simplifies the algorithm and reduces the computational complexity. Furthermore, the variances are not allowed to fall below some minimum value, so that matching does not become unstable in scene regions remaining static for a long period of time.

Only the first D distributions of the pixel x in time t ordered by the decreasing r coefficient value are used as the background model, where D is defined as:

$$D_x^t = \arg\min_d \left(\sum_{i=1}^{d} w_i^t > T \right) \tag{7}$$

The threshold T is the minimum fraction of the background model. If T is small, then the background model is usually unimodal. If T is higher, the background color distribution may be diversified, which could result in more than one color being included in the background model. If the current pixel value does not match any of the first D distributions, it is considered as a part of a foreground object.

Object detection accuracy obtained utilizing this method is satisfactory in many cases. However, in real life scenarios, changing lighting conditions can often cause detection errors. This can be noticed especially for scenes with high illumination variations. Therefore, in the literature some further algorithm improvements, mentioned below, are proposed to solve this problem.

Detection errors for scenes with high illumination variations are related to the distribution adaptation process which cannot update the model fast enough, to compensate the changes. This could be solved by applying a variable learning factor [9]. On the other hand, such a modification can also cause detection errors. Higher α and ρ factors affect the distribution weight, mean and variance adaptation rate. Hence, in case of long-lasting lighting variations, the leading Gaussian distribution can be discarded at its position (considering r factor) due to increasing deviation. This problem can be partially solved by utilizing independent adaptation factors for Gaussian mean and deviation [10]. Another modification of GMM introduces spatial dependencies for the pixel assignment process making it more robust [11]. Kaewtrakulpong and Bowden proposed different adaptation formulas for various processing stages to improve the initial model learning process [12]. These formulas have been implemented in BackgroundSubtractorMOG method contained in the OpenCV library and examined with regards to the research related to this paper along with the algorithm proposed by the authors.

3   Implementation

Three various implementations of the GMM method have been considered for the experiments. Two of them belonged to the Intel's OpenCV 2.4.3 library and utilized Background Subtractor MOG and Background Subtractor MOG2 classes. The first of the above mentioned implementations was based on the algorithm proposed by Kaewtrakulpong and Bowden [12]. The second one utilized the algorithm by Zivkovic [13] which in OpenCV library, compared to BackgroundSubtractorMOG, provided shadow detection and elimination. The third implementation of the GMM method was created by the authors using C++ programming language. Implementing Gaussian Mixture Models using only the native C++ libraries enabled to adjust the method to particular environment conditions by modification of parameters not available for a software developer / user in OpenCV library. It also yielded greater possibilities regarding extending the method with new features. Among such features were included: operating on scaled version of the original video frame at the background modeling level and introducing image postprocessing. Rescaling the original video reduces computational complexity of the algorithm in order to process a video stream in real time. With the default value of scaling factor equal 0.5, the width and height of every video frame is set to half of the original size thus reducing the number of pixels for processing by 4. As a result, the moving object segmentation might be inaccurate by ±1 pixel which does not pose any practical problems. In the scope of the postprocessing elimination of all the objects containing number of pixels smaller than the given threshold was performed. Morphological processing involves finding connecting components in the binary mask that forms the result of background subtraction, removing regions containing less than the required number of pixels, and morphological closing and filling holes in all extracted regions. In the classical GMM method by Stauffer & Grimson [7] each color component is associated with the same value of variance. In the method implemented by the authors three separate values of variance are used, i.e. each color component is represented by its own variance value. In comparison with the implementations contained in the OpenCV library there is no constraint put on the maximum value of variance. Moreover, the algorithm enables to set independent values of α and ρ parameters.

4   Experiments

The quality of hand segmentation was assessed considering two following conditions:

1) no user body in a video stream, stable background,
2) a user visible in a video stream and moving slightly.

Under the condition 2) a user performed slight, random movements with his body and inclined the body from its initial location in the frame at a given moment. In this way a natural position of a user while seated in front of the camera-equipped laptop was simulated. Thus, the algorithms were also examined for images containing varying background (since a user's body is in the background). For both conditions the quality of segmenting open hand shape was assessed. The values of the parameters of the algorithms have been chosen, based on the preliminary experiments and given in Table I. These experiments aimed at obtaining distinct elimination of pixels forming inclined head, within 300 frames used during assessment of hand segmentation quality. Shadow detection and elimination feature of the GMM implementations was turned off as a hand visible in the frame casts no shadow.

Table 1. Values of the GMM algorithms parameters used in the experiments

	K	T	Δ	init var.	min. var.	max var.	α	ρ
MOG	5	0.5	-	-	-	-	-	-
MOG2	5	0.5	2.5	7	6	$9 \cdot 10^2$	-	-
Own GMM	5	0.5	2.5	7	6	-	0.01	0.01

The own implementation of the GMM method was tested considering features not available in OpenCV implementations. Namely, the effect of employing additional image postprocessing phase aiming at combining basic morphological operations was checked. The algorithm was also tested for a feature of rescaling the original video stream to increase the processing efficiency. The scaling factor equal to 0.5 was used.

Considering two testing conditions, three algorithms, and the fact that the own implementation of the GMM was tested for disabled and enabled postprocessing and scaling, four configurations were created. In each regular video stream a hand shape was represented by 300 frames. According to the algorithm basis explained in section

2, the background model in the GMM method was created and its parameters were recalculated with each acquired video frame.

The video streams were recorded indoor (Fig. 1). The resolution equaled 320 x 240 pixels and the frame rate equaled 21 frames per second. In Fig. 2 sample images for condition 2) after applying the background/foreground segmentation algorithms to 50-th, 100-th, 200-th, and 300-th frame are presented.

Fig. 1. Sample frame from the original video stream

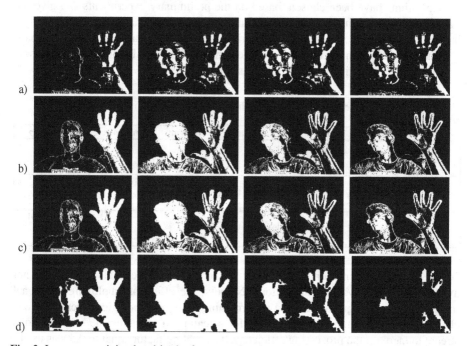

Fig. 2. Images containing hand in the foreground and a user in the background after applying: a) OpenCV MOG, b) OpenCV MOG2, c) own GMM with no postprocessing, d) own GMM with postprocessing and scaling with factor equal 0.5; for 50-th, 100-th, 200-th, and 300-th frame

The ground truth data was prepared which consisted of manually processed binary images of ideally segmented hand shape. The following three measures, based on false negative and false positive errors, were calculated for the assessment of segmentation quality:

$$Precision = \frac{TP}{TP + FP} \tag{8}$$

$$Recall = \frac{TP}{TP + FN} \tag{9}$$

$$Accuracy = \frac{TP + TN}{TP + FP + FN + TN} \tag{10}$$

where:

TP – pixels correctly assigned to foreground (true-positive result),
TN – pixels correctly assigned to background (true-negative),
FP – pixels incorrectly assigned to foreground (false-positive),
FN – pixels incorrectly assigned to background (false-negative).

The precision factor denotes the rate of correct segmentation results in relation to the whole foreground area. The recall parameter marks the degree of relevant segmentations. The accuracy is a more comprehensive measure which shows the overall similarity of the result to the ground truth data. All of these parameters should be maximized for an optimal algorithm. These factors were calculated for the prepared ground truth data and for consecutive video frames. The results have been presented in Figs. 2 – 7.

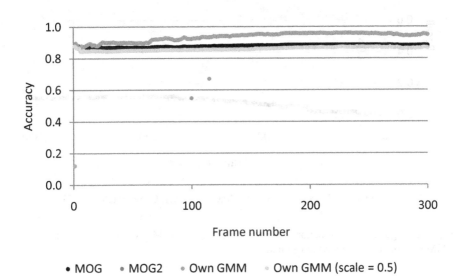

Fig. 3. Change of the accuracy factor with successive frames (the MOG2 curve coincides with own GMM curve); no user in the background

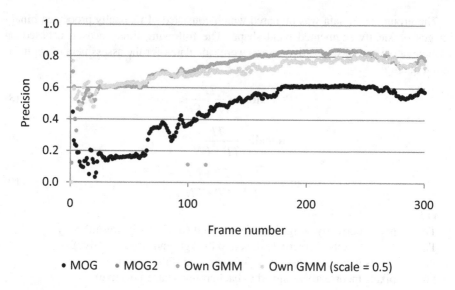

Fig. 4. Change of the precision factor with successive frames (the MOG2 curve coincides with own GMM curve); no user in the background

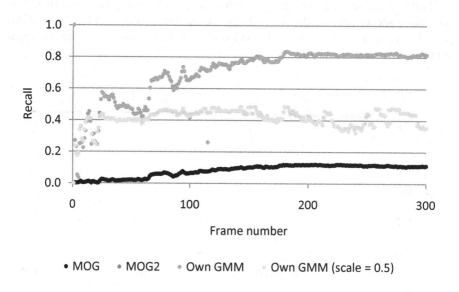

Fig. 5. Change of the recall factor with successive frames (the MOG2 curve coincides with own GMM curve); no user in the background

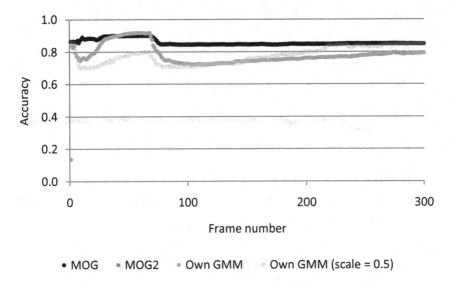

Fig. 6. Change of the accuracy factor with successive frames (the MOG2 curve coincides with own GMM curve); a user in the background

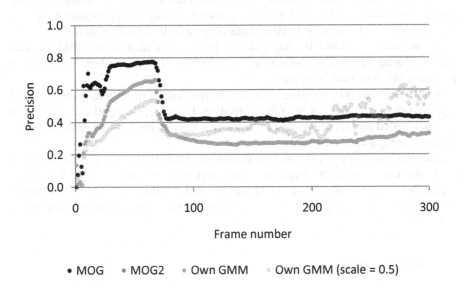

Fig. 7. Change of the precision factor with successive frames (the MOG2 curve coincides with own GMM curve); a user in the background

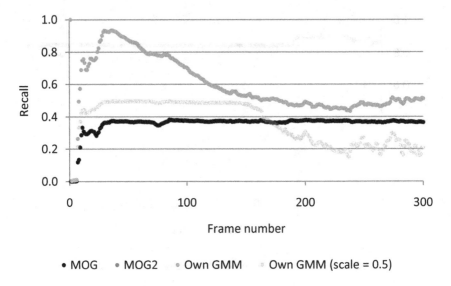

Fig. 8. Change of the recall factor with successive frames (the MOG2 curve coincides with own GMM curve); a user in the background

Variations visible in the beginnings of the charts result from the moment of placing hand in the frame. Rapid change in accuracy and precision chart representations in figs. 5 – 7 between around 80-th and 110-th frames corresponds to the head inclination.

It can be observed that the adaptation to background changes in GMM methods causes reducing pixels of the hand representation with time. It is reflected in the recall feature in Fig. 4 as a sloping curve.

Employing the postprocessing related to morphological operations improves hand representation at the beginning of the adaptation. However, for significant changes in the background and set relatively fast adaptation besides background pixels also pixels constituting a hand are mostly eliminated.

The analysis of charts 2 – 7 and the frames presented in Figs. 1b and 1c enables to state that our own GMM implementation performs similarly to OpenCV BackgroundSubtractorMOG2 algorithm. However, as the authors of above implementation, we gained a better control of the algorithms, making our experiments much more efficient.

5   Conclusions

Basing on the obtained results it can be stated that retrieving hand representation from RGB video stream with a varying background is a particularly complex problem. Utilizing parameters of Gaussian Mixture Models ensuring relatively fast adaptation to background changes, accounts for filtering them out. However, in such a situation, when a user's hand is kept steady in the frame, pixels constituting its representation are eroded in consecutive frames. It seems that Gaussian Mixture Models can make an effective method when applied to scenarios in which background does not change rapidly. An example of such a case can be tracking people and vehicles in a video stream from surveillance cameras [14]. Applying Gaussian Mixture Models to such a problem with parameters providing relatively low adaptation to the background changes, makes it possible to track objects reliably. Utilizing simple foreground segmentation methods based on subtracting successive frames in comparison to advance background modeling results in elimination of inner pixels representing objects.

Acknowledgments. Research funded within the project No. INNOTECH.159382 (In-Tech path), entitled „Spatial Gesture Recognition System with Feedback".

References

1. Van den Bergh, M., Van Gool, L.: Combining RGB and ToF cameras for real-time 3D hand gesture interaction. In: 2011 IEEE Workshop on Applications of Computer Vision (WACV), pp. 66–72 (2011)
2. Yin, X., Guo, D., Xie, M.: Hand image segmentation using color and RCE neural network. Robotics and Autonomous Systems 34(4), 235–250 (2001)
3. Lech, M., Kostek, B., Czyżewski, A.: Virtual Whiteboard: A gesture-controlled pen-free tool emulating school whiteboard. Intelligent Decision Technologies, Multimedia/Multimodal Human-Computer Interaction in Knowledge-based Environments 6(2), 161–169 (2012)
4. Lech, M., Kostek, B.: Testing the novel gesture-based mixing interface. Journal of the Audio Engineering Society 61(5), 301–313 (2013)
5. Bradski, G., Kaehler, A.: Learning OpenCV: Computer Vision with the OpenCV Library. O'Reilly, Sebastopol (2008)
6. Friedman, N., Russell, S.: Image segmentation in video sequences: a probabilistic approach. In: 13th Conf. on Uncertainty in Artificial Intelligence, pp. 175–181 (1997)
7. Stauffer, C., Grimson, W.: Learning patterns of activity using real-time tracking. IEEE Trans. on Pattern Analysis and Machine Intell. 22(8), 747–757 (2000)
8. Laganiere, R.: OpenCV 2 Computer Vision Application Programming Cookbook: Over 50 recipes to master this library of programming functions for real-time computer vision. Packt Publishing (2011)
9. Suo, P., Wang, Y.: An Improved Adaptive Background Modelling Algorithm Based on Gaussian Mixture Model. In: ICSP, pp. 1436–1439 (2008)
10. Chen, G., Yu, Z., Wen, Q., Yu, Y.: Improved Gaussian Mixture Model for Moving Object Detection. In: Deng, H., Miao, D., Lei, J., Wang, F.L. (eds.) AICI 2011, Part I. LNCS, vol. 7002, pp. 179–186. Springer, Heidelberg (2011)
11. Wang, J., Dong, L.: Moving Objects Detection Method Based on a Fast Convergence Gaussian Mixture Model. In: 3rd International Conference on Computer Research and Development, China, pp. 269–273 (2011)
12. Kaewtrakulpong, P., Bowden, R.: An improved adaptive background mixture model for real-time tracking with shadow detection. In: 2nd European Workshop on Advanced Video Based Surveillance Systems (2001)
13. Zivkovic, Z.: Improved adaptive Gausian mixture model for background subtraction. In: International Conference Pattern Recognition, UK, vol. 2, pp. 28–31 (August 2004)
14. Dalka, P.: Multi-camera Vehicle Tracking Using Local Image Features and Neural Networks. In: Dziech, A., Czyżewski, A. (eds.) MCSS 2012. CCIS, vol. 287, pp. 58–67. Springer, Heidelberg (2012)

Modelling Object Behaviour in a Video Surveillance System Using Pawlak's Flowgraph

Karol Lisowski and Andrzej Czyzewski

Gdańsk University of Technology
Department of Multimedia Systems,
Narutowicza 11/12, 80-233 Gdańsk, Poland
{lisowski,andcz}@sound.eti.pg.gda.pl

Abstract. In this paper, methodology of acquisition and processing of video streams for the purpose of modelling object behaviour is presented. Multilevel contextual video processing was also mentioned. The Pawlak's flowgraph is used as a container for the knowledge related to the behaviour of objects in the area supervised by a video surveillance system. Spatio-temporal dependencies in transitions between cameras can be easily changed in real-life situations. In order to cope with such fluctuating conditions, an adaptive algorithm is implemented. Consequently, as it was shown the flowgraph reacts faster to the occurring changes.

Keywords: surveillance systems, Pawlak's fowgraphs, object behaviour.

1 Introduction

Nowadays, video surveillance systems utilize numerous cameras distributed on streets, inside buildings and in other public places. Dozens of cameras can be mounted in an urban district or within a building. Analysis of such a large amount of video data can not be made efficiently by a human. Hence, an automatic analysis must be implemented and the appropriate methods of video processing have to be developed. Modern video surveillance systems use computer analysis in order to obtain the semantic content from a video stream. The video processing operation in a surveillance system is a composite and multistage process which can be divided into layers related to the level of semantic content in the output of a particular stages of processing.

A system such as the one described above generates a large amount of metadata which can be used by various processing algorithms. Each processing layer relies on the results obtained from the previous stage. Therefore, the video processing chain contains the stages listed below:

- background subtraction
- object detection
- object classification
- object tracking within a single camera
- object re-identification

A. Dziech and A. Czyżewski (Eds.): MCSS 2014, CCIS 429, pp. 122–136, 2014.

– object tracking between cameras
– modelling of the object behaviour

After the results of object tracking between pairs of adjacent cameras are obtained, we can calculate a set of paths of objects movement. On this basis, a statistical model is built. The idea of a flowgraph introduced by Pawlak [12,20] is used to reveal dependencies and rules related to the behaviour of objects in a supervised area.

This paper is organized in the following way: in Sec. 2 works related to developing relevant video processing algorithms are mentioned. The method of using flowgraphs to store knowledge about the object behaviour are presented in Sec. 3. Moreover, a flowgraph adapting method is also described in this section. Next, the performed experiments description and comments about the results are encompassed in Sec. 4. In the end, the conclusions related to application of the flowgraphs in the surveillance systems are drawn.

2   Related Works

A considerable effort has been put by various researchers on developing methods of getting a contextual meaning of video streams content from surveillance system cameras. The starting point of video processing is usually the distinction between the stable background and moving objects, as well as shadow removal. The next step is detection of individual moving objects in the mask obtained in the previous step. The next stage is an object tracking within a FOV (Field of View) of a single camera. Additionally, the detected object can be classified as belonging to a specific type (humans, vehicles, etc.) [3,7,25]. Tracking within a single camera provides also information about an objects movement trajectory as well as the time and location of appearing or disappearing. If a number of cameras with non-overlapping FOVs are used, object re-identification methods need to be used to track the movement of objects between cameras. Various methods of object reidentification, based on visual feature descriptors, were developed. An example solution of this problem is based on the analysis of object colour and histogram matching [1]. In a continuously changing environment, where lighting conditions change and differences in white balance of cameras can occur, compensation of colour changes or using colour descriptors independent from these changes are necessary [2,11,13]. Obtaining such visual features of an object is important for efficient re-identification. Another important issue in object tracking between cameras is a topology of the cameras. This information can be obtained either manually or automatically, as a result of topology recovery algorithms [10,17,18,27]. Each object passing through an area supervised by the video surveillance system produces a path which contains a sequence of visited FOVs. Collection of these paths and storing them in a database allows the creation of a statistical model of human behaviour in this area. In other words, such a model contains a statistical route of the object observed by the video surveillance system.

2.1 Multi-level Video Processing

Extraction of the context from video streams can be divided into several stages of video processing (Fig. 1). In the lowest level, the background subtraction provides a binary mask of objects moving within the frame (Fig. 2(b)). From this mask, areas of connected foreground pixels, called blobs, representing contours of the moving objects, are extracted. These blobs are converted into actual objects by a decision making algorithm which uses rules related to object fragmentation or merging, based on the blobs sizes. A majority of methods of background subtraction and object detection are based on the GMM (*Gaussian Mixture Model*) or the Codebook algorithms. More details on this subject can be found in the literature [24,7].

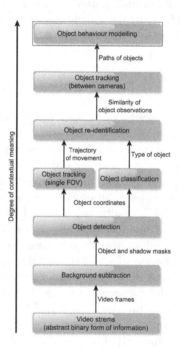

Fig. 1. Multilevel processing of video streams

The subsequent stages of video processing are run when objects are detected and image coordinates (positions in pixels) are assigned to them. These coordinates are needed to initialize the tracking algorithm and to relate the trackers to the detected objects. The trackers are abstract entities used to maintain the data on the tracked objects while they move through the observed area. The tracking algorithm is based on Kalman filters. Descriptors of the object color and texture are computed and stored in the trackers, and the position of each

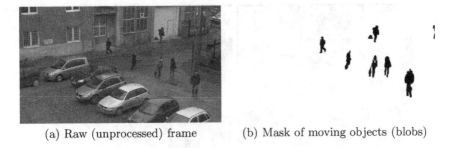

(a) Raw (unprocessed) frame   (b) Mask of moving objects (blobs)

Fig. 2. Backgroung subtraction and object detection

object is predicted from the current frame to the next one. An example of the object tracking results is presented in Fig. 3. The details of the implemented method are avaliable in the literature [26,7].

Fig. 3. Object tracking (images from the PETS 2006 database)

Classification of the detected objects is performed simultaneously with the tracking within a single camera. The classification algorithm is based on shape descriptors. The blob of a detected object is parametrized and classified as a certain type of object. The results are shown in the Fig. 4. The detailed information about this method are also available in the literature [3,7,25].

(a)   (b)

Fig. 4. Object classification

The next processing stages are related to the multi-camera surveillance systems. In this case, object tracking between cameras must be performed. A preliminary process that need to be executed is object re-identification. When an observed object leaves a FOV of the first camera and later a new object appears in another camera, a decision whether the pair of observations represent the same object has to be made. Descriptors of visual features are used to calculate a degree of similarity between the object in a given set of observations. The details of the used method can be found in the literature [9].

In order to construct paths of objects movement, spatio-temporal dependencies related to the topology of camera network should be take into consideration. Various methods and approaches to this issue can be found in the literature [2,1,13,17]. The output of this kind of algorithms is a set of paths passed by the observed objects. In the following section, a method of path analysis oriented on obtaining a model of object behaviour in the observed area, is presented.

In the literature similar approaches to creating additional clues for tracking objects (between non-overlapped cameras) can be found. For instance a dispersion model is used in solution proposed by Leung et al.[14]. In this case determining routes of object are reconstructed basing on the videos from the past.

3   Building Behaviour Model Using Pawlak's Flowgraph

Suppose that a set of cameras is distributed in a certain area. We can define the set of cameras C:

$$C = \{c_a, c_b, \ldots, c_N\} \tag{1}$$

where c_x identifies the particular camera and N is the number of cameras in the whole network. A single path p is defined with the Eq. 2:

$$p = [c_1, c_2, \ldots, c_l] \,, \ c_i \in C \tag{2}$$

where l is the length (the number of steps) of the path p. In other words, an object passing through the supervised area can appear in many cameras and each observation of the object from the consecutive adjacent cameras is considered as a step in the path. Also, a set of paths P which contains all paths observed by a video surveillance system during a certain period can be created (See Eq. 3):

$$P = \{p_1, p_2, \ldots, p_M\} \tag{3}$$

where M is the number of all paths.

The idea of flowgraphs, introduced by Pawlak [12,20], has many implementations in various types of problems [23,15,23,8]. Moreover, extensions of the basic flowgraph concept, which are introduced in order to adjust a flowgraph to a sophisticated challenge, also can be found in the literature[19,4,21,22,28]. In the following part of this paper, such an extension is presented.

The paths collected in the database can be used as the input for the flowgraph, but, using terms introduced by Pawlak in the rough set theory, a set of attributes is needed. Therefore, the set P (Eq. 3) must be converted into the set of transformed paths $\check{P}$ (Eq. 6). An attribute in this case is defined as appearing of an object in the given camera in a strictly determined step of its path. The zeroth step $(j = 0)$ determine a camera in which the object begins its movement through the observer area. The definition of attribute is presented with formula (4):

$$a_{ij} = [c_i, j] \ , \ c_i \in C \ , \ j = 0, 1, \ldots, l_{max} \tag{4}$$

where l_{max} is the length of the longest path. Therefore, an example transformation of the path is defined as shown in Eq. 5:

$$p = [c_a, c_b, c_d, c_c] \rightarrow \check{p} = [a_{a0}, a_{b1}, a_{d2}, a_{c3}, a_{out4}] \tag{5}$$

Applying such transformation to each path in the set P is necessary to input (that is, a set $\check{P}$) this contextual data to the flowgraph. The formula (6) defines the set of transformed paths:

$$\check{P} = \{\check{p}_1, \check{p}_2, \ldots, \check{p}_M\} \tag{6}$$

The next step is utilizing the flowgraph as a container of knowledge about the behaviour of objects within the supervised area. On the basis of the set $\check{P}$, parameters known from the rough set theory must be determined. A group of equations (7) presents formulas needed to perform these calculations:

$$\sigma(a_{ij}) = \frac{\varphi(a_{ij})}{M} \quad , \quad \sigma(a_{ij}, a_{i'(j+1)}) = \frac{\varphi(a_{ij}, a_{i'(j+1)})}{M}$$

$$cer(a_{ij}, a_{i'(j+1)}) = \frac{\sigma(a_{ij}, a_{i'(j+1)})}{\sigma(a_{ij})} \quad , \quad cov(a_{ij}, a_{i'(j+1)}) = \frac{\sigma(a_{ij}, a_{i'(j+1)})}{\sigma(a_{i'(j+1)})} \tag{7}$$

where i and i' are camera identifiers, j and $j+1$ are the indices of two consecutive steps in a path. Additionally, $\sigma(a_{ij})$ is the number of transformed paths that contain the attribute a_{ij}, $\sigma(a_{ij}, a_{i'(j+1)})$ is the number of paths that contain both attributes a_{ij} and $a_{i'(j+1)}$. Value of M is the number of all paths in the set of paths. The parameters *cer* and *cov* are the obtained outputs that have clear interpretation. The parameter $cer\left(a_{ij}, a_{i'(j+1)}\right)$ describes how probable is the situation that the object which appeared in the camera c_i in the step j will appear in the camera $c_{i'}$ in the consecutive step $j + 1$. The parameter *cov* has similar meaning. The parameter $cer\left(a_{ij}, a_{i'(j+1)}\right)$ estimates the probability that the object, which appears in the camera ci0 in step $i + 1$, has been previously observed in the camera c_i. An example flowgraph is presented in Fig. 5

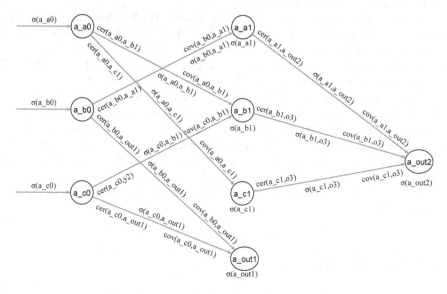

Fig. 5. An example of the flowgraph

Using such constructed flowgraph we can build the probability tree and use it to predict movement of the object. Probabilities that describe this tree can be obtained with the following formula (8):

$$cer[a_{start}, \ldots, a_{end}] = \prod_{i=start}^{i=end} cer(a_i, a_{i+1}) \qquad (8)$$

where *start* determines the vertex from which we start building a probability tree and *end* is the last vertex in probability tree. In Fig. 6 the tree with root in a_{a0}

Flowgraphs, beside many advantages, present also some drawbacks. For example, the flowgraph reacts quite slowly to changes in behaviour of people caused by changes in the topology of a camera network. For example, a new transition between cameras is possible and in this case, the behaviour of objects will also change. Therefore, an adaptation algorithm was applied in the method presented in this paper. In order to adapt a flowgraph to new conditions, measures of the conformity between flowgraphs from different moments were used. Owing to this

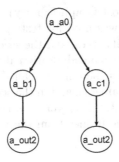

Fig. 6. An example probability tree basing on the flowgraph from Fig. 5

measure we can determine if the flowgraph contains almost the whole knowledge about behaviour of the object. Such situation occurs when new paths do not change structure of the flowgraph in significant way. This flowgraph is considered as a good model of the object behaviour (called a base). The next step of the algorithm is determining if the next paths increase the difference between the base flowgraph and the most recent one. Therefore, two thresholds have to be chosen before the flowgraph starts to operate. The *learning_threshold* is related to making a decision if the flowgraph learned the behaviour of objects, whereas the *adaptive_threshold* is used to decide if a distinct change occured according to the base flowgraph. The measure of confidence is calculated with the following formula (9):

$$D(FG_1, FG_0) = \frac{\sum_{Edges} \left| cer_1(a_{ij}, a_{i'(j+1)}) - cer_0(a_{ij}, a_{i'(j+1)}) \right|}{N} \tag{9}$$

where $Edges$ is set of all edges in the flowgraph FG_0, $(a_{ij}, a_{i'(j+1)})$ identifies the particular edge, N is the number of all edges in the flowgraph FG_0.

Because obtaining a large set of paths is difficult, a method of generating large sets must be implemented. Generation of the large set of paths occurs in the following way:

1. building the flowgraph FG_{real} on the basis of a small (real) set of paths P_{small};
2. generation of paths with a pseudo-random generator [16];
3. collecting the paths into the large set P_{large}.

In the performed experiment, the set P_{large} contains even hundred thousands of paths. In this paper data acquisition and methodology of processing is presented. See previous works of the authors for more details[6,5] related to flowgraphs.

4   Experiments and Results

Methods described in the sections 2 and 3 were implemented in the system used in the experiments. Moreover, flowgraphs and their adaptation algorithm are developed using the BGL (Boost Graph Library). Two path collecting sessions were performed: the first one was used for testing a possibility of building the behaviour model and probability trees, and the second one was oriented on validating the efficiency of the flowgraph adaptation algorithm. The first experiment allowed for collecting 925 paths (hereinafter called the set of paths P_I) from 6 hour video streams from four cameras, and in the second experiment, 1211 paths (hereinafter called the set of paths P_{II}) were observed in ten cameras during 1.5 hours. In the Fig. 7 the sample frames from the video streams used in the experiments is presented.

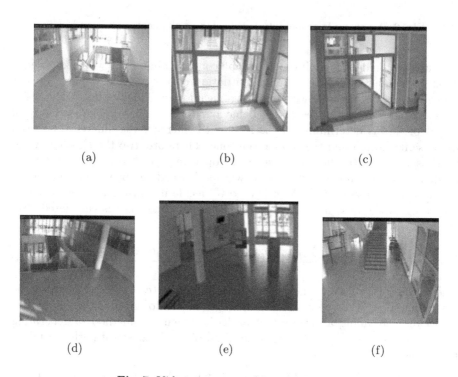

Fig. 7. Video streams used in experiments

On the basis of set P_I, the flowgraph presented in Fig. 8 was obtained. In the Table 1 values of the parameters cer and cov are shown.

Using Eq. 8 we can estimate a probability that an object starting its route in the camera A will go in a given direction (Table 2)

Validation of the flowgraph adaptation method was performed as it is listed below:

1. Building the flowgraph FG_{real} on the basis of a small (real) set of paths;
2. Generation of paths with a pseudo-random generator;
3. Collecting the paths into the large set $P_{generated}$;

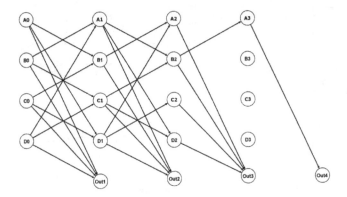

Fig. 8. The flowgraph presenting the obtained model of behaviour

Table 1. The parameters *cer* and *cov* in the flowgraph shown in Fig. 8

Edge	$\sigma()$	$cer()$	Edge	$cer()$	Edge	$cer()$
A0→B1	0.1524	0.4764	D1→A2	0.2190	A2→Out3	1.0000
A0→D1	0.1157	0.3615	D1→C2	0.0714	B2→A3	0.1579
A0→Out1	0.0519	0.1622	A1→B2	0.0287	B2→Out3	0.8421
B0→A1	0.1611	0.6712	A1→D2	0.0656	C2→Out3	1.0000
B0→C1	0.0076	0.0315	A1→Out2	0.9057	D2→Out3	1.0000
B0→Out1	0.0714	0.2973	B1→A2	0.0135	A3→Out4	1.0000
C0→B1	0.0076	0.0398	B1→Out2	0.9865		
C0→D1	0.1114	0.5852	C1→B2	0.1212		
C0→Out1	0.0714	0.3750	C1→D2	0.0303		
D0→A1	0.1027	0.4113	C1→Out2	0.8484		
D0→C1	0.0995	0.3983	D1→Out2	0.7095		
D0→Out1	0.0476	0.1905				

Table 2. The probabilities of various object routes starting from the camera A

Path $[a_{start}, \ldots, a_{end}]$	$cer[a_{start}, \ldots, a_{end}]$
$[A1, B2]$	0.0287
$[A1, B2, A3]$	0.0045
$[A1, B2, A3, Out4]$	0.0045
$[A1, B2, Out3]$	0.0242
$[A1, D2]$	0.0656
$[A1, D2, Out3]$	0.0656
$[A1, Out2]$	0.9057

4. Creating two new flowgraphs (if they are not already created):
   (a) $FG_{reference}$ – a flowgraph that learns from the consecutive paths without the adaptation. The Eqs. 7 are used explicitly (as a new path is add to the flowgraph, the parameters *cer* and *cov* are recalculated)
   (b) $FG_{adaptation}$ – a flowgraph uses the adaptation algorithm

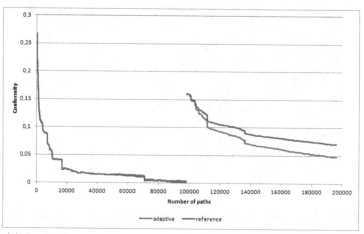

(a) Set P_I, learningTreshold $= 0.0001$, adaptiveTreshhold $= 0.0001$

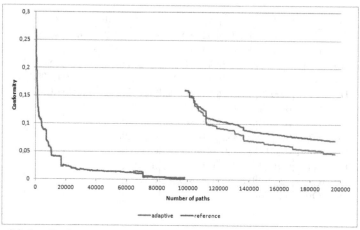

(b) Set P_I, learningTreshold $= 0.0001$, adaptiveTreshhold $= 0.005$

Fig. 9. Changes in conformity between the target flowgraph made on the basis of real set of paths P_I and the flowgraph made from a large set of generated paths

5. Adding new paths (one by one) to the flowgraphs $FG_{reference}$ and $FG_{adaptation}$

6. After each group of a hundred paths, the following conformity measures are calculated: $D_{reference}(FG_{reference}, FG_{real})$ and $D_{adaptation}(FG_{adaptation}, FG_{real})$ with respect to eq. (9)

7. If the first 100 thousand of generated paths are added to the flowgraphs $FG_{reference}$ and $FG_{adaptation}$, then the flowgraph FG_{real} is slightly modified (by adding or removing few edges) and the algorithm goes to step 2. If the second 100 thousand of generated paths are added the algorithm ends.

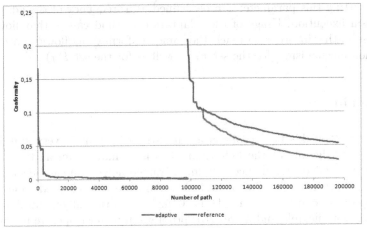

(a) Set P_{II}, learningTreshold $= 0.0001$, adaptiveTreshhold $= 0.0001$

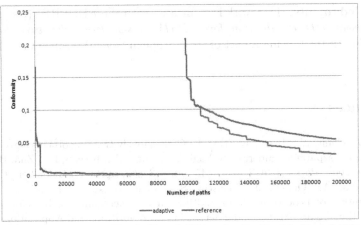

(b) Set P_{II}, learningTreshold $= 0.0001$, adaptiveTreshhold $= 0.005$

Fig. 10. Changes in conformity between the target flowgraph made on the basis of real set of paths $P_I I$ and the flowgraph made from a large set of generated paths

Such validation algorithm of the adaptation method is presented in Fig. 9 and in Fig. 10 for the sets of paths P_I and P_{II}, respectively. As it can be seen that in the half of each chart there is drastic change in conformity measure which is related to simulated change of behaviour. The first part of the chart is used to visualise if adaptation method introduce an unwanted error (lack of conformity). The second part (after 100 thousand paths added) of the chart presents how the adaptation method speeds up learning process of a flowgraph. In other words it describes how fast a flowgraph becomes more coherent with the reality, which is expressed in lower values od D measure (see eq. (9)). Moreover, the impact of changing *adaptive_threshold* is also presented. The easily understandable sense of setting this parameter can be defined as a frequency of the adaptation mechanism execution. Usage of the adaptation method causes that flowgraph needs less paths, in order to reach the same conformity as flowgraph without adaptation mechanisms (for the set P_I as well as for the set P_{II}).

5 Conclusions

The idea of Pawlak's flowgraphs is a data structure that is very suitable for storing knowledge about the behaviour of objects moving inside the area supervised with video surveillance system. A trained flowgraph can be easily used to predict a future movement of the particular object. Such prediction can be also support re-identification methods. Using adaptation algorithm makes the flowgraph more flexible and more error-proof when it must operate in changing conditions.

Acknowledgments. This work is associated with the ADDPRIV (ŞAutomatic Data relevancy Discrimination for a PRIVacy-sensitive video surveillanceŤ) Project No. 261653, being a part of the European Seventh Framework Program (FP7).

References

1. Cai, Y., Chen, W., Huang, K., Tan, T.: Continuously tracking objects across multiple widely separated cameras. In: Yagi, Y., Kang, S.B., Kweon, I.S., Zha, H. (eds.) ACCV 2007, Part I. LNCS, vol. 4843, pp. 843–852. Springer, Heidelberg (2007)

2. Colombo, A., Orwell, J., Velastin, S.: Colour constancy techniques for re-recognition of pedestrians from multiple surveillance cameras. In: Workshop on Multi-Camera and Multi-Modal Sensor Fusion Algorithms and Applications (2008)

3. Dalka, P., Czyżewski, A.: Vehicle classification based on soft computing algorithms. In: Szczuka, M., Kryszkiewicz, M., Ramanna, S., Jensen, R., Hu, Q. (eds.) RSCTC 2010. LNCS, vol. 6086, pp. 70–79. Springer, Heidelberg (2010)

4. Czyżewski, A., Kostek, B.: Musical metadata retrieval with flow graphs. In: Tsumoto, S., Słowiński, R., Komorowski, J., Grzymała-Busse, J.W. (eds.) RSCTC 2004. LNCS (LNAI), vol. 3066, pp. 691–698. Springer, Heidelberg (2004), http://dx.doi.org/10.1007/978-3-540-25929-9_87

5. Czyzewski, A., Lisowski, K.: Adaptive method of adjusting flowgraph for route reconstruction in video surveillance systems. Fundamenta Informaticae 127, 561–576 (2013)

6. Czyzewski, A., Lisowski, K.: Employing flowgraphs for forward route reconstruction in video surveillance system. Journal of Intelligent Information Systems, 1–15 (2013), http://dx.doi.org/10.1007/s10844-013-0253-8

7. Dalka, P., Szwoch, G., Szczuko, P., Czyzewski, A.: Video content analysis in the urban area telemonitoring system. In: Tsihrintzis, G.A., Jain, L.C. (eds.) Multimedia Services in Inteligent Environments. SIST, vol. 3, pp. 241–261. Springer, Heidelberg (2010)

8. Dunin-Keplicz, B., Jankowski, A., Skowron, A., Szczuka, M., Pawlak, Z.: Flow graphs, their fusion and data analysis. In: Monitoring, Security, and Rescue Techniques in Multiagent Systems. Advances in Soft Computing, vol. 28, pp. 3–12. Springer, Heidelberg (2005), http://dx.doi.org/10.1007/3-540-32370-8_1, 10.1007

9. Ellwart, D., Czyżewski, A.: Visual objects description for their re-identification in multi-camera systems. In: Zgrzywa, A., Choroś, K., Siemiński, A. (eds.) Multimedia and Internet Systems: Theory and Practice. AISC, vol. 183, pp. 45–54. Springer, Heidelberg (2013), http://dx.doi.org/10.1007/978-3-642-32335-5_5

10. Farrell, R., Davis, L.S.: Decentralized discovery of camera network topology. IEEE (2008)

11. Gilbert, A., Bowden, R.: Tracking objects across cameras by incrementally learning inter-camera colour calibration and patterns of activity. In: Leonardis, A., Bischof, H., Pinz, A. (eds.) ECCV 2006. LNCS, vol. 3952, pp. 125–136. Springer, Heidelberg (2006)

12. Greco, S., Pawlak, Z., Słowiński, R.: Generalized decision algorithms, rough inference rules, and flow graphs. In: Alpigini, J.J., Peters, J.F., Skowron, A., Zhong, N. (eds.) RSCTC 2002. LNCS (LNAI), vol. 2475, pp. 93–104. Springer, Heidelberg (2002), http://dx.doi.org/10.1007/3-540-45813-1_12

13. Javed, O.: Appearance modeling for tracking in multiple non-overlapping cameras. In: IEEE International Conference on Computer Vision and Pattern Recognition, pp. 26–33 (2005)

14. Leung, V., Orwell, J., Velastin, S.: Performance evaluation of tracking for public transport surveillance. Annals of the BMVA 2010, 1–12 (2010)

15. Liu, H., Sun, J., Zhang, H.: Interpretation of extended pawlak flow graphs using granular computing. In: Peters, J.F., Skowron, A. (eds.) Transactions on Rough Sets VIII. LNCS, vol. 5084, pp. 93–115. Springer, Heidelberg (2008), http://dx.doi.org/10.1007/978-3-540-85064-9_6

16. Matsumoto, M., Nishimura, T.: Mersenne twister: a 623-dimensionally equidistributed uniform pseudo-random number generator. ACM Trans. Model. Comput. Simul. 8(1), 3–30 (1998), http://dx.doi.org/10.1145/272991.272995

17. Nama, Y., Ryu, J., Choi, Y., Cho, W.: Learning spatio-temporal topology of a multi-camera network by tracking multiple people. World Academy of Science - Engieneering and Technology (2007)

18. Niu, C., Grimson, E.: Recovering non-overlapping network topology using far-field vehicle tracking data. In: The 18th International Conference on Pattern Recognition, ICPR 2006 (2006)

19. Pawlak, Z.: Flow graphs and data mining. In: Peters, J.F., Skowron, A. (eds.) Transactions on Rough Sets III. LNCS, vol. 3400, pp. 1–36. Springer, Heidelberg (2005), http://dx.doi.org/10.1007/11427834_1

20. Pawlak, Z.: Rough sets and flow graphs. In: Ślęzak, D., Wang, G., Szczuka, M.S., Düntsch, I., Yao, Y. (eds.) RSFDGrC 2005. LNCS (LNAI), vol. 3641, pp. 1–11. Springer, Heidelberg (2005), http://dx.doi.org/10.1007/11548669_1

21. Pawlak, Z.: Some remarks on conflict analysis. European Journal of Operational Research 166, 649–654 (2005)

22. Pawlak, Z.: Conflicts and negotations. In: Wang, G.-Y., Peters, J.F., Skowron, A., Yao, Y. (eds.) RSKT 2006. LNCS (LNAI), vol. 4062, pp. 12–27. Springer, Heidelberg (2006)

23. Sun, J., Liu, H., Zhang, H.: An extension of pawlak's flow graphs. In: Wang, G.-Y., Peters, J.F., Skowron, A., Yao, Y. (eds.) RSKT 2006. LNCS (LNAI), vol. 4062, pp. 191–199. Springer, Heidelberg (2006), http://dx.doi.org/10.1007/11795131_28

24. Szwoch, G.: Performance evaluation of the parallel codebook algorithm for background subtraction in video stream. In: Dziech, A., Czyżewski, A. (eds.) MCSS 2011. CCIS, vol. 149, pp. 149–157. Springer, Heidelberg (2011)

25. Szwoch, G., Dalka, P., Czyzewski, A.: Objects classification based on their physical sizes for detection of events in camera images. In: NTAV/SPA 2008 Signal Processing: Algorithms, Architectures, Arrangements, and Applications; New Trends in Audio and Video, pp. 15–20 (2008)

26. Szwoch, G., Dalka, P., Czyzewski, A.: Resolving conflicts in object tracking for automatic detection of events in video. Elektronika (2011)

27. Tieu, K., Dalley, G., Grimson, W.E.L.: Inference of non-overlapping camera network topology by measuring statistical dependence. In: Proceedings of the Tenth IEEE International Conference on Computer Vision, ICCV 2005 (2005)

28. Ou Yang, Y.-P., Shieh, H.-M., Tzeng, G.-H., Yen, L., Chan, C.-C.: Business aviation decision-making using rough sets. In: Chan, C.-C., Grzymala-Busse, J.W., Ziarko, W.P. (eds.) RSCTC 2008. LNCS (LNAI), vol. 5306, pp. 329–338. Springer, Heidelberg (2008), http://dx.doi.org/10.1007/978-3-540-88425-5_34

EAR-TUKE: The Acoustic Event Detection System

Martin Lojka, Matúš Pleva, Eva Kiktová, Jozef Juhár, and Anton Čižmár

Technical University of Košice
Dept. of Electronics and Multimedia Communications, FEI TU Košice
Park Komenského 13, 041 20 Košice, Slovak Republic
{martin.lojka,matus.pleva,eva.kiktova,jozef.juhar,anton.cizmar}@tuke.sk
http://www.kemt.fei.tuke.sk

Abstract. This paper introduces acoustic events detection system capable of processing continuous input audio stream in order to detect potentially dangerous acoustic events. The system is representing a light, easy extendable, log-term running and complete solution to acoustic event detection. The system is based on its own approach to detection and classification of acoustic events using modified Viterbi decoding process using in combination with Weighted Finite-State Transducers (WFSTs) to support extensibility and acoustic modeling based on Hidden Markov Models (HMMs). The system is completely programmed in C++ language and was designed to be self sufficient and to not require any additional dependencies. Additionally also a signal preprocessing part for feature extraction of Mel-Frequency Cepstral Coefficient (MFCC), Frequency Bank Coefficient (FBANK) and Mel-Spectral Coefficient (MELSPEC) is included. For robustness increase the system contains Cepstral Mean Normalization (CMN) and our proposed removal of basic coefficients from feature vector.

Keywords: Acoustic Event Detection, Weighted Finite-State Transducers, Continuous Monitoring of Large Urban Areas.

1 Introduction

EAR-TUKE is a lightweight system primarily designed for acoustic events detection from an audio input stream, but not really restricted to this task alone. The gunshot detection in urban areas was a main task initiated in INDECT[1] project work package oriented to intelligent monitoring and automatic detection of threats in urban areas together with our partners from Gdansk University of Technology [1]. The system contains essential functions not only for detection, but also for fast classification of the input audio stream [2]. Its construction supports easy future extension and usage in various other tasks by utilizing weighted finite-state transducers [3]. It is programmed entirely in combination of C language for fast processing and C++ language for logical and easy understandable

---

[1] http://www.indect-project.eu/

A. Dziech and A. Czyżewski (Eds.): MCSS 2014, CCIS 429, pp. 137–148, 2014.

organization of the source code. At the same time the system is made without using additional dependencies making it easier to compile and use on different platforms.

Acoustic events detection system can be of course build from any speech recognition engine available these days [4] [5] or any general purpose toolkits for processing audio signals [7] and classification [6]. These solutions however tend to be unnecessarily complicated and not easy to use for this kind of task. One can say the systems are overcomplicated containing additional and not required functions slowing down the whole system [8]. On top of that, in most cases, they require additional dependencies, with which the user have to count and install before the system or include them while compiling the system.

Based on our past research experiences in acoustic events detection [9] [10], we developed the EAR-TUKE detection system in several iterations successively including new features and functions for accuracy, speed and memory profile enhancement. The result of our effort is described in this paper beginning with a general overview of the system followed by detailed description of its parts. Finally, at the end of the paper, the results of the detection accuracy are presented.

2   EAR-TUKE System Overview

Our effort, as stated in the introduction section, was to create an acoustic event detection system that is not overcomplicated, easy to use and lightweight. This effort was rewarded by the design of EAR-TUKE system. In design process we kept in mind the following requirements:

- Processing of long-term uninterrupted flow of audio stream
- Continuous running of the system
- Easy extensibility of the system
- Low memory profile
- Low computational requirements
- Fast response
- Independent to the environmental changes

The most important requirement that had to be taken into account was the uninterrupted processing of the input audio stream and of course the corresponding continuous running of the whole system. We wanted this system to be used for long-term monitoring of large urban areas for dangerous acoustic events. This also implies the implementation of memory and computational resources saving solutions. All that needed to be combined with fast response of the system. The system should be able to provide results of its detection immediately when the acoustic event happened in sense that the system has little time for computation or confirmation of the result not excluding the real-time processing of the input audio without any significant delay.

The system composition is similar to other systems used in a speech recognition task. The whole system can be broken down into two parts (Fig. 1). The first one is responsible for audio preprocessing combined with feature extraction. The second part is the decoder. Decoder uses search network composed from all available knowledge sources to decode, find, detect and classify desired audio events. The knowledge sources are in this case in contrary to speech recognition simpler and no or little information about sequence of acoustic events is involved. The main part of the knowledge sources is based on the acoustic information about events. This information is statistically described using an acoustic model. The audio preprocessing and decoding, as mentioned before, should be adapted for continuous and uninterrupted processing of input audio signal. As we will describe in this paper later, we were able to achieve such solution.

The EAR-TUKE system is constructed from separable blocks meaning that each block can be separately used without present definition of another block of the system. The implementation of each block is self sufficient and tightly designed, which means that some of the functions of the same block cannot be altered or changed without significant impact to the block itself. Some of the functions are implemented and hardcoded directly into main functions of the block. This is done in favor of fast response and processing of the audio signal. This all imposes limits to the usage of our system, but still we have been able to maintain our desired level of universality.

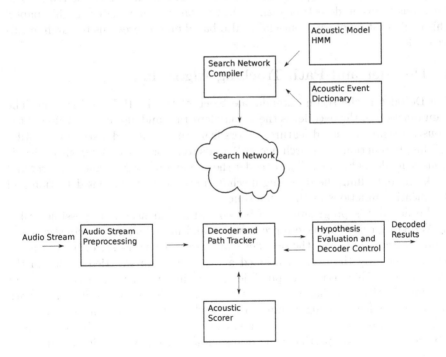

Fig. 1. Internal structure of the EAR-TUKE system

3   Audio Preprocessing and Feature Extraction

The preprocessing part is representing the front-end of our system. It handles audio preprocessing and feature extraction for the next step in acoustic event detection. The front-end is composed to be modular supporting easy implementation and adding new modules. The basic idea behind the front-end is to process audio stream blindly, in sense that no analysis of the input stream is done by the front-end, but the feature extraction. This restriction also applies to any kind of activity detection that cuts out only segments where the acoustic event might be present. All input audio is processed by the front-end and outputted for its whole length.

Currently, the standard Mel-Frequency Cepstral Coefficient (MFCC) can be extracted by our front-end as well as the intermediate results, the Frequency Bank Coefficient (FBANK) and Mel-Spectral Coefficient (MELSPEC) [11]. Additionally energetic and/or zero cepstral coefficient can be included into resulting output feature vector. For each output feature vector the delta and acceleration coefficients can be computed. At the end of the front-end chain preprocessing modules the Cepstral Mean Normalization (CMN) module can be attached. The CMN module is capable of online CMN using sliding window of preset length [12]. Although the CMN is supported, we have found out that it is not required in the acoustic event detection task as it will be described later in this paper. This configuration of the front-end is also based on our previous research in this area [13].

4   Decoder and Path Tracking Algorithm

The Decoder is the second standalone block of the EAR-TUKE system. The main function of the decoder is the actual detection and also classification of the acoustic events extracted feature vectors from the input audio stream. In order to fulfill its function the search network needs to be provided along with suitable acoustic model definitions. The decoder then cooperates with acoustic scorer and block for controlling the decoding mechanism to achieve efficient detection and classification functions at the same time.

The decoder is programmed to be general as much as it is possible utilizing WFSTs for search space representation and interchangeable acoustic scorer representation. This way the decoder can process arbitrary set of input feature vectors, not only the ones mentioned above. Although we tried to design the decoder as much reusable as possible it contains inseparable part: the result tracking algorithm. It handles the retrieval of the decoding result from a path that took the decoding algorithm in the search network. This was done in favor of speed increase and to achieve simpler construction of the decoder. In the next subsections the parts participating in decoding process will be described.

4.1   Search Network

The search network is represented using WFSTs that is a state machine composed with states and transitions between them [14]. Each transition has input and output symbols along with weights. Each search network (see Fig. 2) involves one initial state (marked bold) and one or more final states (marked with double line). The WFSTs are used for their ability to translate input sequence of symbols to output sequence of other symbols, thus from input observations to names of the detected acoustic events [3]. This representation of the search network has its advantages. The first advantage is that the decoder does not need to know about any information provided in the search network as long as the format of the input symbols in the network are coordinated with the acoustic model. This also means that the set of desired events to be detected is easily extendable and we can include any other additional statistical information that needs to be taken into account by the decoding process.

The decoder is based on Hidden Markov Models (HMMs) that are composed from two parts, the topology of the model representing the transition model and from the observations probabilities represented by probability density functions (PDFs) [11] [15]. The WFSTs are used for representation of the topology while the transitions contain probabilities of acoustic model transitions and input symbols are informing about PDFs that needs to be used for scoring the input vectors. The output symbols on the transitions are containing names of the acoustic events. The advantage of representing the topology of HMMs by WFSTs is that the search network can support different topology and number of states for different acoustic events without prior knowledge of the decoder.

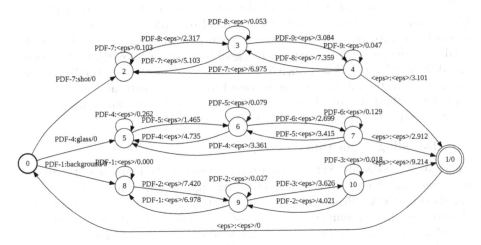

Fig. 2. Weighted Finite-State Transducer Search Network

The search network for our system needs to be generated before the process of detection, meaning that the network representation should be static. As the search network for this kind of task tends to be relatively small (a few dozens of states), the static representation does not imposes any limitation to the usage of the system even on embedded devices with limited resources. The small size of the network also supports fast rearrangement of the network on demand. Another advantage of the static search network is that decoder does not need to bother with the composition of it on-the-fly and so the decoder can work faster [16].

In order to do the detection and classification of an acoustic event the search network contains models not only for acoustic events, but also for background sounds. An example of such search network is on Fig. 2. The network contains three events: gunshot and glass breaking and one background model as can be seen by the output symbols on the transitions. Symbol "$< eps >$" describes empty output symbol. The input symbols are used as information for scoring process and are basically representing the states (Gaussian Mixtures) in HMM acoustic model. The weights on transitions are representing transition probabilities between states also from the HMM acoustic model. This search network is represented by a binary file including the acoustic model information about PDFs allowing us faster loading of all required information into the memory.

4.2 Acoustic Scorer

As mentioned before the decoder requires scorer implementation for scoring input feature vector against the used acoustic model. Our system contains a scorer using PDFs of HMMs and it is working on principle of computing Mahalanobis distance of the feature vector and Gaussian function. The scorer uses information of input symbols provided by the search network in order to know, with which PDFs the input feature vector should be scored.

The scorer is a separate block of the system, so it can be easily replaced with another block that supports another kind of acoustic model or input set of feature vectors. In order to increase robustness of our system in environment conditions changes, such as changes in signal to noise ratio (SNR), we included an additional feature. The principle is to remove a set of basic coefficients of the feature vector during scoring process leaving only delta and acceleration coefficients. We have found out that this important feature works in acoustic event detection task better than using CMN [10].

4.3 Decoding Algorithm

The task of the decoder is to uncover the sequence of the input acoustic events based on input feature vectors extracted from input audio signals. The decoder travels through search network using the feature vectors as guidance in synchronous manner, meaning for each feature vector one step in the search network is performed. Along the path the intermediate scores composed from transition probabilities and acoustic scoring using PDFs are computed. As the result is defined as the most probable path through the search network the Viterbi decoding criterion is used and implemented in form of token passing algorithm, as it is done in Hidden Markov Model Toolkit (HTK) [11]. Token is an object that can travel through the search network and remembers all required intermediate results for representation of the final result. Specifically in our system the token is remembering four elements on its way through the search network:

- Accumulated transition score
- Accumulated acoustic score

- Last found output symbol
- Pointer to token with last non-empty output symbol

When the token travels trough the search network the weight on the transition needs to be accumulated along with total score of the PDFs with incoming feature vector according to the input symbol on the same transition. These accumulated scores together are used for comparing tokens to each other according to Viterbi decoding criterion.

The next information that needs to be tracked along with score are the output symbols on the transitions. In fact the output symbol sequence with the highest score gives us the result of the decoding process. The last two items of the token are used exactly for that purpose. Every token is remembering the last output symbols that it passes on its way through the search network along with the pointer to token with previous passed output symbol. The pointer allows the tokens to chain themselves in order to represent the hypotheses of the decoding process and finally the result of the whole decoding.

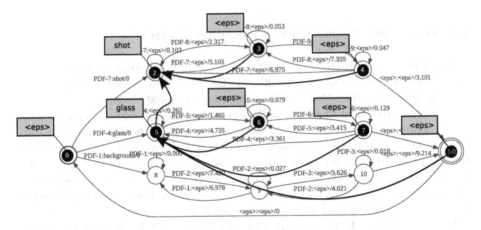

Fig. 3. Decoding process in Weighted Finite-State Transducer Search Network (black bullets are representing tokens, black arrows are representing pointers to previous tokens with non-empty output symbol, gray color is representing search network)

The complete decoding algorithm can be seen on Fig. 3. The black bullets are representing the tokens in the search network, while the black arrows are representing the pointer to token with last non-empty output symbol. At the beginning only one token exists in the search network and it is placed into the initial state. Although logical assumption is to place the tokens where also the information for decoding are, as it is in case of other systems like HTK, in our case the tokens are placed in states despite the information on transitions. The tokens are traveling from state to state. With an incoming input feature vector the tokens are copying themselves to all consecutive states accumulating the total score on the transitions and remembering the output symbols. Each new copy of a token, before passing through a transition, inherits from previous one his score and pointer to a token with last non-empty output symbol, if there was any. If the new token passes non-empty output symbol on its transition to next state, remembers it and so the new tokens copied from this one will inherit a pointer to this token.

By using the pointer to tokens with the last found non-empty output symbol the hypotheses are maintained during the decoding process. When the last token in the chain was from the decoding process according Viterbi decoding criterion removed, the whole hypothesis (the whole chain) should be also removed. Any token in the hypothesis chain can be part of another chain, so each token contains a reference counting. Although the tokens were removed from the search network (does not residue in any state), if there are any other tokens referencing to them, they still exist. If the reference counter drops to zero, the token is then removed from the decoding process completely. When desired, at the end of audio signal or to retrieve partial decoded result, the token from the final state can be taken. The chain, of which the token is the last piece, represents the result of decoding process.

4.4   Hypothesis Evaluation and Decoding Control

This last part of the EAR-TUKE system is a small, but important block. Using this block, the continuous detection and classification is achieved. This block actually does more than that, it also saves computational resources.

As the preprocessing block for audio signal does not provide any information to distinguish acoustic events from background sounds, the detection and followed classification needs to be done in another way. If we use described decoder and the presented search network for processing a recording, the output will be a sequence of acoustic events detected. It is clear that the decoding results are collected at the end of the recording. Unfortunately, for continuous input audio stream this cannot be done as the audio stream does not end.

We have stated at the beginning of this paper that we wanted to design the system to continuously monitor the audio stream. To achieve this, a block for controlling the decoder based on hypothesis evaluation was designed. The function of this block is to look at the end of the current decoding hypothesis (the one represented with token in the final state) after each input feature vector. When the hypothesis meets preset conditions the whole decoding process can be quickly reset meaning that all hypothesis will be removed and all resources released. The new decoding process will start immediately afterwards.

The conditions were chosen so that they take advantage of the background models in the search network. We found out that it is safe to reset the decoder when the most probable hypothesis currently ends with the background model. To be sure that this hypothesis is not a temporary glitch, there is also a condition about the duration of the hypothesis. By testing, the optimal time was finally set to 100 miliseconds. By safe reset of the decoder we are meaning that it does not produce any error or false hypothesis afterwards. In fact the results with the continual reseting the decoder and without it were the same [9].

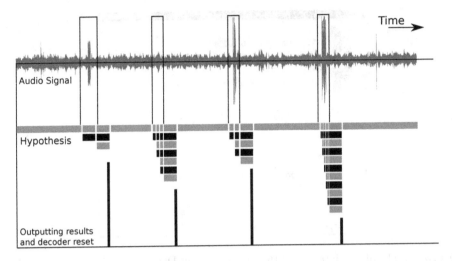

Fig. 4. Example of the Hypothesis evaluation (black color is representing acoustic events hypothesis, gray color is representing background hypothesis)

5 Graphical User Interface

To create easy configuration of our system we included also configuration manager using a configuration file. To support even easier usage, a small graphical user-interface is also provided. It displays the sequence of detected and classified acoustic events. As can be seen in Fig. 5, to each acoustic event the beginning and ending time from the start of the system is provided along with score of each acoustic event.

6 Acoustic Event Detection and Previously Published Results

At the beginning of our development we compared our version of the acoustic event detection with the HTK toolkit. We have used our own database JDAE-TUKE that involved at that time 150 realizations of glass breaking, 463 realizations of gun shots and 53 minutes of background sound (traffic) [17]. From the training part of the database the 2-state HMM model with 4 PDFs on a state using MFCC parametrization including zero, delta and acceleration coefficients was trained and transformed into WFST search network. The training was done using HTK toolkit. The testing part of the database involved 13 gunshot and 46 glass breaking realizations with background sound in the same length. The detection results were the same compared to HTK based system. Both systems from totally 59 reference acoustic events detected 58, thus there was 1 missed alarm. Both systems also included 4 false alarms. This was done by comparing results at the end of the recording, but even with our continual reset of the system based on hypothesis evaluation for long-term monitoring we achieved the

Fig. 5. Graphical user interface of the Acoustic Event Detection System (EAR-TUKE)

Table 1. Development of EAR-TUKE system in comparison to HTK based system

System	Plain Decoding Algorithm Designed	Added Hypothesis Evaluation	Different SNRs	Different SNRs Scorer Modif.
EAR-TUKE	96.32%	96.32%	85.79%	90.99
HTK	96.32%	–	73.33%	–

same results. Accuracy is displayed in Tab. 1 in first two columns. More detailed description and tests can be found in [9].

We have tested our system to robustness against SNR change in environment where the long-term monitoring should be realized. For testing purposes we recorded additional 30 minutes long background recordings to the testing part of the database and mixed them with arbitrary placed acoustic events with different SNRs. We have created test recordings with -3dB, 0dB, 3dB, 6dB, 8dB, 11dB, 14dB, 17dB, and 20dB SNR. We tested all combinations of the models trained and features extracted with and without CMN enabled. The models were from 1 to 3 states HMM with 1 to 1024 PDFs on a state. We have been able to increase the accuracy of our system by changing the acoustic scorer implementation with the basic coefficient of the feature vector removal. We have also conducted similar tests for the HTK based detection system (see accuracy results in Tab. 1 last two columns). We have been able to achieve higher accuracy over HTK without using the scorer modification. With the modification we achieved even better result. More detailed description and more test results are provided in [10].

7 Conclusion

In this paper we have described our system developed for acoustic event detection, the EAR-TUKE system. The system can provide the ability of long-term monitoring task and robustness in acoustic event detection in different environment SNR values. By description of the system development we have also presented our approach to acoustic event detection based on HMMs and utilizing WFST for supporting the extensibility and universality. We have also presented and implemented a method for robustness increase based on the basic coefficient removal from the input feature vector. The presented method has proven to be a better solution to robustness increase than the CMN. For the computational profile enhancement we have described the resource managing system for saving computational resources by continual reseting the system based on current hypotheses monitoring.

As we have stated previously, although the system is focused on acoustic event detection, it can be used in other tasks that are very similar [19]. Using WFSTs in our approach any additional statistical information can be introduced to the search network along with any type of the HMM topology. This also allows the usage of the system in applications like keyword spotting, where also a small search space is used.

The future work will include more robustness, accuracy and speed improvement along with new features extraction implementations including MPEG-7 descriptors.

Acknowledgment. The research presented in this paper was supported by EU R&D Operational Programs funded by the ERDF under the ITMS project 26220220141 (40%) and 26220220155 (40%) and the Ministry of Education of the Slovak Republic under research project VEGA 1/0386/12 (20%).

References

1. Lopatka, K., Kotus, J., Czyzewski, A.: Application of vector sensors to acoustic surveillance of a public interior space. Archives of Acoustics 36, 851–860 (2011)
2. Lopatka, K., Czyzewski, A.: Acceleration of decision making in sound event recognition employing supercomputing cluster. Information Sciences (2013) (article in press)
3. Lojka, M., Juhár, J.: Fast construction of speech recognition network for Slovak language. Journal of Electrical and Electronics Engineering 3(1), 111–114 (2010)
4. Lee, A., Kawahara, T.: Recent Development of Open-Source Speech Recognition Engine Julius. In: Proc. of the Asia-Pacific Signal and Information Processing Association, Annual Summit and Conference, APSIPA ASC 2009, Sapporo, Japan, pp. 131–137 (2009)
5. Lamere, P., Kwok, P., Gouvea, E., Raj, B., Singh, R., Walker, W., Warmuth, M., Wolf, P.: The CMU SPHINX-4 speech recognition system. In: IEEE Intl. Conf. on Acoustics, Speech and Signal Processing (ICASSP 2003), Hong Kong, pp. 2–5 (2003)
6. Schliep, A., Georgi, B., Rungsarityotin, W., Costa, I., Schonhuth, A.: The general Hidden Markov Model library: Analyzing systems with unobservable states. In: Proceedings of the Heinz-Billing-Price, pp. 121–135 (2004)
7. Eyben, F., Weninger, F., Gross, F., Schuller, B.: Recent Developments in openS-MILE, the Munich Open-Source Multimedia Feature Extractor. In: Proc. ACM Multimedia (MM), Barcelona, Spain, pp. 835–838. ACM (2013)

8. Pleva, M., Lojka, M., Juhar, J.: Modified Viterbi decoder for long-term audio events monitoring. Journal of Electrical and Electronics Engineering 5(1), 195–198 (2012)
9. Pleva, M., Lojka, M., Juhar, J., Vozarikova, E.: Evaluating the modified Viterbi decoder for long-term audio events monitoring task. In: Proceedings Elmar - International Symposium Electronics in Marine, pp. 179–182 (2012)
10. Lojka, M., Pleva, M., Juhar, J., Kiktova, E.: Modification of widely used feature vectors for real-time acoustic events detection. In: Proceedings Elmar - International Symposium Electronics in Marine, pp. 199–202 (2013)
11. Young, S., Kershaw, D., Odell, J., Ollason, D., Valtchev, V., Woodland, P.: The HTK Book Version 3.4. Cambridge University Press (2006)
12. Alam, M.J., Ouellet, P., Kenny, P., O'Shaughnessy, D.: Comparative evaluation of feature normalization techniques for speaker verification. In: Travieso-González, C.M., Alonso-Hernández, J.B. (eds.) NOLISP 2011. LNCS, vol. 7015, pp. 246–253. Springer, Heidelberg (2011)
13. Vozáriková, E., Juhár, J., Čižmár, A.: Acoustic events detection using MFCC and MPEG-7 descriptors. In: Dziech, A., Czyżewski, A. (eds.) MCSS 2011. CCIS, vol. 149, pp. 191–197. Springer, Heidelberg (2011)
14. Mohri, M., Pereira, F.C.N., Riley, M.: Speech recognition with weighted finite-state transducers. In: Springer Handbook of Speech Processing, pp. 1–31 (2008)
15. Rabiner, L.: A tutorial on hidden Markov models and selected applications in speech recognition. Proceedings of the IEEE, 257–286 (1989)
16. Dixon, P.R., Hori, C., Kashioka, H.: A comparison of dynamic WFST decoding approaches. In: IEEE International Conference on Acoustics, Speech and Signal Processing (ICASSP), pp. 4209–4212 (2012)
17. Pleva, M., Vozarikova, E., Dobos, L., Cizmar, A.: The joint database of audio events and backgrounds for monitoring of urban areas. Journal of Electrical and Electronics Engineering 4(1), 185–188 (2011)
18. Kiktova, E., Lojka, M., Pleva, M., Juhar, J., Cizmar, A.: Comparison of different feature types for acoustic event detection system. In: Dziech, A., Czyżewski, A. (eds.) MCSS 2013. CCIS, vol. 368, pp. 288–297. Springer, Heidelberg (2013)
19. Sattar, F., Driessen, P.F., Page, W.H.: Automatic event detection for noisy hydrophone data using relevance features. In: Proceedings of the IEEE Pacific RIM Conference on Communications, Computers, and Signal Processing, pp. 383–388 (2013)

Detection of Dialogue in Movie Soundtrack for Speech Intelligibility Enhancement

Kuba Łopatka

Gdansk University of Technology, Faculty of Electronics, Telecommunication
and Informatics, Multimedia Systems Department. Narutowicza 11/12, 80-233 Gdansk, Poland
klopatka@multimed.org

Abstract. A method for detecting dialogue in 5.1 movie soundtrack based on interchannel spectral disparity is presented. The front channel signals (left, right, center) are analyzed in the frequency domain. The selected partials in the center channel signal, which yield high disparity with left and right channels, are detected as dialogue. Subsequently, the dialogue frequency components are boosted to achieve increased dialogue intelligibility. The techniques for reduction of artifacts in the processed signal are also introduced. Smoothing in the time domain and in the frequency domain is applied to reduce unpleasant artifacts. The results of objective tests are provided, which prove that increased dialogue intelligibility is achieved with the aid of the proposed algorithm. The algorithm is particularly applicable in mobile devices while listening in mobile conditions.

Keywords: speech intelligibility, center channel extraction, speech processing, 5.1 downmix.

1   Introduction

Playing a 5.1 movie soundtrack on a device with stereo (2.0) speakers requires a so-called downmix operation. In such case, low intelligibility of movie dialogue is a common problem, especially in mobile listening conditions when noise disturbs the listener or when the movie is played back not in the listener's native language.

In contrast to hitherto existing downmix standards [1-3], we intend to improve dialogue clarity by providing an algorithm which detects the dialogue in movie soundtrack and selectively amplifies the signal components which are related to speech. The dialogue is sought in the center channel of the 5.1 soundtrack. Typically, contrary to a common misconception, the center channel contains not only dialogue. Other sounds, including music and sound effects, are also prominent. However, it is a fair assumption, that once the dialogue is present in the center channel, it is not present in the remaining channels. Therefore, an algorithm based on channel disparity is proposed, which analyzes the spectral content of left, right and center channels and identifies the partials which are related to dialogue. Subsequently, selective

A. Dziech and A. Czyżewski (Eds.): MCSS 2014, CCIS 429, pp. 149–158, 2014.

amplification of dialogue components is applied, which yields improved dialogue intelligibility [4]. This application is focused on speech, and not on singing voice. Albeit the method would also work for singing voice, we find it that the level of voice and instruments in music should not be tampered with.

The problem of dialogue detection in movies was addressed by Kotti et al. [5,6]. Compared to our approach, a much more complicated method was used, employing Support Vector Machines [5] or neural networks [6]. Our algorithm does not require a classifier for detecting dialogue. The problem of voice extraction (or center channel extraction) is known in the field of music signal analysis. Han and Chen [7] proposed a PLCA-based (Probabilistic Latent Component Analysis) algorithm for extracting the main vocal melody from stereophonic music recordings. Lee et al. [8] focus on speech extraction using Blind Source Separation technique based on ICA (Independent Component Analysis). Our algorithm differs by employing a much less complicated method for identification of speech signal, which does not require any statistical processing and is suitable for online operation. Barry et al. [9], on the other hand, proposed a real-time algorithm based on frequency-azimuth analysis, which enables the separation of sound sources in the stereo recording (ADRess algorithm). The method proposed in our work is based on the 5.1 channel layout, which alters the assumptions and the processing required to detect speech in the recording. In our previous work the 5.1 to stereo downmix algorithm with improved dialogue intelligibility was introduced for the first time [10]. In this paper we show how we developed the dialogue detection algorithm by adding signal processing operations which improve the quality of the resulting signal.

2   Overview of the Algorithm

It is assumed that the input of the algorithm is a 5.1 channel movie soundtrack with the channel layout as follows: front left channel - $l(t)$, front right channel - $r(t)$, front center channel - $c(t)$, low frequency channel - $lf(t)$, rear left channel - $l_s(t)$, rear right channel - $r_s(t)$. The low frequency channel, as in most downmix methods, is discarded. In the digital domain the channels are denoted $x[n]$ and their DFT-based (Digital Fourier Transform) spectral representations are denoted $X[k]$. The diagram of the algorithm is presented in Fig. 1. The highlighted blocks pertain to the operations described in detail in this paper. The input channels are analyzed in the frequency domain. The interchannel spectral disparity function $V[k]$ is calculated. Next, the dialogue-related frequency components are detected by applying a voice detection threshold to the disparity function. Thus, a dialogue detection mask $m[k]$ is obtained, which indicates which of the frequency components of the center channel are related to dialogue. Subsequently, energy thresholding is applied to eliminate false positive detections. Finally, smoothing of the dialogue mask is performed in order to reduce the artifacts in the resulting signal.

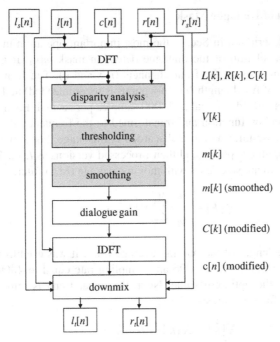

Fig. 1. Block diagram of the algorithm

After the spectral analysis has been completed, the center channel is modified according to Eq. (1),

$$C[k] = C[k] \cdot (1 + g \cdot m[k]) \tag{1}$$

where g is the gain applied to dialogue components. After the modified center channel is transformed back to the time domain, the stereo downmix is obtained according to standard matrix downmix equations:

$$l_t[n] = l[n] + 0.707 \cdot c[n] + 0.5 \cdot l_s[n]$$
$$r_t[n] = r[n] + 0.707 \cdot c[n] + 0.5 \cdot r_s[n] \tag{2}$$

where $l_t[n]$, $r_t[n]$ are the left and right channels of the stereo downmix and the center channel is modified according to Eq. (1).

3   Spectral Analysis

In this section the spectral analysis of the signal is outlined. The result of this processing is a dialogue detection mask, which contains the information about the frequency components, which should be amplified to improve speech intelligibility.

3.1   Calculation of Dialogue Mask

According to the description in Sec. 2, the most important operation in the presented algorithm is the calculation of the dialogue detection mask $m[k]$. It is achieved by spectral disparity analysis of the front channels (l, r and c). The front channels are divided into frames of fixed length N (4096 points is recommended) and 50% overlap. The sampling rate assumed is equal to 48000 samples per second. Each frame is multiplied by Hann window function and transformed to the frequency domain with the use of DFT. The phase information is discarded at this stage. For simplicity, we will denote both the amplitude spectra and their processed versions as $L[k]$, $R[k]$ and $C[k]$. The amplitude spectra are smoothed with moving average (MA) filter,

$$X[k] = \frac{1}{M} \sum_{m=1}^{M} X[k-m]$$ (3)

where M equals the length of the moving average filter. It was established in experiments that $M = 5$, which for $N = 4096$ and sampling rate equal to 48000 S/s corresponds to 60 Hz, is the optimum value. Next, the linear trend is removed from the spectra to facilitate further analysis:

$$X[k] = X[k] - (b - k \cdot a)$$ (4)

where:

$$a = \frac{\sum_k (k \cdot X[k]) - \frac{1}{K} \sum_k k \cdot \sum_k X[k]}{\sum_k k^2 - \frac{1}{K} \left(\sum_k k\right)^2}$$ (5)

$$b = \frac{1}{K} \sum_k X[k] - a \cdot \sum_k k$$

and $K = N/2$. The operations in Eqs. (3-5) are applied to each of the front channels, resulting in the processed spectra $L[k]$, $R[k]$ and $C[k]$. In the next step the spectral disparity function $V[k]$ is calculated.

$$V[k] = \frac{C[k] - L[k]}{C[k] + L[k]} \cdot \frac{C[k] - R[k]}{C[k] + R[k]}$$ (6)

The disparity function is by definition constrained to the interval [-1;1]. The maximum value of disparity indicates that the frequency component is present only in the center channel, whereas the -1 value indicates that the given partial was absent in the center channel and present in the side channels. The dialogue detection mask is defined according to Eq. (7),

$$m[k] = \begin{cases} 1 & \text{if } V[k] \geq t_d \wedge k_1 < k < k_2 \\ 0 & \text{if } V[k] < t_d \end{cases} \tag{7}$$

where t_d is the dialogue threshold and k_1, k_2 are the lower and upper frequency bin limits. We assume that the threshold should be set by the user according to their comfort level. In the experiments we limited dialogue detection to 300-8000 Hz. The *ones* in the dialogue detection mask correspond to the locations of the frequency components which are identified as dialogue.

3.2 Energy Thresholding

The dialogue detection mask $m[k]$ calculated according to Eq. (7) may contain false detections of partials which are not related to speech. It occurs frequently that the current sound frame contains no dialogue, and still some dialogue components are falsely detected. Such false detections are eliminated employing a simple energy criterion. We calculate the energy of the detected dialogue according to Eq. (8),

$$E_d = \sum_{k_1}^{k_2} m[k] \cdot C[k]^2 \tag{8}$$

where $C[k]$ denotes the original center channel spectrum (before processing); and the total energy according to Eq. (9).

$$E_{tot} = \sum_{k_1}^{k_2} C[k]^2 \tag{9}$$

The frames which fail to meet the criterion

$$E_d \geq E_{tot} \cdot t_e \tag{10}$$

where t_e is the energy threshold, are discarded as false detections.

4   Reduction of Artifacts

The reconstruction of the signal from the modified STFT spectrum is prone to two kind of artifacts. The first kind are clicks which are present in the reconstructed signal at time points, in which discontinuities in the spectrum are present. We employ moving average filtration in the frequency domain to smooth the edges of the spectrogram and to reduce such kinds of artifacts. The other sort of distortion is the so-called musical noise. Some of the existing methods for reduction of musical noise employ median filtering [11], or the Ephraim-Malah algorithm [12,13]. We employ smoothing in the time domain (by exponential averaging) to suppress the residual noise in the reconstructed signal.

4.1   Frequency Smoothing

The transients, i.e. clicks in the signal, resulting from spectrogram discontinuities are visible in the spectrogram in Fig. 2. The spectrum of the extracted dialogue channel d is presented, which makes the distortions and the smoothing result more apparent. The spectrum of the dialogue channel is obtained by multiplying the center channel spectrum with the dialogue mask:

$$D[k] = m[k] \cdot C[k] \tag{11}$$

The smoothed dialogue mask is calculated by moving average filtration as defined in Eq. (12),

$$m[k] = \frac{1}{L} \sum_{i=1}^{L_f} m[k - i] \tag{12}$$

where L_f is the length of the MA filter employed for frequency smoothing. In practice, best results are obtained for a filter width equal to 4 spectral bins, which at $N = 4096$ and $SR = 48000$ S/s corresponds to 46.87 Hz. It is worth noting that when the MA filter is too long, dialogue detection becomes less precise. The spectrogram of the signal after frequency smoothing is shown in Fig. 3. It is visible that the frequency smoothing significantly reduces the clicks in the signal.

4.2   Time Smoothing

Time smoothing is employed to reduce both the transient artifacts and the musical noise. Exponential averaging [14] of the dialogue mask is introduced according to the formula:

$$\mathbf{m} = \mathbf{m}_{new} \cdot \alpha + \mathbf{m}_{old} \cdot (1 - \alpha) \tag{13}$$

where $\mathbf{m}_{new}$ is the mask calculated only from the current frame (according to Eq. (7)), $\mathbf{m}_{old}$ is the $\mathbf{m}$ from the previous frame and α is the exponential averaging constant, which relates to the time constant:

$$T_c = \frac{N}{SR \cdot \alpha} \tag{14}$$

It was found during experiments that the optimum time constant lies in the range from 100 to 200 ms. If the time averaging constant is too long, the dialogue detection mask becomes smeared and the algorithm is less precise. The effect of time smoothing is shown in Fig. 4. Time smoothing helps to significantly reduce the musical noise and also suppresses some of the clicks. However, applying exponential smoothing yields to a decrease in dialogue amplification. Due to the operation expressedin Eq. (13) the values in $\mathbf{m}$ are usually much less than 1, which affects the dialogue boost introduced in Eq. (1). It was established that after time smoothing the energy of the detected dialogue is at least 6 dB, lower. Therefore, 6 dB additional gain is applied to make up for this effect.

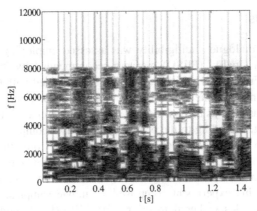

Fig. 2. Spectrogram of the detected dialogue without smoothing

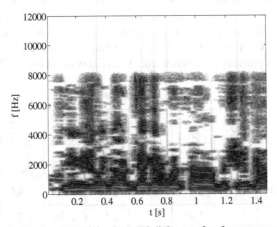

Fig. 3. Spectrogram of the detected dialogue after frequency smoothing

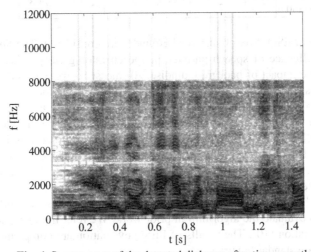

Fig. 4. Spectrogram of the detected dialogue after time smoothing

5   Experiments

The improvement of dialogue intelligibility was assessed employing the Perceptual Evaluation of Speech Quality (PESQ) measure recommended by the International Telecommunication Union (ITU) [15]. The tests were conducted with Opticom Opera software [16]. The center channel was used as a reference track and the downmixed signal (see Eq. (2)) was used as the test signal [17]. The downmix with dialogue intelligibility enhancement, according to the proposed method, is compared with standard downmix methods: ATSC (Advanced Television Systems Committee) [18], ETSI (European Telecommunications Standards Institute) [1], ISO/IEC (International Standards Organization / International Electrotechnical Commission) [2] and ITU [3]. The test set employed in this experiment comprised 12 movie samples, chosen from a database of movie samples gathered in prior work [10,17]. All samples contained actors' speech and different background sounds, such as music, loud sound effects (shots, motor noise) or urban noise. The proposed algorithm was evaluated with 10 dB boost and with 6 dB boost. The energy threshold was equal to -10 dB and the dialogue threshold was equal to 0.3. No time smoothing and no frequency smoothing was introduced in this particular measurement. The results are shown in Tab. 1.

Table 1. Results of PESQ evaluation [17]

	ATSC	ETSI	IEC	ITU	proposed (6 dB)	proposed (10 dB)
PESQ	2.52	2.17	2.67	2.65	**2.85**	2.85
Speech	2.39	1.95	2.57	2.54	**2.76**	2.77
Back-ground	2.94	2.74	3.03	3.01	**3.15**	3.08

The measures PESQ, Speech and Background were considered. The *Speech* factor depicts the influence of speech partials on speech intelligibility, whereas *Background* reflects the impact of background noise. All measures were considered better when high values are obtained. The average value from evaluation of 12 different signal samples from different movies are presented. It is visible that the proposed algorithm outperforms the standard downmix methods as far as speech intelligibility is concerned. Such a result was also proven in subjective listening tests in our previous work [10]. The difference between the 10 dB and 6 dB version of the proposed algorithm is rather subtle. The *Background* metrics is higher for the 6 dB version, since larger gain leads to an increase in distortions, i.a. musical noise.

Apart from the PESQ evaluation, standard detection measures (TP, FP, MSER) were also used to evaluate the algorithm in prior work. We refer the interested reader to the prior publication [10]. The results of PESQ evaluation are compliant with the evaluation based on standard metrics.

6   Conclusions

A method for detection of movie dialogue in 5.1 soundtrack was presented. The results of dialogue detection are used to enhance speech intelligibility of the movie soundtrack. The results of objective tests employing PESQ measure were presented, which prove the effectiveness of the algorithm.

The methods for reduction of artifacts based on frequency smoothing and temporal smoothing were introduced. The effect of these operations will be evaluated in the future work by means of subjective listening tests. In future research we also aim to implement mechanisms for the automatic adjustment of dialogue detection threshold t_d.

Acknowledgements. This work was supported by the grant no. PBS1/B3/16/2012 entitled „Multimodal system supporting acoustic communication with computers" financed by the Polish National Centre for Research and Development and the company Intel Technology Poland. Special thanks to Adrian Stabiński for conducting the PESQ measurements.

References

1. Technical Specification: ETSI TS 102 563 V1.2.1, European Telecommunication Standards Institute (2010)
2. Technical standard: ISO/IEC 14496-3:2009, Information technology – Coding of audio-visual objects – Part 3: Audio, International Standards Organization (2009)
3. Technical standard: ITU-R B S.775-3 - Multichannel stereophonic sound system with and without accompanying picture. International Telecommunication Union (2006)
4. Lopatka, K., Czyzewski, A.: Method and apparatus for speech clarity enhancement in multichannel multimedia signal, especially audio-visual signal. Polish patent application no. P.402373 (January 7, 2013)
5. Kotti, M., Ververidis, D., Evangelopoulos, G., Panagakis, I., Kotropoulos, C., Maragos, P., Pita, I.: Audio-Assisted Movie Dialogue Detection. IEEE Transactions on Circuits and Systems for Video Technology 18(11), 1618–1627 (2008)
6. Kotti, M., Benetos, E., Kotropoulos, C., Pitas, I.: A neural network approach to audio-assisted movie dialogue detection. Neurocomputing 71(1-3), 157–166 (2007)
7. Han, J., Chen, C.-W.: Improving melody extraction using Probabilistic Latent Component Analysis. In: 2011 IEEE International Conference on Acoustics, Speech and Signal Processing (ICASSP), May 22-27, pp. 33–36. IEEE, Prague (2011)
8. Lee, T.-W., Lewicki, M.S., Girolami, M., Sejnowski, T.J.: Blind source separation of more sources than mixtures using overcomplete representations. Signal Processing Letters 6(4), 87–90 (1999)
9. Barry, D., Lawlor, R., Coyle, E.: Real-time sound source separation: Azimuth discrimination and resynthesis. In: 117th Audio Engineering Society Convention. AES, San Francisco (2004)
10. Lopatka, K., Kunka, B., Czyzewski, A.: Novel 5.1 downmix algorithm with improved dialogue intelligibility. In: 134th Audio Engineering Society Convention, May 4-7. AES, Rome (2013)

11. Goh, Z., Tan, K.C., Tan, T.G.: Postprocessing method for suppressing musical noise generated by spectral subtraction. IEEE Transactions on Speech and Audio Processing 6(3), 287–292 (1998)
12. Cappe, O.: Elimination of the musical noise phenomenon with the Ephraim and Malah noise suppressor. IEEE Transactions on Speech and Audio Processing 2(2), 345–349 (1994)
13. Ephraim, Y., Malah, D.: Speech enhancement using a minimum-mean square error short-time spectral amplitude estimator. IEEE Transactions on Acoustics, Speech and Signal Processing 32(6), 1109–1121 (1984)
14. Yager, R.: Exponential smoothing with credibility weighted observations. Information Sciences 252, 96–105 (2013)
15. ITU-T Recommendation P.800, Methods for Subjective Determination of Transmission Quality, ITU (1996)
16. Opticom software homepage (2013), http://www.opticom.de
17. Stabinski, A.: Multimedia database for evaluation of downmix quality, Master thesis, Gdansk University of Technology (2013)
18. Digital Audio Compression Standard (AC-3, E-AC-3), ATSC (2010)

Fuzzy Classification Method for Knife Detection Problem

Aleksandra Maksimova[1], Andrzej Matiolański[2], and Jakob Wassermann[3]

[1] Institute of Applied Mathematics and Mechanics, National Academy of Science of Ukraine,
Donetsk, Ukraine
`maximova.alexandra@mail.ru`
[2] Department of Telecommunication, AGH University of Science and Technology,
Krakow, Poland
`matiolanski@kt.agh.edu.pl`
[3] Department of Electronic Engineering, University of Applied Sciences Technikum Wien,
Wien, Austria
`jakob.wassermann@technikum-wien.at`

Abstract. In this paper we propose a new approach for pattern recognition problems with non-uniform classes of images. The main idea of this classification method is to describe classes of images with their fuzzy portraits. This approach provides good generalizing ability of algorithm. The fuzzy set is calculated as a preliminary result of algorithm before crisp decision or rejecting that allows to solve a problem of uncertainly at the boundaries of classes. We use the method to solve the problem of knife detection in still images. The main idea of this study is to test fuzzy classification with features vectors in real environment. As a feature vectors we decided to use selected MPEG-7 descriptors schemes. The described method was experimentally validated on dataset with over 12 thousands images. The article contains results of five experiments which confirm good accuracy of the proposed method.

Keywords: pattern recognition, fuzzy classifier, fuzzy inference, data analysis, knife detection, feature descriptor.

1   Introduction

This paper deals with analyzing the video in CCTV systems. There are various problems associated with analyzing such dangerous situations. The knife in the human hand is an example of a signal of danger. Our motivation is to solve the problem of knife recognition in frames from camera video sequences.

There are several known approaches to knife detection: using Haar cascades [1], Active Appearance Model [2] and Geometrical Approach [3]. Those methods work with images pixel by pixel, which in many cases could be inefficient. The way of representing the image as a set of feature vectors is using descriptors MPEG-7, are introduced in this paper.

In prior studies the adequate algorithm accuracy could be achieved only for simple examples, when the knife is clearly observed in the image. For more difficult situations,

A. Dziech and A. Czyżewski (Eds.): MCSS 2014, CCIS 429, pp. 159–169, 2014.

when the blade of the knife reflects light, reducing the visibility, or if the knife is turned edgewise to the frame, the quality of the algorithm is poor.

Methods of object identification on the image are distinguished by great percent of false alarms. The quality rate can be estimated more effectively by multi-valued truth-space is used in fuzzy logic theory [4]. In such case the result of classification algorithm is information vector with degree of confidence with the object assigned to a particular class. Methods for pattern recognition, that use fuzzy sets, are called fuzzy classifiers [5]. There are some approaches for fuzzy classifiers creation: tuning knowledge database by evolutionary methods [6], applying FuzzyLVQ and FSOM networks [7], and using fuzzy clustering methods [8]. We will use fuzzy clustering approach extended for pattern recognition problem.

The paper is organized as follows. Section 2 describes used feature vectors, section 3 introduces inference model based on fuzzy classification method. Section 4 contains experimental verification of proposed approach, section 5 is a conclusion.

2   MPEG-7 Feature Vectors

The cropped images are obtained from CCTV cameras. The image is scanned with a sliding window of size $W \times H$, so let us solve the problem for these $W \times H$ fragments of original image. We will threat the problem as a pattern recognition one. Database consists of two classes of images. Let us consider two types of images: positive examples (PE) if there is a knife on the image (Fig. 1 a), and about negative examples (NE) otherwise (Fig. 1 b). The images was taken indoor or through car window (because holding knife at street is forbidden in Poland).

a)   b)

Fig. 1. Exemplary images: a) positive example, b) negative example

Modern literature described many different visual descriptors with their advantages and disadvantages [9]. Among them we decided to use visual descriptors from MPEG-7 standard. Because of specific knifes image pattern we chose two descriptors: Edge Histogram [10] and Homogeneous Texture [11]. The first one contains information about various kinds of edges on the image. It is a numerical vector contains counted eighty edges types. The second describes specific image pattern. It describes directionality, coarseness and regularity of patterns in image. Those two descriptors give us entire information about features characteristic for knives. We avoid using color and shape descriptors because of light reflections and the great number of knife types. The described feature vectors are used to build the model, which presented in this work.

3   Fuzzy Classification Model

To create a model for knife detection it was taken into account the peculiarities of the problem and the presentation of image using MPEG-7. Let us discuss solving the pattern recognition problem in the face of uncertainty [12], where the object of the real world (e ∈ O) is represented as a vector of informative features:

$$x = (x_1, x_2, \dots, x_m),\tag{1}$$

where $x_i = f_i(e)$, f_i – is measuring method for i feature of real object:

$$f_i: O \rightarrow X_i,\tag{2}$$

where X_i – admitted region for the feature, due to the nature of the object and its measurement method, $X_i \subset \mathcal{R}$, where $\mathcal{R}$ is the set of real numbers.

Let Ω be an alphabet of classes of images for patter recognition problem:

$$\Omega = \{\omega_j\}_{j=1}^{k},\tag{3}$$

where ω_j – is the name of class of images and k –is their number.

It is known finite set of   samples:

$$Z = \{(e_i, o_i)\}_{i=1}^{n}\tag{4}$$

where e_i –   is   real   object,   described   by   feature   vector x (1),   and $o_i \in \Omega$ – is his label.

Let us construct a classifier as a mapping:

$$D: X \mapsto \tilde{\Omega}\tag{5}$$

where Ω – an alphabet of classes of images (3), $\tilde{\Omega}$ – the set of fuzzy subsets over alphabet of classes, a $X = X_1 \times X_2 \times \dots \times X_m$ – region of admissible values in the features vectors space of object x, specified in (1). As a classification result in this situation will be fuzzy set:

$$\tilde{\alpha} = \sum_{i=1}^{k} \alpha_i / \omega_i,\tag{6}$$

where α_i – the degree of similarity between the object x and class of images ω_i. To improve the method validity the final decision about object belonging to class of images is performed by analyzing the obtained fuzzy set $\tilde{\alpha}$,specified in (6).

3.1   The Clustering Algorithm with an Unknown Number of Classes

In this paper it is proposed to carry out a preliminary analysis of the data in order to establish the intra-structure for each class of images. For these purposes are encouraged to use FCM-fuzzy clustering algorithm [8]. Result of the algorithm is fuzzy c −partition as matrix $U = [u_{ik}]_{n \times c}$, where u_{ik} − is degree of membership x_i to cluster k, and c − number of clusters, which is a parameter of the algorithm. There are two types of c-partition, it is used further in the work:

$$M_{fcn} = \{U \in M_{pcn} | \forall k \ \Sigma_{i=1}^{c} u_{ik} = 1\}, \tag{7}$$

$$M_{hcn} = \{U \in M_{fcn} | \forall k, i \ u_{ik} \in \{0,1\}\}, \tag{8}$$

where M_{pcn} − possibilistic, M_{fcn} − fuzzy and M_{hcn} − crisp c-partition.

Besides c−partition $U \in M_{fcn}$, results of algorithm are geometrical centers of clusters $G = \{g_i, g_2, ..., g_c\} \subset \mathcal{R}^m$. FCM-algorithm minimizes the Bezdek-Dann functional:

$$J_{\gamma}^{FCM}(U, G; X) = \Sigma_{k=1}^{n} \Sigma_{i=1}^{c} u_{ik}^{\gamma} d^2(x_k, g_i) \rightarrow \min_{\{U,G\}} \tag{9}$$

under the constraints:

$$\Sigma_{i=1}^{c} u_{ik} = 1, \forall x_k , k = \overline{1, n}, \tag{10}$$

where γ − fuzziness coefficient, and $d^2(x, g)$ − square of the distance between the element x and the center of the cluster g. Here it is used Euclidean distance. The method of altering-optimization is used in FCM-algorithm. It is calculated at each step by the centers of the cluster membership degrees u_{ik} for object x_k:

$$u_{ik} = \left(\Sigma_{j=1}^{c} \left(\frac{d(x_k, g_i)}{d(x_k, g_j)}\right)^{\frac{2}{\gamma-1}}\right)^{-1}, \tag{11}$$

where $1 \leq i \leq c, 1 \leq k \leq n$, and then new centers of clusters by u_{ik}:

$$g_k = \frac{\Sigma_{k=1}^{n}(u_{ik}^{\gamma} \cdot x_k)}{\Sigma_{k=1}^{n} u_{ik}^{\gamma}}, \tag{12}$$

To initializing the algorithm it is determined initial values of cluster prototypes. It is calculated minimal p_{1f_i} and maximal p_{2f_i} values for every feature f_i, $i = \overline{1, m}$, specified in (2) by samples Z, specified in (4):

$$g_k = p_1 + \frac{k(p_2 - p_1)}{(c+1)}, \tag{13}$$

where $p_1 = (p_{1f_1}, p_{1f_2}, ..., p_{1f_m})$, and $p_2 = (p_{2f_1}, p_{2f_2}, ..., p_{2f_m})$, $1 \leq k \leq c$, c− the number of clusters.

The main disadvantage of FCM-algorithm is the necessity to set as a parameter of the algorithm the number of clusters that in the study of data structures is unknown in advance. To solve the problem in finding the optimal number of clusters the criterion of the adequacy of clusters is used. This criterion can be informally described as "the most appropriate cluster structure", which for each task will be different. It implicates the fact, that the choice of criteria will also be different.

There are some criterion on cluster validity. For proposed fuzzy model is considered the next one. Bezdek`s partition coefficient is [11]:

$$v_{PC}(U) = \frac{\sum_{k=1}^{n} \sum_{i=1}^{c} u_{ik}^2}{n}, \tag{14}$$

where U - fuzzy c-partition, c – the number of clusters, n– the number of samples elements. The next properties is v_{PC}:

$$v_{PC} = 1 \Leftrightarrow U \in M_{hcn},$$

$$v_{PC} = \frac{1}{c} \Leftrightarrow U = \left[\frac{1}{c}\right] = \overline{U},$$

where M_{hcn} is specified in (9), $\overline{U}$ – is the «fuzziest» partition you can get, science it assigns every point in X with equal membership values $\frac{1}{c}$ to all c classes. Bezdek`s partition coefficient belongs to class of criterion, that use only information about U, but no information about data itself, like G и X.

The Xie-Beni index v_{XB} [11] belongs to class of validity criterions, that are used whole information $(U, G; X)$:

$$v_{XB}(U, G; X) = \frac{\sum_{i=1}^{c} \sum_{k=1}^{n} u_{ik}^2 \|x_k - g_i\|^2}{n \left(\min_{i \neq j}\{\|g_i - g_j\|^2\}\right)} = \left[\frac{\left(\frac{\sigma}{n}\right)}{sep(G)}\right], \tag{15}$$

where σ– is the ration of the total variation of (U, G), and the separation $sep(G)$ of the vectors G:

$$\sigma(U, G; X) = \sum_{i=1}^{c}\left(\sum_{k=1}^{n} u_{ik}^2 \|x_k - g_i\|^2\right),$$

$$sep(G) = \min_{i \neq j}\left\{\|g_i - g_j\|^2\right\}.$$

The smaller value v_{XB}, specified in (18) indicates the better partition on X, what is right for $\gamma = 2$ [13]. Studies of the influence of fuzziness coefficient on Xi-Beni index (12) points to his instability for large values of γ [13].

To find the optimal number of classes a method, based on scheme presented in Fig.2 is proposed in [14]. Result is presented as fuzzy model $FP^{\omega} = <U, G, X, c>$, that will be called fuzzy portrait of class of images [15] within the general concept proposed by the author, where ω is class of images from alphabet Ω, specified in (3).

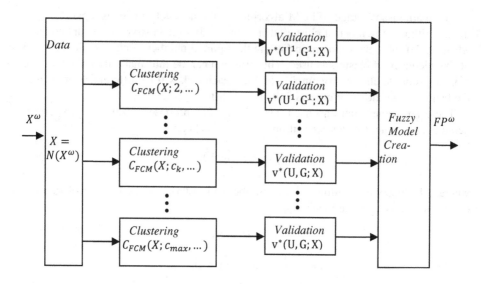

Fig. 2. The general scheme of fuzzy model creation

On the scheme $X^\omega \subset \mathcal{R}^m$ corresponds to part of input data Z, specified in (4), for elements with $o_i = \omega$; $N(X^\omega): \mathcal{R}^m \mapsto [0,1]^m$ – normalization procedure for sample ; C_{FCM} – clustering algorithm presented as function $C_{FCM}(X; c, \dots): \mathcal{R}^{n \times m} \mapsto M_{fcn}$, where n – is the number of sample elements, M_{fcn} – is specified in (9), c – is the parameter of algorithm, that specifies the number of clusters, and other possible options of FCM-algorithm [8,13]; v^* – is the validity criterion like (14) or (15), and

$$U^1 = \left(\underbrace{1,1,\dots,1}_{n}\right)^T$$ – unit vector, $G^1 = \{g_1\}$, where g_1 is calculated by (12) pro-

viding that $U = U^1$. The range of values is $c = 2,3,\dots,c_{max}$, with $c_{max} \leq \sqrt{n}$, where n – cardinality of the set X^ω. In the fuzzy models creation step the validity criterions are analyzed. For criterion (18) the best partition is at minimal value.

The proposed scheme of intra-class analysis and fuzzy model FP^ω creation will be used as a part of classification method (5). It is the set of samples Z (4), which elements are grouped by membership to classes of Ω like $X^{\omega i} = \{(x_1, x_2, \dots, x_m) |$ $(x_1 x_2, \dots, x_m, \omega_i) \in Z\}$, $\forall i = \overline{1, K}$. For every class of images a local fuzzy model is created. A special method to combine all local models in one fuzzy model is used:

$$FM = <\{FP^{\omega_i}\}_{i=1}^{K}, D>, \tag{16}$$

where D – algorithm if decision making (5). Next, we define D and show how the problem of pattern recognition will be solved under uncertainty using only the information of the model (16).

3.2 Method of Decision Making

As a result of algorithm D for object x under conditions of uncertainty according to the statement of the problem considered is a fuzzy set $\tilde{\alpha} \in \tilde{\Omega}$, specified in (6).

The main idea for this method is following. The tuning of classification model is carried out for each class of images separately, but for decision making is used data on all classes of images together. The advantages of this approach are the transparency of the model and the ability of the method for adaptation to new data. It will be considered the method for decision making $D(x^*; FM, \Lambda, \varepsilon) = \tilde{\alpha}$, where FM is the model (20), $\tilde{\alpha}$ in the form (6), $\Lambda = \left\{\left(p_{1f_i}, p_{2f_i}\right)\right\}_{i=1}^{m}$ – the set of pairs minimal p_{1f_i} and maximal p_{2f_i} values, are used for normalization of data, f_i – feature of object, $i = \overline{1, m}$, m – the number of features, ε– the threshold value; and x^* – the new recognizable object. Let us denote the set of cluster centers corresponding to model FP^{ω_i} as G^{ω_i} and their number as c^{ω_i}.

Step 1. Transform x^* using Λ with formula:

$$x = \frac{x^* - p_1}{p_2 - p_1},\tag{17}$$

where p_1 and p_2 as in formula (13).

Step 2. Calculate α_i for every $\omega_i, i = \overline{1, K}$ to have $\tilde{\alpha}$ in a form (6). Set $\omega = \omega_i, \alpha = \alpha_i$, $FP = FP^{\omega_i}$. Calculate the distance from x to the nearest center of cluster for class ω by model FP:

$$l = \min_{g \in G^\omega}(d(x, g)),\tag{18}$$

where d is the distance.
Determine B^ω, which consist of the centers of whole clusters of model, except class ω:

$$B^\omega = \bigcup_{\substack{j=1 \\ j \neq i}}^{k} G^{\omega_k},\tag{19}$$

where i – the index of class ω. Calculate α by formula:

$$\alpha = \left(1 + \sum_{g \in B^\omega} \frac{l^2}{d^2(x,g)}\right)^{-1},\tag{20}$$

where l is calculated by (22), B^ω is determined in (23), and d is distance. Form the result $\tilde{\alpha}$ in the form (6) from α (24) for every class.

Step 3. Change $\tilde{\alpha}$ excluding from consideration the classes with small membership α_i replacing it by α–cut:

$$\alpha_i = \begin{cases} 0, \text{if } \alpha < \varepsilon \\ 1, \text{if } \alpha \geq \varepsilon \end{cases},\tag{21}$$

where ε – is the parameter of classification method, corresponding to threshold.

Step 4. Calculate the result class of images:

$$H(\tilde{\alpha}) = \begin{cases} \omega_i, \text{if } \exists! \ i: \alpha_i = 1, \\ \omega_0, \text{otherwise.} \end{cases} \tag{22}$$

where ω_0 —is unknown class if images affiliation to which denotes rejection option.

4   Experimental Verification

As a practical implementation of the method, proposed in this article, a standalone application was developed. The special library for fuzzy classification was developed in C++ and used in this application to create classification algorithm D, specified as (5). The application supports learning and test modes of operation. In the experiments two sets of samples are used:

- learn samples, which are used for creation the model in learn mode,
- test samples, which are used to estimate the quality of classification in test mode.

The dataset of 12899 examples of images: 9340 NE and 3559 PE was prepared. The alphabet of classes of images is $\Omega = \{NE, PE\}$. The Edge Histogram (EH) and Homogeneous Textures (HT) descriptors were calculated for a whole dataset. The statistical analysis of the set of samples presented with HT descriptors shows that this HT descriptor can't be used to share classes of images. The classification was carried out with EH descriptor due to good results of statistical analysis of the images described by EH descriptor.

Let us consider the confusion matrix Q to evaluate the quality of algorithm D. There are in cell q_{ij} of confusion matrix the number of elements from test sample, for which ω_i is right class, whereas classification result is ω_j. There is an example of the confusion matrix for the problem with two classes in table 1. Artificial class ω_0 is used for rejection option as on step 4 of decision making algorithm.

Table 1. Confusion matrix

Method Model	ω_0	ω_1	ω_2
ω_1	q_{10}	q_{11}	q_{12}
ω_2	q_{20}	q_{21}	q_{22}

Let p_i be the priori probability for class ω_i, $i = \overline{1, K}$, $\sum_{i=1}^{K} p_i = 1$. To calculate the probability of event, that algorithm classifies the object belonging to class ω_i as object of class ω_j, $i = \overline{1, K}, j = \overline{0, K}$ is used formula:

$$p_{ij} = \frac{q_{ij}}{\sum_{k=0}^{K} q_{ik}}, \tag{23}$$

where q_{ij} – element of confusion matrix.

Two types of error for algorithm with rejection function are considered. The error of the first type calculated as:

$$A^I = \sum_{i=1}^{K} p_i \left(\sum_{\substack{j=1 \\ j\neq i}}^{K} p_{ij} \right),$$ (24)

where p_i is probability of class ω_i and p_{ij} is calculated by (23). To calculate the probability of an event:

$$R = \sum_{i=1}^{K} p_i p_{i0},$$ (25)

where p_i, p_{i0} like in (24). The error of the second type includes the first type error and rejection and is calculated as:

$$A^{II} = A^I + R.$$ (26)

The series of experiments for prepared set of samples was done. The quality of negative examples has less effect on the result (24-26).

There are not only good examples in whole set of samples. Thence every image was analyzed by operator and the good examples were selected. As a result 573 good positive examples and 431 good negative examples were selected. Figure 3 present examples for images.

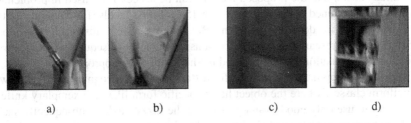

a)   b)   c)   d)

Fig. 3. Exemplary images: a) good positive example, b) bad positive example, c) good negative example, d) bad negative example

Five collections of samples were drown up for experiments. Their numerical descriptions are presented in Table 2. Type of examples is shown like «good» if we use selected examples and «all» if we use all examples we have. For every example a set of samples is divided in the ratio of two to one.

Table 2. Learn and test sets for experiments are held

		Exp.1		Exp.2		Exp.3		Exp.4		Exp.5	
		Num	Desc.	Num	Desc.	Num	Desc.	Num	Desc.	Num	Desc.
Learn	PE	378	Good	378	Good	573	Good	573	Good	2348	All
samples	NE	6164	All	284	All	6164	All	431	Good	6164	All
Test	PE	195	Good	195	Good	3026	All	3026	All	1211	All
samples	NE	3176	All	147	All	3176	All	8909	All	3176	All

The results of experiments in Table 3 show that the best characteristic has fuzzy models created on sets, which contain only good positive examples. This is experiment 3 and experiment 4 with 14% of errors on test samples. It was thus established that model need to train on good positive examples only. The quality of negative examples less affected on the result.

Table 3.   Experiment results

Knife detection		Exp1	Exp2	Exp3	Exp4	Exp5
Learn	A^I	27,74%	25,47%	**14,30%**	**13,90%**	17,16%
	R	01,23%	01,53%	00,49%	00,53%	00,87%
	A^{II}	26,50%	27,00%	14,78%	14,42%	17,92%
Test	A^I	27,02%	26,76%	**14,32%**	**14,59%**	17,46%
	R	01,53%	00,70%	00,64%	00,66%	00,84%
	A^{II}	28,56%	27,46%	14,96%	15,25%	18,30%

5   Conclusion

The article presents fuzzy model for knife detection. As a feature for pattern recognition problem were selected elements from MPEG-7 descriptor. The experimental verification shows, that the proposed method can be successfully used in problematic situations. The obtained result with less than 15% of miss labels (for whole dataset) is pretty good result for described problem. But for real system this results have to be improved. Further research will be aimed at assessing a set of sequential images from video, and a combination of the proposed method with other approaches.

The described approach can be used for different pattern recognition problems with non-uniform classes, where the object has a specific form like the exemplary knife. It is necessary to use only good examples to train the fuzzy model. Subsequently such a model can be applied to examples with less clear images.

Acknowledgment. Research was partially supported within the project under Grant INDECT No. FP7-218086. Work has been co-financed by the European Regional Development Fund under the Innovative Economy Operational Programme, INSIGMA project No. POIG.01.01.02-00-062/09. Development of the model has been fund by INDECT project. Implementation, tests and result analysis have been fund by INSIGMA project.

References

1. Żywicki, M., Matiolański, A., Orzechowski, T.M., Dziech, A.: Knife detection as a subset of object detection approach based on Haar cascades. In: Proceedings of 11th International Conference on Pattern Recognition and Information Processing, Minsk, Belarus, pp. 139–142 (2011)
2. Glowacz, A., Kmieć, M., Dziech, A.: Visual Detection of Knives in Security Applications using Active Appearance Models. Multimedia Tools and Applications (2013)

3. Maksimova, A.: Knife Detection Scheme Based on Possibilistic Shell Clustering. In: Dziech, A., Czyżewski, A. (eds.) MCSS 2013. CCIS, vol. 368, pp. 144–152. Springer, Heidelberg (2013)
4. Konor, A.: Computational Intelligence: Principles, Techniques and Applications. Springer, Heidelberg (2005)
5. Kuncheva, L.I.: Fuzzy Classifier Design. Physica-Verlag, Heidelberg (2005)
6. Ishibuchi, H., Nakashima, T., Nii, M.: Classification and Modeling with Linguistic Information Granules. Springer (2005)
7. Chen, N.: Fuzzy Classification Using Self-Organizing Map and Learning Vector Quantization. In: Shi, Y., Xu, W., Chen, Z. (eds.) CASDMKM 2004. LNCS (LNAI), vol. 3327, pp. 41–50. Springer, Heidelberg (2005)
8. Bezdek, J.C., Keller, J., Krisnapuram, R., Pal, R.: Fuzzy Models and Algorithms for Pattern Recognition and Image Processing. Springer, New York (2005)
9. Baran, R., Glowacz, A., Matiolanski, A.: The efficient real- and non-real-time make and model recognition of cars. Multimedia Tools and Applications (2013)
10. Information Won, C.S., Park, D.K., Park, S.-J.: Efficient Use of MPEG-7 Edge Histogramm. ETRI J. 24(1), 23–30 (2002)
11. Ro, Y.M., Kim, M., Kang, H.K., Manjunath, B.S., Kim, J.: MPEG-7 Homogeneous Texture Descriptor. ETRI Journal 23(2), 41–51 (2001)
12. Yu, M.A., Kozlovskii, V.A.: Algorithm of Pattern Recognition with intra-class clustering. In: Proceedings of 11th International Conference on Pattern Recognition and Processing, Minsk, pp. 54–57 (2011)
13. Pal, N.R., Bezdek, J.C.: On Cluster Validity for the Fuzzy c-Means Model. J. IEEE Transactions on Fuzzy Systems 3(3), 370–379 (1995)
14. Maksimova, A.: Decision Making Method for Classifying Models Based on Intra-class Clustering on FCM-algorithm. Artificial Intelligent J. 3(61), 171–178 (2013) (in Russian)
15. Maksimova, A.: The Model of Data Presentation with Fuzzy Portraits for Pattern Recognition. Int. J. of Computing 11(1), 17–24 (1995)

Methods for Face Localization in Static Colour Images with an Unknown Background

Mariusz Marzec[1], Aleksander Lamża[1], Zygmunt Wróbel[1], and Andrzej Dziech[2]

[1] Department of Computer Biomedical Systems, Institute of Computer Science,
University of Silesia, ul. Będzińska 39, 41-200 Sosnowiec, Poland
[2] AGH University of Science and Technology,
Faculty of Mining Surveying and Environmental Engineering,
Al. A. Mickiewicza 30, 30-059 Kraków

Abstract. This paper analyses the practical application of the methods for face and head localization in colour images with varying background. The Haar Cascade Classifier and Local Binary Pattern were selected as basic methods because of their high efficiency in this type of applications. The results obtained in the test set of images prompted the authors to choose the Haar Cascade Classifier. This method was then implemented in the face detection module, which is part of a comprehensive system for determining the forbidden regions.

1 Introduction

The studies presented in this paper are designed to prepare an algorithm enabling automatic designation of a mask covering the human silhouette area. This task will allow to add text information to the test image in such a way so that it will not distort the information contained therein or it will distort it minimally. In summary, additional information should be added (superimposed) to the test image in such a way so as not to cover the face or torso of the person present in the image, which means that it should be deployed outside the designated mask areas.

The first element of the presented system is the face and head detection block. A very important part of the research is implementation of the described algorithms and solutions in the real system. The system for searching forbidden regions is created within the framework of the project IMCOP.

From a human point of view, the correct determination of the position and area of the silhouette of a person in a static image is an easy task that does not require much effort. Human senses perform this operation automatically and, as a result, the regions of interest are selected without any problems, regardless of the image colour, texture or brightness. From the point of view of a computer and image analysis and processing, this task does not seem to be so easy. There appear typical problems that the algorithm has to deal with:

- Correct separation and elimination of the background
- Determination of the silhouette area homogeneity with regard to texture and colour

A. Dziech and A. Czyżewski (Eds.): MCSS 2014, CCIS 429, pp. 170–181, 2014.

- Determination of the area taking into consideration the orientation and position of the head and arms
- Classification of areas in order to select the most important area (people in the foreground)

Fig. 1. Example of area designation and text information addition performed manually by the authors

The afore-mentioned operations were carried out in Fig. 1 manually so as to present the assumptions and purpose of the research in graphical form. It can be observed that despite the addition of a large amount of descriptive information, the head and torso of the person in the image are still clearly visible (she is still recognizable). The added text did not distort or obscure the important areas of the image (covered by masks), which are marked in red. Moreover, a high degree of background complexity (variety of colours and textures) and the presence of many faces can be observed in the image. The task of the algorithm described herein is to obtain approximate results with complete automation of image processing.

2   Overview of Face Detection Methods

In order to develop initial assumptions and select specific solutions, it was necessary to consult the available literature on the issue of face localization.

Face Localization
Face localization methods can be found very often in the literature related to image processing and analysis. This task has a wide variety of solutions [1],[2],[3] which can be divided into several basic groups.

The first group of methods is based on knowledge of the image ("knowledge-based") that researchers possess and which they have put in the form of a set of rules and relationships that describe a typical face. The face is described as a set of characteristic points or areas linked together by relations such as distance, mutual position, etc. These methods work best for face images in the anterior projection and in the case of uncomplicated background. An example can be found in [4], where the authors proposed a face detection method based on geometric relationships of characteristic areas of the face such as the eyes and mouth.

The second group of methods ("feature invariant approaches") includes algorithms whose task is to look for the basic features of the image ("invariants") such as edges, colours, shapes, areas of a certain colour or texture. They are characterized by insensitivity to the position, orientation, inclination of the face, point of view or lighting conditions. Examples of solutions based on colour segmentation are presented in [1],[5],[6]. However, the authors point out the difficulties in obtaining adequate sensitivity of such solutions in the actual image acquisition conditions which are related to the impact of lighting.

Another group of methods concerns matching templates ("template matching"). In this case, specially prepared patterns describing the face as a whole or its individual features (i.e. eyes, nose, mouth) separately are used for face detection. These patterns are prepared by experts on the basis of knowledge of the test image. After matching the patterns to the image, the correlation between individual patterns is calculated. Based on the correlation value, the result of the localization process is determined. These methods are relatively easy to implement. An example can be found in [7], where the authors propose the use of a deformed model representing the shape of the face and its most important elements to determine the face position. Another method from this group, which is also often used, is the Hough transform which allows to determine the orientation of the head contour approximated with the use of an ellipse of a certain size and orientation. The first stage most often involves edge detection which is followed by relevant analysis. Examples of this method are presented in [8].

The last group of methods ("appearance-based methods" or "learning-based methods") are algorithms that use models, templates or patterns resulting from the learning process. Proper operation requires a training set on the basis of which the algorithm learns to recognize and creates a corresponding pattern. An important factor influencing the effectiveness of this group is an appropriate choice of the training set (images containing correct and incorrect examples) as well as learning and classification methods. Most commonly the algorithms based on neural networks are applied here. An example can be found in [9], where the authors propose the use of a one-way feed-forward network for face detection based on skin colour.

New solutions most often belong to the last group of methods and have appeared in the past few years due to the rapid increase in computing power. "Learning-based" algorithms are gaining a greater advantage in face localization systems [2] in relation to the three previous groups. Methods based on the Local Binary Pattern [10],[11] and Haar-like methods [12],[13],[14] are some of the most commonly implemented solutions at present.

To localize the face, the authors in [10] proposed a method based on image features which, in the literature, are referred to as "Local Binary Pattern features." They allow to achieve good results in a wide variety of applications (classification and segmentation of textures, extraction of images), and therefore they also operate effectively in the case of face localization. After determining LBP features for the test image, the algorithm classifies and selects them with the use of the trained Gentle AdaBoost classifier. The authors did not present the measurement results of face localization effectiveness paying attention to only about half of the time of the algorithm operation (3.2 compared to 6.3 seconds).

In [12], in the first stage of the algorithm operation, the image features referred to as "Haar-like features" were used, which allow to encode the differences in intensity between two adjacent rectangular areas in different scales and, what is essential, they enable to extract effectively a texture regardless of the absolute image intensity. The characteristics determined in such a way underwent classification using the AdaBoost. In order to optimize calculations, a cascade of classifiers was used. The effectiveness of face localization ranged from 76.1% to 93.9% depending on the allowable number of false detections. After analysing the above methods, it was concluded that application of one of the last two methods will be considered in the face localization task discussed in this paper.

3   Assumptions and Research Material

3.1   Initial Assumptions

For the method proposed here, it was assumed that the face of a person in a static colour image would be the first element localized automatically by the system. Determination of the head area at this stage seems to be easier than designation of the entire body / torso of a person taking into account the diversity of colours and textures that can occur in the region of the observed person's torso.

Moreover, some assumptions regarding the importance of information transmitted by certain areas of the image were made. From the point of view of the task, the most important information can be found in the face and torso areas – Fig. 1. Therefore, these areas should be designated in such a way so that the added descriptive content will not distort the information in the image.

It is equally important that the algorithm should also eliminate irrelevant faces so that the determined masks of the face and torso represent only the person (people) located in the foreground. Fig. 2 shows how the algorithm should behave in accordance with the assumptions and how the algorithm behaves without the possibility of identifying the most significant person in the image.

Fig. 2. Assumptions for proper designation of the head mask and the problem with locating many people

Due to the above-mentioned assumptions, it was found that at the current stage of research:

- The analysis process will be divided into two stages, the first one will involve operation of the face localization block, and then the torso localization block will be developed;
- For the proper operation of the system, it will be most important to designate the head area in the form of a rectangular area including the face, hair;
- Due to the nature of the images (people are in typical positions), it is assumed that the head orientation is similar to the vertical;
- It is also assumed that the most important people in the image are in the foreground. Head sizes in this case are the biggest.

The paper describes the face and head detection block under the above assumptions.

Research Material and Tools

A set of 128 colour images of varying sizes was used as research material. For each image, a binary mask was manually created containing areas representing the heads of people in the image (Fig. 3b). For the purpose of specific tests of the head and torso area identification, a group of 18 representative images was selected.

a)   b)

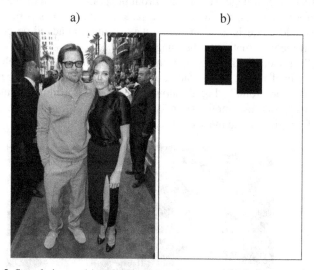

Fig. 3. Sample image (a) and a binary mask prepared for it (b) - negative

Then, all of the test images were analysed in order to obtain the results of automatic separation of masks using the proposed algorithm.

In order to choose a particular method of head localization, the algorithm operations were compared for two cases where:

1. Local Binary Pattern was used in the localization block
2. Haar Cascade Classifier was used in the localization block

The algorithm and the user interface were implemented in Java using OpenCV package [15].

For the purpose of testing the developed algorithm, a tool (*MaskTester*) was prepared which is used to compare the masks. The tool accepts two graphic files (in PNG format, monochrome images) containing respectively the reference mask and the mask obtained from the present algorithm.

To obtain meaningful results, a method of comparing masks was proposed which is based on the common part. Mask compatibility coefficient (S) is determined from the following relationship:

$$S = \frac{M_1 \cap M_2}{M_1 \cup M_2},$$

where M1 is the reference mask, and M2 – the resulting one. The compatibility coefficient is calculated for all the values occurring in the mask images. In the case of binary masks (Fig. 3b), there will be two values.

4   Comparison of the Proposed Methods for Face Localization

The tests of face localization algorithms were carried out on a set of 128 images, separately for both methods of face detection: Local Binary Pattern (LBP) and Haar method.

The main difference between these methods is the detection time. The results are presented in Table 1 (tests were performed on a computer with an Intel Core2 Duo T7700@2.40GHz and 4 GB of RAM).

Table 1. Comparison of the mean times of face detection

	LBP	Haar
t_{mean} [ms]	406	2045
t_{min} [ms]	20	136
t_{max} [ms]	3924	19 936

It can be observed that the face detection time in the case of the method based on the Haar cascade is more than five times greater than for LBP.

It remains to be considered whether the prolongation of execution time brings tangible benefits in terms of improved quality of detection. Fig. 4 shows a graph presenting the comparison of the number of faces detected in the two discussed methods.

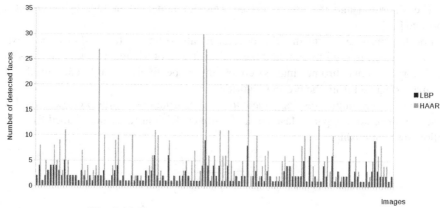

Fig. 4. Number of detected faces using LBP and HAAR

The number of detected faces is consistent in both methods in only 36 percent, and more faces are detected in the case of the Haar method (the number of detections is higher in 96 percent). However, what should be taken into account is the need to choose those detected areas that are important from the point of view of the developed algorithm. As mentioned before, only the biggest masks are selected from the set of detected face masks.

After taking into consideration the algorithm which excludes irrelevant masks, the results shown in the graph in Fig.5 were obtained.

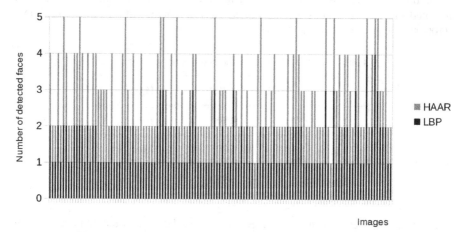

Fig. 5. Number of created face masks for LBP and HAAR method

In 22 percent of cases in the Haar method the number of masks was higher. This does not mean, however, that the final results, i.e. the compatibility of designated masks with the masks created manually, are higher. This is due to the fact that in the Haar method there are often multiple detections of the same face, and thus redundant masks are formed, or face masks are detected within the torso of a given person. Examples of such situations are illustrated in Figure 6.

Fig. 6. Multiple face masks and masks within the torso

Detailed studies carried out on the selected set of 18 representative images suggest that the use of the Haar method increases the accuracy of the head area detection by only 5 percent. However, it should be borne in mind that the application of the Haar method instead of LBP leads to a fivefold increase in the processing time.

When testing the full set of 128 images using LBP, it occurred twice that no face was detected. Whereas using the Haar method, the face was detected each time. In view of the fact that the Haar method results in a greater number of detected faces, in the final algorithm a solution may be used, wherein LBP-based detection bringing no face detection is followed by re-detection using the Haar method. In this way, a higher compatibility coefficient can be obtained.

5 Proposed Method

5.1 Determination of the Position and Area of the Face and Head

The authors of this paper assumed that the face localization block is the first stage of the proposed algorithm. As mentioned in the introduction, the methods of head / face localization are widely used and their efficiency is over 90%. This fact prompted the authors to use such a method of solving the problem. This is a slightly different approach in relation to the methods where the mask covering the test object (e.g. the whole person in the image) is designated directly.

5.1.1 Face Detection

A cascade classifier implemented in the OpenCV library in the `CascadeClassifier` class was used to detect faces. The use of the classifier results in a list of square masks which determine the areas of detected faces. In the subsequent step, they are sorted in descending order with respect to their size. In order to eliminate less essential faces (i.e. smaller as it was initially assumed), filtering with a defined size threshold can be applied. The value of 60% of the largest mask size was selected experimentally.

5.1.2 Head Area Determination

The head area is determined on the basis of the face area obtained in the previous step. The easiest method, i.e. the geometric method, was proposed. Based on the analysis of the areas returned by the face detector, correction coefficients K were determined, which enable to estimate the expected head area.

$$K = \left(k_x, k_y, k_w, k_h \right),$$

where the subsequent coefficients are responsible for: the x coordinate, y coordinate, width and height. The head area is designated according to the following relationships:

$$H_x = F_x - k_x F_w,$$

$$H_y = F_y - k_y F_h,$$

$$H_w = k_w F_w,$$

$$H_h = k_h F_h.$$

The performed tests resulted in the optimum values of the coefficients: $K = \left(0.05, 0.35, 1.1, 1.5 \right).$

Fig. 7 shows two slices of sample images after applying the method described above. The smaller square is the face area resulting from the face detection method, whereas the larger rectangle is the estimated head area.

Fig. 7. Examples of detected face masks and head areas determined with the geometric method

6   Results

A detailed study on the compatibility of the head masks was performed on a set of 20 selected images. For each image, a mask was prepared (Fig. 3) containing the head area (in white) and the background marked in black. To compare their compatibility with the masks derived from the present algorithm, the tool mentioned in the section "Research material and tools" was used. The comparison resulted in coefficients S denoting the compatibility degree of both masks.

Test of the head area determination effectiveness
The first study analysed the determined head and background masks. A summary of the results is presented in Table 2 and the values for individual images in Fig. 8.

Table 2. Summary of the compatibility results of the head and background masks

	Compatibility of background masks S(g)	Compatibility of head masks S(h)
mean	0,84	0,70
min	0,65	0,36
max	1,00	0,90

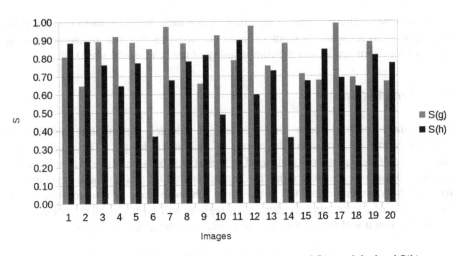

Fig. 8. Mask compatibility coefficients for the background $S(g)$ and the head $S(h)$

The results indicate low scores for images 6 and 14. The results obtained stem from the fact that faces were not properly detected, and thus the head areas were not determined (Fig.9).

Fig. 9. Images for which low mask compatibility coefficients were obtained (images 6 and 14)

As mentioned above in the comparison of the face detection methods, the Haar method may increase the number of detected faces. In the case discussed here, it occurred for the image 14 and the compatibility of the head masks was 0.69.

7   Conclusions

The obtained results indicate that the initially adopted assumptions and applied methods enable to determine the masks of people in images. The analysis and comparison of the known methods used in these types of issues aiming at solving the practical task allowed to determine the current capabilities and potential development paths of the algorithm presented in the paper. The next stage of research devoted to the problem of determining the forbidden regions will be to develop the discussed solution so that it will enable the location of human silhouettes in images.

References

1. Beigzadeh, M., Mafadoost, M.: Detection of Face and Facial Features in digital Images and Video Frames. In: Cairo International Biomedical Engineering Conference, CIBEC 2008, pp. 1–4 (2008)
2. Zhang, C., Zhang, Z.: A Survey of Recent Advances in Face Detection. Technical report, Microsoft Research, 577 (2010)

3. Yang, M., Kriegman, J., Ahuja, N.: Detecting faces in images: A survey. IEEE Transaction on Pattern Analysis and Machine Intelligence 24(1), 34–58 (2002)
4. Miao, J., Gao, W., Chen, Y., Lu, J.: Gravity-center template based human face feature detection. In: Tan, T., Shi, Y., Gao, W. (eds.) ICMI 2000. LNCS, vol. 1948, pp. 207–214. Springer, Heidelberg (2000)
5. Hsu, R.L., Abdel-Mottaleb, M., Jain, A.K.: Face detection in color images. IEEE Pattern Analysis and Machine Intelligence 24, 696–706 (2002)
6. Phung, S.L., Bouzerdoum, A., Chai, D., Kuczborski, W.: A color-based approach to automatic face detection. In: Proceedings of the 3rd IEEE International Symposium on Signal Processing and Information Technology, pp. 531–534 (2003)
7. Lanitis, A., Taylor, C., Cootes, T.F.: An Automatic Face Identification System Using Flexible Appearance Models. Image and Vision Computing 13(5), 392–401 (1995)
8. Chan, Y.H., Bakar, S.A., Rahman, S.A.: Face Detection System Based on Feature-Based Chrominance Colour Information. In: International Conference on Computer Graphics, Imaging and Visualization, pp. 153–158 (2004)
9. Mostafa, L., Abdelazeem, S.: Face detection Based on Skin Color using Neural Network. In: GVIP 2005 Conference, Cairo, Egypt, pp. 53–58 (December 2005)
10. Jo, C.-Y.: Face detection using lbp features. Tech. Rep., Stanford University. CS 229 Final Project Report (December 2008)
11. Zhang, L., Chu, R., Xiang, S., Liao, S., Li, S.Z.: Face Detection Based on Multi-Block LBP Representation. In: Lee, S.-W., Li, S.Z. (eds.) ICB 2007. LNCS, vol. 4642, pp. 11–18. Springer, Heidelberg (2007)
12. Viola, P., Jones, M.: Rapid object detection using a boosted cascade of simple features. In: Proceedings of 2001 IEEE International Conference on Computer Vision and Pattern Recognition, pp. 511–518 (2001)
13. Padilla, R., Costa Filho, C.F.F., Costa, M.G.F.: Evaluation of Haar Cascade Classifiers Designed for Face Detection. World Academy of Science, Engineering and Technology 64 (2012)
14. Ramirez, G.A., Fuentes, O.: Multi-Pose Face Detection with Asymmetric Haar Features. In: IEEE Workshop on Applications of Computer Vision, WACV 2008, pp. 1–6 (2008)
15. http://opencv.org/opencv-java-api.html

Creating Covert Channel Using SIP

Miralem Mehić, Martin Mikulec, Miroslav Voznak, and Lukas Kapicak

VŠB-Technical University of Ostrava 17.listopadu 15,
708 00 Ostrava-Poruba, Czech Republic
{miralem.mehic.st,martin.mikulec,lukas.kapicak}@vsb.cz,
voznak@ieee.org

Abstract. Sending VoIP (Voice Over IP) by default requires two protocols:SIP and RTP. First one is used for establishing and changing the settings of the session and second one for exchanging voice packets. The main aim of this paper is to calculate the maximum number and type of SIP messages that can be transferred during established VoIP call without detection and raising an alarm from IDS (Intrusion detection system). Finally, we calculated Steganography bandwidth, amount of data in these messages that can be used for transfer of hidden content. Also, this paper deals with Snort IDS settings for raising alarm, traditional ones by using hard-coded rules and usage of anomaly detection plugin. Results of experiment are provided.

Keywords: Steganography, VoIP, Security, SIP.

1 Introduction

VoIP is the most popular service in IP networks and as such it is of interest for new ventures and experiments. Securing network with new and inventive traffic flows is the hard task and requires permanent and uninterrupted monitoring of the network health. This can be achieved using IDS (Intrusion Detection System) with hard-coded network rules that will define limits for the network traffic or usage anomaly detection solution that will constantly monitor current network traffic and compare it with previously recorded one. Second solution gives a higher risk of raising false alarms since detecting of the stealth attack on the network is a hard request.

Steganography is method of hiding data inside of existing channels of communications. Usually it means hiding data within existing, ordinary messages, so no one except sender and receiver can't detect them. Steganography as new rising threat in telecommunications requests from the attacker a good knowledge of communications methods and protocols, and as such presents a new challenge for network administrators and operators.

There are two main protocols used in VoIP call: SIP (Session Initiation Protocol) used for establishing, changing parameters and termination of an established call, and RTP (Real Time Protocol) used for transferring voice data. In this paper, we are interested in number and type of SIP messages that can be sent in a call without raising the

A. Dziech and A. Czyżewski (Eds.): MCSS 2014, CCIS 429, pp. 182–192, 2014.

alarm. These messages then can be used further to transfer hidden data, so we calculated available bandwidth for hiding data is these messages.

2   State of the Art

There are several types of Steganographic techniques in VoIP networks according to Mazurczyk and Szczypiorski [2] but all of them can be categorized in following three:

- Packet modification steganography
- PDUs time relations
- Technique that require hardware modification of uses device

First one represents the technique based on using unused fields in protocol, mostly in IP, UDP, TCP or even RTP and RTCP packets. This method is susceptible to detection by Intrusion detection system (IDS), but it requires very precise rules for monitoring of network. Instead of using a separate RTCP flow authors proposed embedding the control information into the actual RTP flow. Unused bits in the IP/UDP/RTP headers signal the type of parameters, whereas the parameter values are embedded as a watermark in the voice data[3,4].

Second method is based on the deliberate data delay, since the VoIP content is very sensitive to delay and jitter variations. This method is related to LACK (Lost Audio Packet Steganographic Method) that is based on deliberate delays of the VoIP packets since receiver will consider only packets that are delivered on time and discard packets that are delayed. Using this technique receiver will instead of discarding delayed packets read them for steganographic purpose. This method is quite hard to identify in network, but it is also hard to achieve. There are also variations of this technique such as affecting the order of packets, modifying inter-packet delay or introducing intentional losses [7].

Third method is based on usage modified hardware for Steganographic purpose. One of the most researched techniques is HICCUPS (Hidden Communication System for Corrupted Networks) for VoWLAN (Voice over Wireless LAN) specific environment. However this Steganographic method is quite difficult to implement as it requires modification to network cards [8]. Also, there is a possibility of usage retransmission technique as it is explained in [9] on example of TCP protocol The main idea of this technique is in deliberately dropping some packets and resending new ones but this time with hidden data.

An anonymous author proposed an indirect covert channel over the DNS protocol [1, 6] and gave us an idea to try to implement a similar method in VoIP networks. The main idea of that proposal is usage of network resources without registration with covert behavior. Since VoIP calls require registration in order to create a call, we will analyze usage of SIP messages as convert channel during regular voice call.

This article is organized as follows: third section presents available methods for detecting anomalies and attacks in SIP, while, in the fourth section, we present results of the experiment and finally calculate allowable steganographic bandwidth. Conclusion and discussion on future work are in fifth six.

3   Our Contribution

3.1   Defining Limits

Steganography means communication in hidden channels and the best way to define available steganography bandwidth is to search for limits that are defined as a threat in that channel. For this purpose, we searched for VoIP anomalies and its detection, since we need to know the total number of messages that can be transferred during regular VoIP call. The basic idea for detecting flooding attacks is directly monitoring the traffic volume/rate, where alarms are raised if the traffic volume in one time interval is larger than an adaptive threshold estimated based on historical traffic conditions.

Jin Tang defines in his paper [11] the minimum number of messages that may be considered as a flood attack and that number is 15 messages per second and using proposed technique it is possible to detect this flood attack with probability up to 88%. Also, Jin explains usage of integrated sketch technique with Hellinger distance (HD) in order to find differences in network probability distributions. But Jin also quotes that used method will become ineffective if the 4 SIP messages are proportionally flooded simultaneously. Jin refer to such an attack as multi-attribute attack. We used this fact to organize our steganographic method further. One particular kind of attack is called the stealthy SIP flooding attack, where intelligent attackers deliberately increase the flooding rates in a slow pace [12]. It is easy to find that techniques with Hellingers distance approach are not able to identify changes in traffic efficiently. Jin claims that with the usage of Wavelet Based Detection technique is possible to detect this kind of attacks, so we can't increase once defined burst of data that need to be sent if we wish to stay undetected.

There are two ways of detection attack and anomaly in the network. One is based on signatures where counting technique is used, and results are compared with already defined rules. This method is the detection of all that is declared as invalid, and everything else is assumed as valid traffic. And second technique is based on the detection of an anomaly in the network. It is done by comparing current network traffic with traffic that is recorded in the previous period. In this approach everything that is not already known is assumed as invalid. This technique is vulnerable on stealth attack, and it is described in Jin's papers [12].

SNORT is one of most popular network tools for detecting attacks and anomalies in network. It is primarily designed to work as signature-based IDS system, and administrator should define the signatures that will trigger the alarm. Rules for triggering alarm are defined mostly by counting number of packages with specific header field in a particular period of time. Since Snort can process only one package in time, usage of other plugins for processing results are recommended, like fwSnort or SnortSam that use Snort's output in order to change IPTables firewall rules. We investigated network operators rule and fetch theirs commonly used rules. Some of most popular rules for preventing SIP flood attack are listed in table 1.

Table 1. Snort hard-coded rules for detection of SIP flood attack

1.	`alert ip any any -> any 5060 (msg:"COMMUNITY SIP INVITE message flooding"; con-tent:"INVITE"; depth:6; threshold: type both, track by_src, count 100, seconds 60; class-type:attempted-dos; sid:100000158; rev:2;)`
2.	`alert ip any any -> any 5060 (msg:"COMMUNITY SIP TCP/IP message flooding directed to SIP proxy"; threshold: type both, track by_src, count 300, seconds 60; class-type:attempted-dos; sid:100000160; rev:2;)`

The first rule count number of INVITE messages in one minute and as long as the number of messages is less than the number that is specified, the alarm will not be raised. The second rule is very strictly, and it means that Snort will raise an alarm if the number of any messages that use TCP transport protocol is higher than 300 in a minute.

Anomaly is something that we do not occur in a common environment. SNORT had a few plugins that are available for detecting anomaly in the network. One of most popular plugin was SPADE (Statistical Packet Analysis and Detection Engine), the project that was founded by DARPA (American Defence Advanced Research Projects Agency) but after commercialization it was developed under the name Spice and abandoned in 2003. Currently, there is one anomaly detection plugin for snort called SNORT.AD [16] and we used it for this purpose. Current version (3.0) is programmed for Snort 2.9.4.5. and it can monitor following network parameters : total number of TCP, UDP, and ICMP packets, number of outgoing TCP, UDP, and ICMP packets, number of incoming TCP, UDP, and ICMP packets, number of TCP, UDP, and ICMP packets from current subnet, number of TCP packets with SYN/ACK flags, number of outgoing and incoming WWW packets – TCP on port 80, number of outgoing and incoming DNS packets – UDP outgoing on port 53, number of ARP-request and ARP-reply packets, number of non TCP/IP stacks packets, the total number of packets, TCP, WWW, UDP, and DNS upload and download speed [kBps].

The main idea is to record traffic using AD Snort preprocessor to log file, then using Profile Generator create profile.csv with predicted traffic. This file is then used to compare current network traffic with predicted one. Profile Generator is based on R language / environment (The R Project for Statistical Computing) [18] and currently

Table 2. Profile generator methods

Moving average	$$\widehat{y}_t = \frac{\sum\limits_{i=t-k}^{t-1} y_i}{k}$$
Naive model	$\widehat{y}_t = y_{t-T}$

implements five method of profile file generation: the moving average, the naive method, autoregressive time series model, Holt-Winters model and Brutlags version of HW model [19, 20]. We used only Naïve and Moving average methods and the values of depending variables are calculated using formulas displayed in table 2.

It is recommended to record network traffic for three weeks in order to get the correct image of network traffic and then use Profile generator methods for defining boundaries for network traffic. Naive and AVG methods implement three type of prediction : LAST, DAILY and WEEKLY. Difference between them is in duration of the interval used for computing values for used model : last existing values, values grouped per hours of the last day and values grouped per day of the week, respectively.

3.2   Experiment Setup

We are focused on calculating number of SIP messages that are exchanged during regular VoIP call. With the purpose of simpler computation of exchanged messages, we used Asterisk as a middle point in the conversation, since Asterisk is the most used PBX software in the world. We want to calculate the number of SIP messages that can be exchanged during the call without raising an alarm, so we assume that both VoIP clients are successfully registered on registrar. There is a possibility for clients to communicate without any B2BUA (Back-to-back User Agent), but for now we assume all data is going through Asterisk 11.

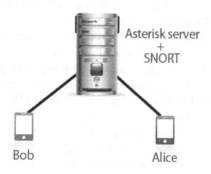

Fig. 1. Network scheme

Also, when the call is established, it is possible to send INVITE messages with parameters that will indicate a change of call settings or to send OPTIONS messages to query the capabilities of the other side or to send INFO messages with DTMF tones that will not change session state.

VoIP call has been established through Asterisk11 server using two X-LITE VoIP clients. Asterisk is used as the middle point for counting messages sent during regular VoIP call. Snort IDS is used to raise the alarm if the number of messages exceeds defined limit of messages. First we installed Snort AD plugin and generated profile shape of traffic. Since we are interested only in investigating a limits for one specific call in a short period of time, we generated few calls in 7 minutes interval and applied different AVG and Naive Profile generator methods on recorded traffic. This traffic shape is presented in figure 2. After that, we reinstalled snort and this time we applied the hard-coded rules from table 1. Monitoring of Network monitored was performed using tcpdump.

In order to test the established environments, we needed some type of generator of additional SIP messages. First idea was to use SIPp but soon we noticed that SIPp has its software limits. It was reflected by the number of messages per second that SIPp was able to fire. Usage this tool on computer with stronger performances didn't give a huge improvement. Second option is to use our own script. NET:SIP module for PERL has been used for writing Perl script to simulate flow of SIP messages. This module depends on the Lag Net::SIP::Leg wrapper for the socket which is used to send and receive messages and it supports both, TCP and UDP. We sent randomly INFO/INVITE/OPTION message from one client to Asterisk. Since we are right now interested in the number of messages and not its content, we are not focused on the impact of these messages to Asterisk. We assumed that the average duration of VoIP call is 1 minute.

4   Results

4.1   Calculation of Number of Messages in VoIP Call

From our experiment, we found out that the average number of exchanged messages during phase of establishing and call termination, without using any additional generator of SIP messages is less than 30 messages in 60 second. Snort will not raise alarms for this amount of messages, since this number is the minimum of messages for establishing authenticated VoIP call. Messages are not sent in a burst so they can't be observed as attack and this number is not enough to be observed as a stealthy SIP attack. RTP messages take the main part of communication in VoIP call since they carry all data information and SIP messages are in the regular call reduced to a minimum. In the following table, we present number of messages transferred in a regular call plus the SIP messages that are generated artificially using PERL script.

Table 1. Number of transmitted messages

Number of additionally generated SIP messages per second	Number of RTP messages in one minute	Number of SIP messages in one minute
0 (Regular VoIP call)	6068	27
1	6069	84
2	6062	144
3	6067	203
4	6976	265
5	6012	324
9	6857	566
13	6031	800

From the data presented, we can see that if we generate at least one additional SIP message per second, the total number of SIP messages in one call is increased almost three times comparing to the number of SIP message in regular VoIP call.

Now, let us compare these results with rules defined in table 1. Since we are not generating only INVITE messages, we are unnoticeable by the first rule. Following second rule, we can't sent more than 300 SIP messages in one call so we can generate additionally 4 SIP messages per second as the maximum.

There are three SIP usage cases: over UDP (User Datagram Protocol) with authentication, over TCP (Transmission Control Protocol) with authentication and TLS (Transport Layer Security) [10]. By default, most SIP devices use the first option, SIP over UDP as their main protocol. RTP messages are also sent via UDP protocol. So, since we are sending all files via UDP on transport layer AD Snort will use the sum of all packages (SIP and RTP) to calculate the maximum and minimum number of messages and on that way define boundaries for network traffic shape.

It is very important to underline that in the case when the SIP messages are sent over UPD, the second rules from table 1 does not apply since it counts only number of messages that are transferred using TCP transfer protocol.

Figure 2. shows the area in which the network traffic should move. If the network traffic is below the minimum or above maximum boundaries alarm will be raised. We can see that using an AVG method provides very broadly while NAIVE method gives very strict boundaries. The line for regular VoIP call is almost lying on minimum for NAIVE method and all two other lines for VoIP call are outside of allowed NAIVE area.

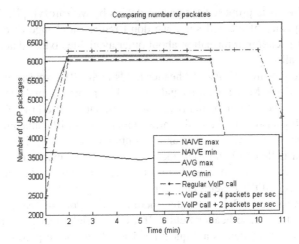

Fig. 2. Comparing UDP (SIP+RTP) network traffic

During the process of establishing a call UDP traffic is quite small, since there are no RTP messages, only SIP for arranging call parameters as it can be seen on Figure 2 in the first minute of recorded traffic. During the phase of establishing or tearing down the call, Snort AD will raise an alarm because of "unusually low UDP traffic".

So it is obvious that the usage of NAIVE method for generating profile file will give very strict limits for alarm but because of its constancy it is possible to expect a lot of false alarms. If the network administrator uses this method for detecting anomalies, we can't sent more than 1 SIP message per second while usage of the AVG method allows usage more than 4 messages per second.

4.2   Calculation of Steganographic Bandwidth

Steganographic Bandwidth represents the total amount that of bits that can be used for transmission of steganography content during one time unit [bps] by usage of all steganographic techniques. It is different from regular bandwidth which represents the total number of bits that can be transferred from one side to another.

Once we know the number of messages we can send in convert channel we can calculate total steganography bandwidth. If we use the approach as multi-attribute attack, we can send SIP messages in circle schedule. And if we calculate the total number of fields that can be changed in each SDP packet that is a vital part of each SIP packet, we can calculate the total bandwidth we dispose. If we look on SDP content of INVITE message we will see that there are Session description fields, Media description fields and Time description fields that are mandatory.

Let assume that we don't want to change the quality of established call, so in that case we will not change parameters that can disturb the call by itself. One of that field, for example, is used media codec, so we can change for i.e. the order of available codecs. For example if there are 5 available codecs and its order is changing with ascending order, this order can present steganography bit "1" or "0" if a descending order is used, like it is proposed for packet delays by Mazurczyk [7]. This will have no impact on quality of the call since we don't request a change of codec currently used, we are just sending information about other available codecs that can be used in an established call.

RFC 3261 defines mandatory SIP header fields in all SIP requests and they are To, From, CSeq, Call-ID, Max-Forwards and Via. SIP supports in total 115 header fields, so it means there are 109 more fields that are optional to use [14]. SIP packet may contain the SDP packet with the basic parameters of the VoIP connection. SDP specifies 5 mandatory fields : v, o, s, m, t and 15 optional fields [15]. If we sum these all fields, the result is that SIP and SDP message contains 11 mandatory fields and 124 optional fields. From this data, it is obvious that we can create code scheme and existing or absence each of these fields can represent code symbol.

RFC 3261 in section 7.3.2. states that there are two types of header fields, request header fields and response header fields. If a header field appears in a message not matching its category (such as a request header field in the response), it must be ignored. Also in section 18.1.1 RFC 3261 states that SIP implementations over UDP must be able to handle messages up to 65,535 bytes, including IP and UDP headers, or 60,507 bytes without them.

Since each message needs to have previously mentioned mandatory fields we can't use whole message for steganographic purpose, but this number can be estimated to 58 kbytes.

Finally, if we use one message per second the available Steganographic bandwidth is about 464kbps, and if we use 4 messages per second this number is increased to 1856kbps.

5   Conclusion and Future Work

Security policy that is implemented in the network defines what bandwidth of convert channel can be poses a threat. USA DoD (Department of Defense) specifies [13] that any covert channel with bandwidth higher than 100 bps must be considered insecure for average security requirements, because 100 bits per second is the approximate rate at which many computer terminals are run. For security requirements, it should not exceed 1bps.

Asterisk in previous versions had problems with support the amount of data in regular SIP messages that are specified in RFC 3261, for i.e. messages with large encryption keys and similar [23], but the current version worked without a problem. Here we need to underline that Asterisk works like B2BUA and it will not forward original messages from one client to another since it need to adopt these messages for its compatibilities. The only message that can be sent through Asterisk is SIP message MESSAGE used in Instant Messaging, but hiding data in regular MESSAGE doesn't have too much sense. So, it means we can't send hidden data through Asterisk (except regular Instant Message) but it is possible to send SIP message directly from one UAC to other UAC or sent messages through other implementation of SIP server, like Kamailio, that will forward this messages. In that scenario, it is necessary to configure

SNORT to monitor the whole network instead of one point in the network, but its implementation is out of scope of this paper.

Also, it is necessary to underline possibilities of sending different types of SIP messages for Steganographic purpose. After sending INVITE message, there are two additional SIP messages, one 200 OK from receiver and ACK additional message from the sender to confirm it. INFO and OPTION messages produce only one additional message, 200 OK, so usage of these messages for steganographic purpose is better because it will decrease the number of total exchanged SIP messages during the call.

From Steganographic point of view usage of flooding technique for SIP messages will not provide extra wide bandwidth, but since the SIP and SDP message are consisted of a large number of fields it is possible to send one message with a lot of information included. In an environment with regular Snort rules applied using multiple SIP messages with different field values can produce much broader bandwidth. Finally, the results show it is possible to send 4 messages per second as the maximum without raising Snorts alarm. Four messages if these messages are sent over TCP or if the AVG method for anomaly detection is used and messages are sent over UDP.

Detection of anomalies in VoIP calls is a demanding task, and it is still in the phase of the investigation. This can be concluded from the fact that currently there is a restricted number of available software for this purpose. We saw, for example, that usage of NAIVE method for predicting network traffic would raise an alarm if the user sent more than one message per second.

The contributions of this paper lies in showing communication channels and calculating its bandwidth that can be used to send hidden data and thus undermine the security of the network.

Our future work will consist of detecting network anomalies in VoIP calls using other Profile generator methods and using other ways of generating lower or higher rate of hidden network traffic in VoIP call.

References

1. Zander, S., Armitage, G., Branch, P.: A Survey of Covert Channels and Countermeasures in Computer Network Protocols. IEEE Communications Surveys & Tutorials 9(3), 44–57 (2007) (cited on page 7)
2. Mazurczyk, W., Szczypiorski, K.: Steganography of VoIP Streams. In: Meersman, R., Tari, Z. (eds.) OTM 2008, Part II. LNCS, vol. 5332, pp. 1001–1018. Springer, Heidelberg (2008)
3. Janicki, A., Mazurczyk, W., Szczypiorski, K.: Steganalysis of transcoding steganography. Ann. Telecommun., doi:10.1007/s12243-013-0385-4
4. Mazurczyk, W., Kotulski, Z.: New VoIP Traffic Security Scheme with Digital Watermarking. In: Górski, J. (ed.) SAFECOMP 2006. LNCS, vol. 4166, pp. 170–181. Springer, Heidelberg (2006)
5. Mazurczyk, W., Szaga, P., Szczypiorski, K.: Using transcoding for hidden communication in IP telephony. Multimed. Tools Appl., doi:10.1007/s11042-012-1224-8

6. Anonymous, DNS Covert Channels and Bouncing Techniques (2005),
   http://www.archives.neohapsis.com/archives/fulldisclosure/
   2005-07/att-0472/p63_dns_worm_covert_channel.txt
7. Berk, V., Giani, A., Cybenko, G.: Detection of covert channel encoding in network packet
   delays (Tech. Rep. TR2005-536). Department of Computer Science, Dartmouth College
   (November 2005)
8. Szczypiorski, K.: HICCUPS: Hidden Communication System for Corrupted Networks. In:
   Proc. of ACS 2003, Międzyzdroje, Poland, October 22-24, pp. 31–40 (2003)
9. Mazurczyk, W., Smolarczyk, M., Szczypiorski, K.: Hiding Information in Retransmis-
   sions. Telecommunication Systems 52(2), 1113–1121 (2013)
10. Kulin, M., Kazaz, T., Mrdović, S.: SIP Server Security with TLS: Relative Performance,
    Evaluation. In: 2012 IX International Symposium on Telecommunications (BIHTEL). Fac.
    of Electr. Eng., Univ. of Sarajevo, Sarajevo, Bosnia-Herzegovina, pp. 1–6. IEEE (2012)
11. Tang, J., Cheng, Y., Hao, Y.: Detection and prevention of SIP flooding attacks in voice
    over IP networks. In: 2012 Proceedings IEEE INFOCOM. IEEE (2012)
12. Tang, J., Cheng, Y.: Quick detection of stealthy sip flooding attacks in voip networks. In:
    2011 IEEE International Conference on Communications (ICC), pp. 1–5. IEEE (June
    2011)
13. US Department of Defense – Department of Defense Trusted Computer System Evaluation
    Criteria, DOD 5200.28-STD (The Orange Book) (1985)
14. Session Initiation Protocol (SIP) Parameters,
    http://iana.org/assignments/sip-parameters/sip-
    parameters.xhtml
15. [RFC3261] [RFC3261][RFC3427][RFC5727]
16. SDP: Session Description Protocol, http://ietf.org/rfc/rfc2327.txt
17. Snort.AD - Snort(tm) preprocessor based on traffic anomalies detection,
    http://anomalydetection.info
18. Szmit, M., Adamus, S., Bugala, S., Szmit, A.: Implementation of Brutlag's algorithm in
    Anomaly Detection 3.0. In: FedCSIS, pp. 685–691 (September 2012)
19. The R Project for Statistical Computing, http://r-project.org
20. Szmit, M., Szmit, A.: Usage of Modified Holt-Winters Method in The Anomaly Detection
    of Network Traffic. Case Studies. Journal of Computer Networks and Communication (ar-
    ticle in press)
21. Brutlag, J.D.: Aberrant Behavior Detection in Time Series for Network Monitoring. In:
    14th System Administration Conference Proceedings, New Orleans, pp. 139–146 (2000)
22. Szmit, M., Szmit, A., Bugala, S.: Usage of Holt-Winters Model and Multilayer Perceptron
    in Network Traffic Modelling and Anomaly Detection. Informatica (03505596) 36(4)
    (2012)
23. Digium/Asterisk JIRA – Asterisk Issues,
    http://issues.asterisk.org/jira/browse/ASTERISK-8320
24. Open Source SIP Server, http://www.kamailio.org/w

Statistical Assessment of Retrieved Images and Videos Using the INACT Tool

Libor Michalek[1], Michał Grega[2], Mikołaj Leszczuk[2], Damian Bryk[2],
Bartłomiej Grabowski[2], Radek Turon[3], and Petr Oprsal[3]

[1] Department of Telecommunications, FEECS, VSB–Technical University of Ostrava,
17. listopadu 15, 708 33 Ostrava–Poruba, Czech Republic
[2] AGH University of Science and Technology,
al. Mickiewicza 30, 30-059 Krakow, Poland
[3] Police of the Czech Republic, Directorate of Czech Police for the Moravian and
Silesian Region, The Service of Criminal Police and Investigation, 30. dubna 24, 729
21 Ostrava, Czech Republic

Abstract. The INACT tool is designed to be used by police forces in
cases of prosecution for the production, distribution, and possession of
child pornography (CP). The INACT tool is being developed under the
INDECT research project. [1] We performed a statistical assessment of
results in order to determine success and performance in the process of
searching. We focused on the size of the confidence interval, which is
based on the values of first hit times. The aim of the experiments was
to confirm that the INACT application is functional and performs well
enough to be used by police forces in searching for CP. The paper also
describes progress in the development of the INACT application with
respect to the indexing and searching of movies.

1 Introduction

Child Pornography (CP) is a term which broadly describes all multimedia and
writings that depict sexual activities involving a child. Possession of CP images
is considered a crime in most countries. This law applies not only to regular
citizens, but also to police units - due to local regulations, police officers have
to destroy all evidence after an investigation is completed. This significantly
complicates the gathering and presenting of evidence in police investigations. All
these procedures require a tool which could overcome this problem. The result
of our research and development, performed in close cooperation with police end
users, is the INACT (INDECT Advanced Image Catalogue Tool) software [1,2].

This article follows up [3] by providing a more thorough and complex statistical assessment. The assessment is based on the results of experiments which
have been performed with the cooperation of the Service of Criminal Police and

---

[1] The research leading to these results has received funding from the European Community's Seventh Framework Programme (FP7/2007-2013) under grant agreement
no. 218086 – INDECT project.

A. Dziech and A. Czyżewski (Eds.): MCSS 2014, CCIS 429, pp. 193–201, 2014.
© Springer International Publishing Switzerland 2014

Investigation of the Czech Police. It must be stressed that the experiments performed by the Service of Criminal Police and Investigation with the INACT application were conducted with the use of sensitive content. These are the first published results, as the team working on the application did not have access to such content for legal reasons.

The rest of the paper is structured as follows. The second section describes the functions of the INACT application itself. In the third section, function for video indexing is introduced. The fourth section focuses on the practical experiments and statistical evaluation. In the conclusion, the statistical analysis is evaluated, and some further recommendations are made.

2   Application

The INACT tool is used for the detection of child pornography. INACT compares images from a previously created digital catalogue of descriptions of pictures (the equivalent of fingerprints) collected during previously conducted investigation operations. The result of such a search can be used to prove that the suspect is in possession of banned content, actively shares it, or creates it. The image catalogue can be created using a number of sources on the Web, based on the patterns that are there, thus, in a distributed mode.

In the European Union, the Codes of Criminal Procedure and regulation governing the police define access rights for police forces and the local processing of data sets using specialised tools. The police have the right, both at the crime scene and at police facilities, to conduct analytical work with material retained on the basis of a relevant order.

In any case, there is an obligation to produce appropriate protocols documenting the operation performed. Securing digital storage media (e.g. hard disk, flash drive) and browsing it is then carried out in accordance with the law. Such activities allow the police to demonstrate possession of prohibited files and prosecute the offence under the Criminal Code. Applicable laws in Poland are similar to the legislation in force in the EU and other countries [2].

To test the overall performance of the INACT tool, the first experiment was conducted using a PC with an Intel Core 2 Duo T5600 1.83 GHz with two cores, operating under the control of the Ubuntu 11.04 operating system. The average time needed to find the first illegal photography was 1 min 47 sec. By comparison, the search when reviewing each file individually lasted 13 minutes 40 seconds - an order of magnitude slower. For further testing, and in particular because of the needs of police officers, a Windows version of the tool has been developed.

To achieve a better result from the above, the authors investigated the possibility of optimisation by decreasing the image resolution. Images are reduced to an average of 0.065 megapixels, which, in total, speeds up the search process by a factor of 12 [3].

It should be pointed out that the process may be accelerated further, including the pre-selection of folders (e.g. containing temporary Internet files) before beginning the search, or by providing a mechanism which, also before searching, will increase the priority of the previously selected folders (in a graphical user interface, by interacting with the person using the tool). It should be noted that the usefulness of this method is not limited to image searches, since it can also be used to search for similarities in any structures, also in computer networks.

In future, it is expected that the application will have a function (plug-in) which implements the ability of automated detection of child pornography based on nudity and age classification of the image processed. The present child pornography classifier function is still under development, although initial tests have been performed [1].

In order to test the overall performance of the INACT automated CP detection plug-in, we conducted an experiment on a set of test samples containing 7,151 photos totalling 11,227 MB from free, publicly available databases, which are commonly used for research purposes. The current version of the plug-in achieves an accuracy which allows it to reject approx. 90 percent of faces of adults and to find approx. 70 percent of children's faces. In addition, it correctly recognises 90 percent of images of nude figures. The false positive rate is around 15 per-cent [3].

Finally, the authors began work on cataloguing and searching for movies (described in Section 3).

3   Video Indexing

While the INACT tool is extremely useful in the search for CP content in suspect file systems due to its fully automated operation, it must be noted that video content also poses a serious and common threat. Due to the expansion of CP as a crime, the end users testing the INACT application requested that it would be able to process video files.

The simple approach is to treat a video as a sequence of images. This approach is far from being effective, as consecutive frames of a video are very similar to each other, and both indexing and searching within them is redundant. Therefore, it was decided that each movie which is indexed and searched should be represented by a set of significant frames. These frames, extracted automatically, represent the most informative parts of the movie. We refer to such frames as *key frames* - not to be confused with 'key frames' used in movie compression algorithms.

In order to assess available key frame selection algorithms, we tested several closed- and open-source solutions. Closed-source solutions could not be used due to integration issues and licensing. The most promising results were provided by GPL-licensed *ffmpegthumbnailer* [4]. The most significant drawback of this software is that it returns only one frame per movie file. Instead of adapting ffmpegthumbnailer, we decided to come up with a dedicated solution. We decided to design and apply our own algorithm based on automated shot boundary detection. This algorithm as its first step converts a frame to an 8 bit RGB colour space. In the second step, a difference between histograms of consecutive frames is calculated. This makes it possible to identify shot boundaries in the video. We assume that the key frames are coming from the beginning of a shot in the video. Moreover, we require the key frame to be informative, meaning that the algorithm should avoid selecting out-of-focus or under- or over-exposed frames as key frames. For that purpose, the third stage of the algorithm is used, which employs edge detection. The algorithm rejects a frame with a low number of edges as non-informative.

Indexing of movies in the INACT INDEXER application is semi-automatic. The software automatically identifies movie files and performs key frame detection. Before the application calculates the descriptors for key frames, the key frames have to be confirmed to be informative and representative by the operator. This stage is necessary because although our key frame detection algorithm performs well, in rare cases it returns non-informative frames as key frames. As it is of the highest priority to keep only informative CP data in the INACT database, confirmation by an operator is required.

Operation of the SEARCHER application in the case of movies is simple. When a movie is found in the suspect file system, it is analysed with the same key frame detection algorithm as used in the INDEXER. Descriptors of the identified key frames are compared against the database of hashes. The comparision of descriptors is performed using metrics best suited for each descriptor, based on the experiments performed by the authors. If identical or similar frames are detected, the operator is informed, and the suspect key frame is displayed in the interface. Algorithms for movie analysis and search are depicted in Figure 1.

4 Practical Experiments

The INACT tool is, above all, being developed for CP searching and detection by police forces. For this reason, there is a need to perform a set of practical experiments based on images and video files containing CP. In [3], we presented the performance evaluation of experiments which consisted of 10 sets, each set consisting of over 400 images with a very high resolution. A more complex set of experiments has now been performed for determining the statistical parameters. The aim of the experiments was to show the real situation which occurs when the impounded hardware is being searched for suspect content. The experiment has been divided into two crucial parts. The first part focuses on testing of images, while the second part focuses on testing the video files.

For this experiment we created a test file system. The structure of the files and directories is a real structure from a HDD seized by police. This structure was filled by us with additional data. We have used approx. 10,000 natural images. For each of the experiments we have also used a number of real CP images or videos.

The INACT SEARCHER application implements a bee optimisation algorithm which implements random behaviour [1]. In order to provide a reliable result, we have repeated the experiments multiple times. The results presented were obtained by averaging multiple test results of small and defined variance. For such series of data, we can apply the Central Limit Theorem [5] and assume normal distribution for the test runs.

All experiments were performed by and at the premises of the Czech Police, in line with current law regulations.

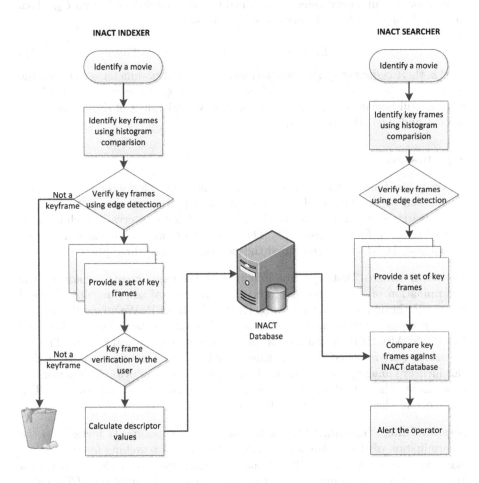

Fig. 1. Algorithms of INACT movie processing for INACT INDEXER and INACT SEARCHER

4.1   Conditions for Statistical Assessment

To evaluate the success of a search, we have to estimate the interval in which the first hit time values will vary. Confidence interval is a widely used and appropriate parameter for statistical evaluation. A Confidence interval gives an estimated range of values which is likely to include an unknown parameter, the estimated range being calculated from a given set of sample data - the first hit time.

Interval estimation defines a numerical range in which the actual value of the parameter Θ is found with a specified probability of P. In the case of interval estimation, the unknown value Θ is defined by two limit values L_1 and L_2, which are called the Confidence Interval - see Equation (1).

$$P = (L_1 < \Theta < L_2) = (1 - \alpha) \quad \alpha \in (0, 1). \tag{1}$$

P is the *Coefficient of Reliability* (probability) and parameter α is called the *Significance Level*. In our case, Θ is first hit time for that the value of confidence interval will be calculated. The most commonly used values of significance level are *0.1* and *0.05* respectively [6,7].

4.2   Results

To verify the functionality of the INACT application, a large number of experiments had to be performed. The aim of the experiments was, in the case of image searching, to determine the size of the confidence interval, which is based on the values of first hit times [3]. The experiments were performed on a copy of real suspect HDD. We separated the experiments into three parts.

Identical Image Testing. The first part of the experiments focused on the determination of the confidence interval in the case of searching for identical images. Eight images were indexed by INACT INDEXER. We mixed those identical CP images with a 10,000+ set of natural images in the filesystem. We used INACT SEARCHER to find the CP images among the natural images. The experiments were repeated for many times. We focused on the time needed to find this identical image (first hit time). Figure 2 shows the results for each performed experiment. The dotted line expresses the median value for all experiments. The median value has been calculated to 935.3 s.

Similar Image Testing. The second part of the experiments focused on the determination of the confidence interval in the case of searching for similar images. As before, we indexed 10 CP images. Again, we used a filesystem with a 10,000+ set of general natural images, into which the 10 additional CP images were randomly added. Unlike the previous experiment, the CP files added to

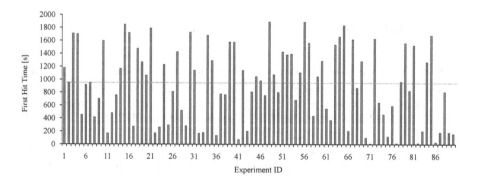

Fig. 2. First hit time for identical image for each experiment

the test set were not identical to those indexed. They were only visually similar (e.g. coming from the same photographic session). Using INACT SEARCHER, we focused on the first hit time for each found similar image (see Figure 3). The dotted line expresses the median value for all experiments. The value has been calculated to 742.9 s.

For the first and second part of the experiments, the statistical parameters have been calculated (see Tab. 1). We focused on a confidence interval which gives an estimated time range for time to first hit. The estimated range has been calculated from a given set of experiment data and is related to the mean value for all experiments. Confidence intervals are calculated for coefficient reliability equal to 90% and 95% [8].

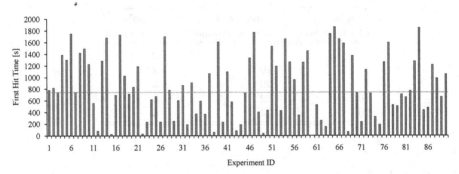

Fig. 3. First hit time for similar image for each experiment

Table 1. Statistical information for image experiments

	Identical	Similar
Number of Experiments	30	30
Confidence Interval (P=0.90) [s]	976.1 ±168.4	885.2 ±158.1
Confidence Interval (P=0.95) [s]	976.1 ±200.6	885.2 ±188.4
Number of Experiments	60	60
Confidence Interval (P=0.90) [s]	964.2 ±114.5	855.4 ±119.8
Confidence Interval (P=0.95) [s]	964.2 ±136.4	885.4 ±142.8
Number of Experiments	90	90
Confidence Interval (P=0.90) [s]	915.6 ±100.6	844.5 ±93.4
Confidence Interval (P=0.95) [s]	915.6 ±119.9	844.5 ±111.3

Video File Testing. The third and last part of the experiment focused on video files. Since the movie search is key frame-based, it was necessary to choose and index a few CP key frames from CP movies. This was done manually using the INACT INDEXER tool. As the INACT SEARCHER has been developed for searching suspect movies which could contain CP content, this time we focused only on how successful the tool was in this process. We did not focus on the first hit time since, in the case of movie searching, we assume only to find or potentially separate from other video files those which contain the CP content. Moreover, the values of first hit time are not meaningful due to the large dependency on the size of video files.

During the experiment, we used a file system with a 1,000+ set of natural movies. Among them, we randomly added 5 video files with CP content. We used the INACT SEARCHER to find these movies. Several tests were performed, while the number of indexed files was increased. It was proved that increasing the number of indexed files increased the number of found files with CP (see Tab. 2).

Table 2. Statistical information for video experiments

Number of files indexed	Number of total keyframes	Number of files found
1	6	2
2	10	2
5	26	3
10	32	3
20	74	4

5   Conclusion

This paper describes progress in the development of the INACT application. A new function for indexing and searching movie sequences has been introduced and tested.

The main part of the paper focuses on a description of experiments and their statistical evaluation. The aim of the performed experiments was to determine the applicability of the INACT tool. It should be emphasised that all experiments were performed on real data, i.e. data seized by police forces as suspect. This cooperation was crucial, as due to the legal regulations the developers of the algorithms and software did not have access to any CP content. It is obvious that the direct cooperation with Czech Police has been essential and fruitful.

Detailed statistical evaluation has been done which proved that the range of the confidence interval gives us information on how the first hit time could vary according to the number of experiments. The large width of the confidence interval indicates that more experiments have to be done for a definite result is determined. Nevertheless, according to the mean value, the value of the confidence interval is significantly lower. Furthermore, it has been proved that the confidence interval does not change significantly with the number of experiments. Therefore, we can claim that the result of the first experiment is convincing, and further experiments are not necessary.

The experiments, followed by the statistical evaluation, confirmed that the INACT application is fully functional and can be used in law enforcement operations on a daily basis. The functionality of movie indexing and searching has been proved, since the INACT INSEARCHER application found the video files with CP content in a real filesystem.

Currently, the main goal of INACT development will focus on optimising the INACT performance and polishing the user interface.

Acknowledgements. The research leading to these results has received funding from the European Community's Seventh Framework Programme (FP7/2007-2013) under grant agreement no. 218086 – INDECT project. Development of systems has been co-financed in Poland by the European Regional Development Fund under the Innovative Economy Operational Programme, INSIGMA project no. POIG.01.01.02-00-062/09.

References

1. Grega, M., Bryk, D., Napora, M.: INACT – INDECT advanced image cataloguing tool. Multimedia Tools and Applications, 1–16 (2012)
2. Grega, M., Bryk, D., Napora, M., Gusta, M.: INACT — INDECT advanced image cataloguing tool. In: Dziech, A., Czyżewski, A. (eds.) MCSS 2011. CCIS, vol. 149, pp. 28–36. Springer, Heidelberg (2011),
   http://www.springerlink.com/index/JH87416833611825.pdf
3. Michalek, L., Grega, M., Bryk, D., Grabowski, B.: Performance evaluation of INACT – INDECT advanced image cataloguing tool. Advances in Electrical and Electronic Engineering 10(4), 308–311 (2012)
4. Boer, D.V.: Ffmpegthumbnailer – lightweight video thumbnailer that can be used by file managers, http://code.google.com/p/ffmpegthumbnailer/
5. Rice, J.A.: Mathematical statistics and data analysis, 2nd edn. Duxbury, Belmont (1995)
6. Mendenhall, W., Beaver, R., Beaver, B.: Introduction to probability and statistics. Duxbury Press (2012)
7. Grinstead, C.M., Snell, J.L.: Introduction to Probability. American Mathematical Society (1997)
8. Harmon, M.: Confidence Intervals in Excel – The Excel Statistical Master. Excel Master Series (2011)

Framework for Opinion Spammers Detection

Andrzej Opalinski and Grzegorz Dobrowolski

AGH University of Science and Technology, Krakow, Poland
{andrzej.opalinski,grzela}@agh.edu.pl

Abstract. Evolution of the WEB and high anonymity of virtual identities result in positive and negative impact on society. One of the negative effects is a problem of false spam opinions, which are distributed throughout WEB forums and recommendation portals. Researches in this area mainly concern detection of particular examples of spam opinions. Nevertheless, an idea of detecting virtual multi-identities, created by a single person, still seems to be lacking effective solutions. Presented article describes a system which allows to search virtual multi-identities, created in order to generate spam opinions. The system bases on a combination of features from various domains: natural language processing, time-activity analysis and related to common objects. Series of tests evaluated system's efficiency in the area of detecting virtual multi-identities from recommendation portal.

Keywords: virtual identities, opinion spam, cybercrime.

1   Introduction

According to the recent surveys, almost 2,4 billion people has an access to Internet network. In Europe, this rate reaches 63% and in North America 78% of society. The increase, comparing to the beginning of the century rised to more than 500% [6][14]. Another indicator of evolution of the WEB is the number of active webpages, which exceeds 633 millions. Significant reasons of this phenomenon are miniaturization and price drop of hardware followed by increasing access to the Internet access services. Great impact on this state stem from the evolution of the Internet to the WEB2.0 model, where any user can create, publish and modify his own content within the framework of the WEB. Migration of successive human's life areas into the WEB, results in emergence of the cybersociety, where real people are represented by their virtual identities [16].

Existing relations and activities are mapped to structures and functionalities of the Internet's social networks, but the mapping does not include all aspects of reality. First important reason of this problem is limited structure of Internet social networks. Additionally, it is to observe the phenomenon of unrestricted ability of creation and verification of features of virtual identities, representing a person in virtual world[28]. Relatively high freedom in creating many virtual identities, characterized by various features, and their low verification leads to the number of consequences.

A. Dziech and A. Czyżewski (Eds.): MCSS 2014, CCIS 429, pp. 202–213, 2014.
© Springer International Publishing Switzerland 2014

Positive aspects of that status are for example: facilitating personal relations for people with low self-esteem, experiences' exchange and support within the group of people with similar problems, experimenting with personal behaviors that would not be accepted by the real-life environment[3]. Moreover, it promotes freedom of speech in countries, where it is limited due to religious or political reasons.

Unfortunately, there are also negative aspects of this phenomenon. These are inter alia: racial or religious hatred, sexual deviations like pedophilia, black PR (compromising informations or photos), broad meaning of cybercrime as trafficking in illicit goods, coordination of criminal or terrorist groups[22]. Another example of harmful impact of the WEB evolution is deceptive opinion spam, posted on recommendation portals or Internet forums. This issue may refer to objects, brands, companies or services, and it can occur in positive or negative connotation. Those opinions are frequently generated by a single real person, who use several virtual identities. There are also some crowdsourcing WEB portals, where one's can outsource such services[7][2].

Widespread of deceptive opinion spam resulted in the evolution of researches in this domain. Some of surveys concern detection of a spam opinion based on its text content, another detects users, who create those messages. However, the problem of detecting virtual multi-identities, created and used by single person, seems to be still unresolved.

The article presents the concept of a model and a system crated on its basis, which facilitate searching for multi-identities of single person. It is noticeable that model use various features coming from the domain of natural language processing, user's time activity and structural features of text messages. Furthermore, the system maintains effectiveness with increasing number of virtual identities, what happens in case of most of similar systems from this research domain.

The second section of the article presents status of reseaches in this science's area, the third one applies to its specific issues.The fourth presents system's architecture. Fifth section includes experiments and test results, and the last section express conclusions and plans for further research's directions and their evolution.

2   Related Works

The problem of detecting multi-identities, hidden in Internet's social networks is relatively young research domain, rapidly developing since last few years. In order to create solution for this problem, it is necessary to aggregate methods from various cognate disciplines. The essential approach could be based on models from two classical research domains: matching duplicated identity from databases[24] or text authorship analysis[20][9]. Unfortunately, both approaches are not directly applicable, due to source differences. Methods derived from duplicated identities detection are based mainly on personal data, which are rarely available in content generated by hidden multi-identities. As it comes to classical text authorship's analysis methods, it applies to the relatively small number of authors, characterized by large text's corpses, while deceptive opinion spam sources provide with different data.

There are several surveys in the area of text authorship's analysis, which refers to sources from the WEB. Stamatos presented approach based on n-gram char chains [19], which were efficient for about 50 authors. This method was also applicable for plagiarism detection in textual documents[21]. Style markers, text structure and keywords were also used for detecting criminal activities based on the Web's resources[33]. Furthermore, emails[34] and Internet forums[18] were also used as a source for analysis of a text's authorship, but all the approaches were significantly loosing effectiveness with increasing numbers of authors.

Another research area, which provides with useful solutions, is classical spam detection from the WEB sources[7]. Those surveys applied to recommendation portals, Internet forums or social networks[25][15]. A disadvantage of those methods is that they act as a binary classifier, who separate spam from non-spam messages or users. Those approaches does not support detecting pairs of multi-identities or multi-messages of a single person.

A social context and relations were also applied to identify virtual identities from the WEB resources[12]. Social roles and activity types were used to detect multi-identities in sources referring to the criminal files [31]. However those approaches used personal data as a key feature of its solution.

There were carried out surveys, which relay on user's time activity and rating polarization, in order to detect group of spam users from recommendation portals[30]. However, this approach does not consider text's content and it detects spamming groups, instead of pairs of multi-identities. User's time-activity was also a basic feature for monitoring real time Internet's communicators[1]. Those approaches require large data source with high time resolution and also does not base on contents of text messages.

The analysis of current state of the topic of virtual multi-identity researches indicates a few deficiencies in this area. Solutions from multi-identity detection are based mostly on the personal data. Text's authorship analysis approaches based on classical classifier models remains efficient just for small number of authors. As it comes to spam detection systems, they function as a binary classifier, detecting spam users or messages. The system which is described in this paper intends to resolve those deficiencies, by aggregating features from various domains, and by facilitating detecting pairs of multi-identities of a single person, without decreasing effectiveness with increasing number of virtual identities.

3   Domain Related Research Issues

There is a one key problem related to researches from domain of deceptive opinion spam and virtual multi-identity detection. It is a lack of gold standard data, that could be used for an evaluation of the effectiveness of proposed model's effectiveness[17][8]. Obtaining such a data from their authors, is for obvious reasons virtually impossible.

Due to the gold standard data deficiency, there are some other solutions that are commonly used to verify experiment's results. First approach consist on receiving deceptive opinion spam, by outsourcing this task to one of the crowd-sourcing web portals, for instance MTurk [1][17][5]. People creating those opinions are unaware of creating data for research purposes, so it tends to simulate original opinion spam generating process.

Another method of assessing results is selection of false opinions or multi-identities based on certain criterion. In one of surveys, author worked for some time as a crowdsourcer and he used gained knowledge to select a set of potential spamming virtual identities and messages[2]. Another criterion used to select a set of multi-identities was presented in a survey of Wang[26]. Authors selected profiles, whose personal photos where highly indexed by Google Image Search services and the accounts were blocked by administrators. Those conditions indicated profiles that was considered as false or spamming.

Assessing results by human judges is another approach commonly applied in researches on deceptive opinion spam and multi-identity detections[32][27][10]. The degree of efficiency of assessing results, for different type of judges, was examined in one of the researches[26]. Improvement of evaluation of the efficiency was acknowledged by approach that used human group classification's methods[11]. One of the commonly chosen examples of those techniques, is a model of "skeptic judge"[17], which relies on the majority of voting human arbitrators. Discussed approach reduces FalseNegative error, which is typical in human judging techniques[29].

These methods are substitutes for a gold standard data, in order to evaluate efficiency of models for researches in domains of deceptive opinion spam and multi-identities detection. A choice of particular method depends on source's type, its characteristic and law conditions.

4   A Framework Architecture

To facilitate researches on multi-identities detection, author proposed a model and developed a system, presented on Fig.1. Main system modules are described in a successive parts of this section.

4.1   Data Acquisition Module

First system component, considering the data processing aspect, is the crawl and data storage module. It provides the functionality of crawling the source domains and extracting potentially valuable data, that could be used afterwards. In order to accomplish this task, author used a crawling and data indexing tool, described in previous author's publications[23]. The extraction of important information requires analysis of site's HTML structure and implementation of dedicated parser, for each source of data. Selected information is stored in the system's database.

---

[1] www.mturk.com

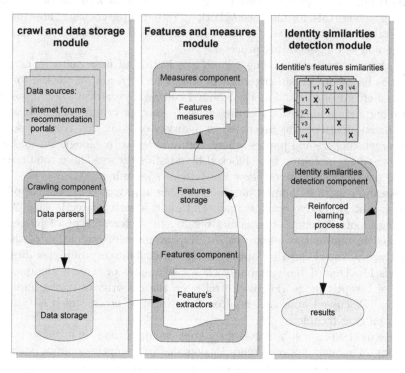

Fig. 1. System overview architecture

4.2   Features and Metrics Module

A module of features and metrics is the core of the system and it process the data, related to all virtual identities found in data sources. The module contains algorithms which generate all types of characteristics for every virtual identity in the system, and stores them in the tables in database.

Those characteristics are basis for metrics algorithms from measures component, which compares by pairs all types of characteristics for all pairs of virtual identities existing in the system.

There are about 20 various types of characteristics and metrics based on it, implemented into the system. They could be divided basing on source data's type into :

- Based on text features
  - Total and average number of characters, digits, special chars, words, sentences, posts;
  - Frequency of occurrences of special chars and words containing: % ~ @ # $ ^ & * - _ + = ¡ ¿ { } / [ ] —;
  - Common function words, based on text authorship's analysis approaches[34];

- Frequency of punctuation marks;
- Content related words[4];
- Text sentiment (emotional polarization), calculated by Cluo library[13];
- Based on common time activity points - compares dates of users activities. Granularity of time periods depends on the source's characteristic. (weekly, daily, hourly,...);
- Based on common object's links
  - Based on a structure's specific object, connecting virtual identities (threads on forum, commonly commented products, et cetera)
  - Based on commonly outgoing links included in user's messages

Metrics are functions that base on similarity measure, dedicated and implemented for each type of characteristic. Single metric compute similarity of pair of characteristics, corresponding to pair of virtual identities. The result of the metric is a similarity value of two virtual identities considering particular feature (described by the characteristic). The similarity value returned by metrics is a floating-point number in the range from 0 to 1. 0 result indicates total lack of similarity and 1 indicates the identity of virtual identities (considering only one particular feature).

For numerical values, similarity is computed by a measure presented in Eq.1.

$$Sim_m(i,j) = 1 - \frac{|f_m(i) - f_m(j)|}{max(f_m) - min(f_m)} \tag{1}$$

For sets and the categorical values, similarity is computed by Jaccard's measure, as in Eq.2.

$$J(A,B) = \frac{|A \cap B|}{|A \cup B|} \tag{2}$$

Computed similarities of pairs of virtual identities, based on a single feature, are stored in the virtual identities similarity matrices. Each feature is represented by a single matrix, and the size of the matrix is the number of virtual identities stored in the system.

4.3 Identities' Similarities Detection Module

The last stage of the process is being accomplished by the identity similarities detection module. The primary algorithm of a detection of identities' similarities is based on weighted sets of a similarity measures, and it is presented on Eq.3.

$$a_p(t_i, t_j) = \sqrt{\frac{\sum_{\forall w_a \in Ws} w_a * m_a(ch_i, ch_j)^2}{|Ws|}} \tag{3}$$

where:
W - set of weights for features, $w_a \in W$
Ws - relevant set of weights, that:
$\forall w_a \in Ws : w_a \in W, w_a > 0,1$

Weights from Eq.3 are established during supervised learning process, under system's administrator verification. The process schema is presented on Fig.2.

Supervisor of the learning process assesses the correctness of returned similarities value of virtual pair of identities. During this assessment process, system presents all text data for both compared virtual identities, characteristics for both virtual identities and their similarity measure's value. At the end, system presents similarity value of the pair of the virtual identities.

Function of estimation for current algorithm's efficiency returns true, if supervisor will asses the similarities result for 10 times in the row. If the result assessment of supervisor is false, the counter is reseted to 0, and supervisor selects the incorrect weights (features) to be raised or lowered. Weights values are corrected by 10% of their values, up or down, depending on the supervisor's decision.

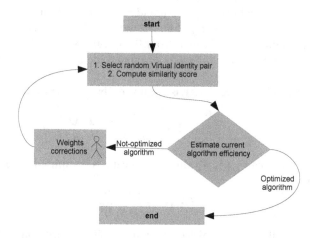

Fig. 2. Supervised learning algorithm schema

After the series of empirical test author established a feature threshold value on 0,1. If during the supervised learning process any of weights reaches the threshold value or lower, it will be removed from further stages of process and it will not be considered in Eq.3. It is a simplified version of feature extraction and dimension reduction step, which increase significantly system performance.

5 Testbed and Experiment Results

In order to evaluate the concept and its efficiency, there was performed a series of tests. The objective of the test was to find multi-virtual identities based on the WEB resources, and evaluate system's effectiveness.

5.1 Data Source

For testing purposes, author selected a Polish tourism recommendation portal Oceniacz.pl[2] and its part, corresponding to travel agencies. Data extracted from the website contained 2034 comments, referring to 93 travel agencies, generated by 1784 virtual identities.

5.2 Evaluation Method and Experiment Plan

Evaluation Method - Skeptic judge model[17], described in previous section was applied to evaluate system efficiency. Judges group was constituted by 4 volunteers and model response was based on minimum 3 agreed votes. 2 vs 2 answer samples was treated as unresolved and rejected. System presented to arbiters pairs of virtual identities, followed by their text messages, characteristics based on them, features' similarity values and total similarity value. Judges answered "Yes" or "No" for question: "Does presented pair of virtual identities indicate significant features of single person multi-identity ?"

Experiment Plan - For testing purposes, all characteristics implemented within the system were generated for 1784 virtual identities. Afterwards, similarities for all feature's matrices were computed.

Subsequent tests were performed in three series, varying between features sets content, used for computing total value of identity's similarity:

- Series 1 - based on a text features,
- Series 2 - based on a text features + based on common object's links,
- Series 3 - based on a text features + based on common object's links + based on common time activity points.

For all three series, the test schema was as presented below:

- Execution of supervised learning process,
- Computing total similarity based on Eq.3 for all 1590436 pairs of virtual identities. Average computing duration of this process was about 2 days for PC-class computer with 4GB RAM and 2-core 2,4GHz CPU,
- All virtual identities' pairs were sorted basing on their total similarity score,
- Parameter P (value of total similarity) was established to divide set of pairs into two subsets: similar and different pairs,
- Value of P parameter was changed from 0,8 to 1 with step of 0,025 and following test was performed in a loop:
  - Drawing of 20 pairs from both subsets,
  - All 40 pairs were presented to arbiters in random order. Skeptic judge model evaluated each pair,
  - Skeptic judge model result was compared to the system's result (considered as binary classifier).
- For each P value TruePositive, TrueNegative, FalsePositive i FalseNegative factors were computed, followed by F-measure - commonly applied in evaluation of classification method[4][33].

---

[2] www.oceniacz.pl

5.3   Test Results

Evaluation of system's efficiency for all three series by F-measure is presented for different values of P-parameters on Fig.3

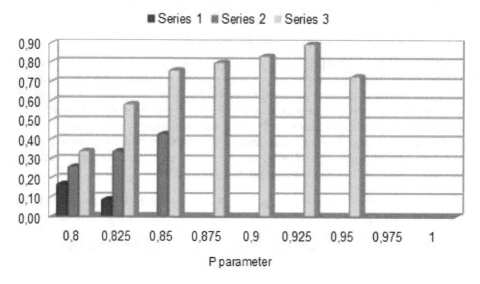

Fig. 3. Values of F-measure

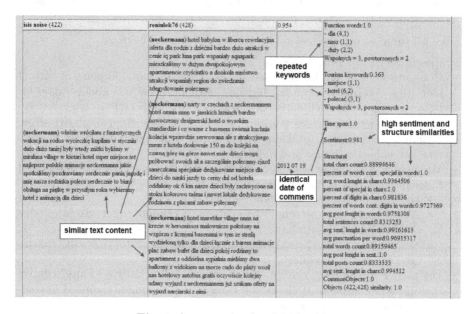

Fig. 4. An example of multi-identities

Main conclusions based on the experiment's results are:

- Similarities detection based on test features (Series 1) and text features + common object's links (Series 2) returns low quality results, even for lower P parameters values
- There are no pairs of virtual identities that received similarity value higher than 0,85 for Series 1 and 0,875 for Series 2
- Extending features set by characteristics based on common time activity points significantly improved classification efficiency. Best results (considering F-measure) were obtained for 0,925 P-parameter value
- Presented system is able to detect multi-identites. An example of two detected multi-identities is presented on Fig.4

6 Conclusions and Future Works

Results of the experiments proves, that it is possible to search and find virtual multi-identities from Internet social networks. Presented system integrates various types of features. Additionally it does not require personal data and maintains efficiency for large number of virtual identities. Obviously, the system would not provide with 100% effectiveness, and there are some techniques (as operating in different time periods or modification of stylometric text's characteristics) that will cause avoidance of detection. However, for most popular opinion spam deception examples, presented solution is efficient enough.

Presented system could be used in the future, for developing techniques of virtual identity similarities detection. It can be adapted for applying new, advanced solutions from domains of natural language processing domain, user time activity or social network analysis. Domain specific elements are required to be considered, for generating new characteristics for every new data source.

The other research directions, that can be examined with presented model are also methods of identities' similarities detection based on classical classification approaches. However, on the basis of WEB resources, it would require applying more complex features; extraction and dimension's reduction techniques, to enable parsing number of virtual identities.

Summarizing, presented system proved its usefulness, and that it is promising framework for further research development in area of virtual identity detection based on Internet social networks.

Acknowledgments. The research leading to these results has received funding from the European Communitys Seventh Framework Program (FP7/2007-2013) under grant agreement nr 218086.

References

1. Chen, H.-C., Goldberg, M., Magdon-Ismail, M.: Identifying multi-ID users in open forums. In: Chen, H., Moore, R., Zeng, D.D., Leavitt, J. (eds.) ISI 2004. LNCS, vol. 3073, pp. 176–186. Springer, Heidelberg (2004)

2. Chen, C., Wu, K., Srinivasan, V., Zhang, X.: Battling the internet water army: Detection of hidden paid posters. arXiv preprint:1111.4297 (2011)

3. Christopherson, K.M.: The positive and negative implications of anonymity in Internet social interactions: On the Internet, nobody knows you're a dog. Computers in Human Behavior 23(6), 3038–3056 (2007)

4. De Vel, O., Anderson, A., Corney, M., Mohay, G.: Mining e-mail content for author identification forensics. ACM Sigmod Record 30(4), 55–64 (2001)

5. Harris, C.G.: Detecting Deceptive Opinion Spam Using Human Computation. In: Workshops at the Twenty-Sixth AAAI Conference on Artificial Intelligence (2012)

6. International Telecommunication Union: Measuring the Information Society 2012, Place des Nations, CH-1211 Geneva Switzerland (2012) ISBN 978-92-61-14071-7

7. Jindal, N., Liu, B.: Analyzing and Detecting Review Spam. In: Data Mining, ICDM 2007, October 28-31, pp. 547–552 (2007)

8. Jindal, N., Liu, B.: Opinion spam and analysis. In: Proceedings of the International Conference on Web Search and Web Data Mining, pp. 219–230 (2008)

9. Juola, P.: Authorship attribution. Foundations and Trends in Information Retrieval 1(3), 233–334 (2007)

10. Kim, S.M., Pantel, P., Chklovski, T., Pennacchiotti, M.: Automatically assessing review helpfulness. In: Proc. of the 2006 Conference on Empirical Methods in Natural Language Processing, pp. 423–430 (2006)

11. Le, J., Edmonds, A., Hester, V., Biewald, L.: Ensuring quality in crowdsourced search relevance evaluation: The effects of training question distribution. In: SIGIR 2010 Workshop on Crowdsourcing for Search Evaluation, pp. 21–26 (2010)

12. Li, J., Wang, G.A., Chen, H.: Identity matching using personal and social identity features. Information Systems Frontiers 13(1), 101–113 (2010)

13. Maciolek, P., Dobrowolski, G.: CLUO: Web-Scale Text Mining System for Open Source Intelligence Purposes. Computer Science 14(1), 45 (2013), doi:10.7494

14. Miniwatts Marketing Group: World internet usage and population statistics (June 30, 2012), http://www.internetworldstats.com

15. Mukherjee, A., Liu, B., Glance, N.: Spotting Fake reviewer groups in consumer reviews. In: Proc. of the 21st Int. Conf. on WWW, pp. 191–200. ACM (2012)

16. Musial, K., Kazienko, P.: Social networks on the internet. World Wide Web, 1–42 (2012)

17. Ott, M., Choi, Y., Cardie, C., Hancock, J.T.: Finding deceptive opinion spam by any stretch of the imagination. arXiv preprint:1107.4557 (2011)

18. Pillay, S.R., Solorio, T.: Authorship attribution of web forum posts. In: eCrime Researchers Summit (eCrime), pp. 1–7. IEEE (2010)

19. Stamatatos, E.: Author identification using imbalanced and limited training texts. In: 18th International Workshop on DEXA 2007, pp. 237–241. IEEE (2007)

20. Stamatatos, E.: A survey of modern authorship attribution methods. Journal of the American Society for information Science and Technology 60(3), 538–556 (2009)

21. Stamatatos, E.: Intrinsic plagiarism detection using character n-gram profiles. In: 3rd PAN Workshop on Uncovering Plagiarism, Authorship and Social Software Misuse, vol. 2, p. 38 (2009)

22. Thomas, D., Loader, B.: Cybercrime: Security and surveillance in the information age. Routledge (2000)

23. Turek, W., Opalinski, A., Kisiel-Dorohinicki, M.: Extensible web crawler – towards multimedia material analysis. In: Dziech, A., Czyżewski, A. (eds.) MCSS 2011. CCIS, vol. 149, pp. 183–190. Springer, Heidelberg (2011)

24. Wang, A.G., Atabakhsh, H., Petersen, T., Chen, H.: Discovering identity problems: A case study. In: Kantor, P., Muresan, G., Roberts, F., Zeng, D.D., Wang, F.-Y., Chen, H., Merkle, R.C. (eds.) ISI 2005. LNCS, vol. 3495, pp. 368–373. Springer, Heidelberg (2005)

25. Wang, D., Irani, D., Pu, C.: A social-spam detection framework. In: Proceedings of the 8th Annual Collaboration, Electronic Messaging, Anti-Abuse and Spam Conference, pp. 46–54 (2011)

26. Wang, G., Mohanlal, M., Wilson, C., Wang, X., Metzger, M., Zheng, H., Zhao, B.: Social Turing Tests: Crowdsourcing Sybil Detection. arXiv preprint:1205.3856 (2012)

27. Weimer, M., Gurevych, I., Mühlhäuser, M.: Automatically assessing the post quality in online discussions on software. In: Proceedings of the 45th Annual Meeting of the ACL, pp. 125–128 (2007)

28. van Kokswijk, J.: Granting Personality to a Virtual Identity. International Journal of Human and Social Sciences 2(4) (2010)

29. Vrij, A.: Detecting lies and deceit: Pitfalls and opportunities. Wiley Interscience (2008)

30. Xie, S., Wang, G., Lin, S., Yu, P.S.: Review spam detection via temporal pattern discovery. In: Proceedings of the 18th ACM SIGKDD, pp. 823–831 (2012)

31. Xu, J., Chau, M., Wang, G.A., Li, J.: Complex problem solving: identity matching based on social contextual information. Journal of the Association for Information Systems 8(10), 525–545 (2007)

32. Yang, Y.C., Padmanabhan, B.: Toward user patterns for online security: Observation time and user identification. Decision Support Systems 48(4), 548–558 (2010)

33. Zheng, R., Qin, Y., Huang, Z., Chen, H.: Authorship analysis in cybercrime investigation. In: Chen, H., Miranda, R., Zeng, D.D., Demchak, C.C., Schroeder, J., Madhusudan, T. (eds.) ISI 2003. LNCS, vol. 2665, pp. 59–73. Springer, Heidelberg (2003)

34. Zheng, R., Li, J., Chen, H., Huang, Z.: A framework for authorship identification of online messages: Writing-style features and classification techniques. Journal of the American Society for Information Science and Technology 57(3), 378–393 (2005)

A Bloom Filter-Based Monitoring Station for a Lawful Interception Platform

Gerson Rodríguez de los Santos, Jose Alberto Hernández,
Manuel Urueña, and Alfonso Muñoz

Universidad Carlos III de Madrid
Avda Universidad 30, 28911 Leganés, Madrid, Spain
{gsantos,jahgutie,muruenya,ammunoz}@it.uc3m.es
http://www.it.uc3m.es/

Abstract. Lawful Interception (LI) is a fundamental tool in today's Police investigations.Therefore, it is important to make it as quickly and securely as possible as well as a reasonable cost per suspect. This makes traffic capture in aggregation links quite attractive, although this implies high wirespeeds which require the use of specific hardware-based architectures. This paper proposes a novel Bloom Filter-based monitoring station architecture for efficient packet capture in aggregation links. With said Bloom filter, we filter out most of the packets in the link and capture only those belonging to lawful interception wiretaps. Next, we present an FPGA-based implementation of said architecture and obtain the maximum capture rate achievable by injecting traffic through four parallel Gigabit Ethernet lines. Finally, we identify the limitations of our current design and suggest the possibility of further extending it to higher wirespeeds.

Keywords: Lawful Interception, FPGA, Bloom filter, Packet Capture.

1 Introduction

Criminality is, and is likely to be at all times, a great problem in our society. The first task in solving a criminal case concerns the collection of evidence and the investigation of suspects. In some occasions, the Police forces need to lawfully intercept the communications (phone, computers, etc) of suspects, especially in severe crimes like terrorism, child pornography, political corruption and organised crime in general. On the other hand, the secrecy of communications is recognised as a fundamental right in most countries, therefore a wiretap warrant, issued by a judge, is necessary to intercept communications.

A usual approach for Lawful Interception (LI) involves wiretapping directly the suspect's subscriber loop, typically cable (xDSL, HFC), fibre-based (FTTx) or wireless (WiFi). However, individual wiretapping poses serious scalability problems, especially concerning cost. Besides, wiretapping at aggregation points, where the traffic of thousands of users is aggregated, is technologically challenging, but possibly more cost-effective. Such a large-scale monitorisation requires

A. Dziech and A. Czyżewski (Eds.): MCSS 2014, CCIS 429, pp. 214–228, 2014.

fast traffic capturing (at the line rate), and high-speed filtering out of non-suspicious traffic while ensuring that 100% of the suspects' traffic is captured. To accomplish these goals, specialised monitoring hardware is required, for instance FPGA (Field Programmable Gate Array)- or GPU (Graphics Processing Unit)-based systems.

Because high processing speeds are required in these environments, the use of data structures that provide low latency is required as well as specialised hardware. One possible solution which has been the subject of study in recent years is the use of Bloom Filters [1] (BF). These data structures permit to quickly check if a binary string belongs to a registered set of elements with a reasonable false positive probability.

In this light, this paper proposes an FPGA-based monitoring station architecture for the high-speed collection of suspects' traffic in multi-Gbit/s links. Additionally, we present an implementation based on a NetFPGA with 4x 1 Gbit/s input ports where traffic is captured, filtered and forwarded to other output port(s). Inside the monitoring station, the source and destination IP addresses of every incoming IP packet are checked against a list of suspect's IP addresses which are stored in a Bloom Filter and implemented in hardware. This implementation allows the monitoring station to operate at wirespeed, showing its applicability in realistic investigation scenarios.

The rest of the paper is organised as follows: Section 2 reviews previous work related with high-speed packet processing, GPUs, multicore processors and FPGA based systems. Section 3 overviews the fundamentals of Bloom Filters. The whole Lawful Interception scenario and the inner hardware architecture are described in Section 4. Finally, Section 5 shows introduces the FPGA platform used in the implementation of our prototype, as well as a number of experiments demonstrating the feasibility and performance of our prototype. Section 6 concludes this paper with a summary of its main contributions.

2   Related Work

While guaranteeing real-time processing and null network information loss is a tall order, there are several technologies appointed for this demanding task, namely GPUs, Multicore processors and FPGAs.

2.1   GPUs

GPUs provide a massive amount of small computational elements, which are very suitable for tasks that can be parellelised at a reduced cost.

GPUs have been used to provide parallelisation to a wide variety of networking tasks. In [2], a GPU-based routing implementation with Deep Packet Inspection (DPI) capabilities is presented. Such a DPI is both implemented using a Finite State Automata (FSA) and a Bloom Filter paradigm, and are subsequently compared showing that Bloom Filters provide the best performance.

GPUs in the routing context were first presented in [2] and further extended in [3]. In this work, the authors show a direct table lookup (with up to 2^{24}

entries) for routing which highly minimises memory access in comparison with other data structures such as Tries.

In [4], an architecture for packet signature matching is examined and implemented in a GPU. A comparison between Deterministic Finite Automata (DFA) and eXtended Finite Automata (XFA) based architectures is provided. Both of them are analysed and implemented for comparison showing a better performance and less memory usage coming from XFA implementations.

In [5], another GPU-based packet regular expresion matching engine is introduced. With three optimisation techniques aimed at improving memory access, the implementation is able to reach 128.6*Gbps* rate.

GPUs have also been a subject of research in the design of Intrusion Detection Systems (IDS). In [6], a GPU parallelised architecture based on the Wu-Manber algorithm is shown. The work in [6] was subsequently improved in [7], where a hierarchical parallel machine architecture on GPU was used to address some of the shortcomings revealed in [6], mainly the problem of state explosion that appears when it is necessary to search for complex regular expressions.

2.2 Multicore Processors

Another means of parallelisation comes from multipurpose, multicore processors. In this field, extensive research efforts have been conducted in the parallelisation of packet processing, especially pattern matching, see [8,9,10]. As a consequence, DPI has been the most recurring topic in this area. In [11] a parallelisation of the L7 filter [12], a DPI extension for Linux Netfilter is presented. Finally, [13] proposes a pre-filtering algorithm to ignore unwanted matches for L7 filter. This allows the L7 filter to get a better efficiency for the L7 rule matching algorithm.

2.3 FPGAs/ASICs

FPGAs and ASICs allow full task customisation and implementation in hardware.

FPGAs have been used to overcome the limitation of pure software environments for traditional networking tasks such as IP forwarding [14]. The most popular application of FPGAs in the networking area comprises those related with pattern and string matching for IDS and Intrusion Protection Systems (IPS). In [15,16,17,18] a parallel Bloom Filter based architecture is presented and subsequently improved. Another approach for IDS implementation in FPGA is the Finite State Machine (FSM) paradigm [19,20], which has different pros and cons with the Bloom Filter approach [21]. Additionally, in [22], an FPGA implementation of a Deep Packet Inspection architecture with Regular Expression Detection is shown. In [23], a parallel pattern matching architecture based on a compact reconfigurable filter and a coprocessor for FPGA is presented.

Finally, there has also been research regarding hardware implementations of firewalls. In [24], [25] two different firewall implementations are shown. There are also some combined proposals like [26], which suggest a combination of Firewall, IDS and rate limiting in the same implementation.

The main contribution of our paper consists in the design of a hardware Bloom Filter packet monitoring station architecture for Lawful Interception.

3 Bloom Filters Background

A Bloom Filter [1] (BF) is a data structure used to test whether an element belongs to a certain set or not. A BF is characterised by a number k of hash functions and a binary array N of bits initially set to zero, as shown in Fig. 1.

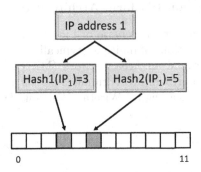

Fig. 1. Bloom Filter example

Now, consider we wish to store n elements in the array, say for instance the list of IP addresses from suspects to be monitored. In this light, the k hash functions are applied to each element in the IP list producing a number of positions in the binary array, which are then set to one. In the example, $k = 2$ hash functions are applied to the first IP address, setting the third and fifth position of the binary array to unity (note that the binary array has 12 positions, starting from 0 until 11). After the n IP addresses are stored, the binary array contains a number of ones which characterises the list of n IP addresses to be monitored. This is often referred to as the *training phase* of the Bloom Filter.

The average number of ones in the binary array is:

$$E(W) = N \left[1 - \left(1 - \frac{1}{N} \right)^{kn} \right] \approx N \left(1 - e^{-\frac{kn}{N}} \right) \tag{1}$$

where $E(W)$ is often referred to as the *weight* of the BF.

This structure allows to fast check whether an IP address belongs to the set of suspicious IPs stored in the array, just by computing the k hashes and checking the associated positions.

However, the BF may produce false positives, that is, a certain IP address may not have been programmed in the binary array, but still the hash functions applied to it may point at positions set to one. This occurs with the following probability [1]:

$$P_{fp} = \left(\frac{E(W)}{N} \right)^k \approx \left(1 - e^{-\frac{kn}{N}} \right)^k \tag{2}$$

The false-positive probability reduces for large values of N. Nevertheless, filtering is required to remove the false positives from the actual positives. Given the fact that a Lawful Interception platform must not store traffic that does not belong to the wiretapped suspects, this issue has been addressed in our design and is further explained in section 4.1.

4   System Design and Architeture

4.1   Lawful Interception Platform Architecture

Consider the lawful interception scenario of Fig. 2, further explained in in [27], where the Internet connections of multiple (typically thousands) *subscribers* are aggregated at the Metropolitan Area Network (MAN). We assume that some (very few) of these subscribers are criminal *Suspects* under investigation. To investigate these suspects, a Digital Wiretap Warrant (DWW) [28] issued by a judge is mandatory.

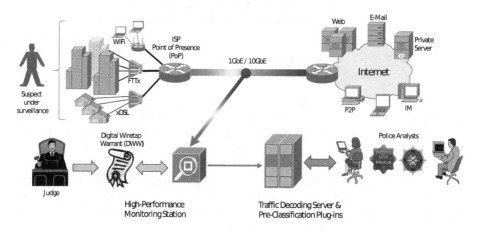

Fig. 2. Lawful Interception scenario

In this scenario, our *monitoring station* collects the traffic of thousands of users traversing its ports. A DWW is required for any capturing process. This means that the monitoring station will not capture any traffic from that suspect unless a valid DWW is provided in order to prevent misuse by the Police, the ISP or any other unauthorised third party. The monitoring station has a list of IP addresses (of the suspects under a wiretap warrant) loaded in its internal Bloom Filter to decide which packets are to be captured and stored for further investigation by the Police forces. Because Bloom Filters have false positives, packets are filtered at software level at the monitoring station. This ensures that any packet which does not belong to a suspect is never stored. Additionally, zero-loss packet capturing is mandatory for the suspects' traffic.

The captured traffic is then sent to the *Traffic Decoding Server* [27], which takes the capture files produced by the Monitoring Station to reconstruct the files and contents that the suspect has transmitted or received.

4.2 Traffic Inspector Module Architecture

Fig. 3 shows the architecture of the Bloom Filter traffic inspection module, which comprises:

- Two FIFO queues to regulate input/output to the module, called Input and Output FIFO respectively.
- A Packet Buffer in which some packet words are copied for inspection.
- An Inspector module which checks both source and destination IP addresses to be inspected.
- User-Space Bloom Filter Interaction module (USBI), which communicates the User Space software and the Bloom Filter. This module allows to add/remove/update IP addresses in the Bloom Filter dynamically.
- A Bloom Filter, which is queried by the inspector module twice per packet. The Bloom Filter is implemented using the FPGA's BRAM (Block Random Access Memory). The read and write access to the Bloom Filter is managed by a priority-encoded controller, which gives priority to the Inspector over the User Space Bloom Filter Interaction module.

To illustrate how our hardware architecture operates, consider the arrival of a packet at the Input FIFO (step 1 in Fig. 3). The first bytes of the packet are stored in a Packet Buffer (step 2), and simultaneously they are copied to the Output FIFO. Next, the inspector obtains the bytes that contain the source and destination IP addresses of the packet (step 3), and checks whether or not there is a positive matching in the Bloom Filter (step 4). If there is a positive match, then the packet is captured by the monitoring station by changing certain bits in the control header of the packet (step 5). Otherwise, the packet is simply not stored.

Once the first word of the packet is allowed to exit the module, then its next words are automatically forwarded without further checks. After the first word of this packet exit the Inspector module, the next packet in the queue can be analysed.

The priority encoding of the Bloom Filter guarantees that any operation from user space which involves the Bloom Filter (reading or writing) will be delayed if the inspector needs to check the Bloom filter to classify a packet. A simple request-response protocol is implemented between the USBI and the Bloom Filter and also between the USBI and the user space to indicate when low-priority operations have been attended by the Bloom Filter. Software tools are used at user space to ensure that the Bloom Filter is properly recalculated each time a new IP address is added or deleted from the list.

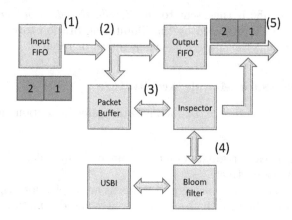

Fig. 3. Block architecture of the traffic inspection module

Two different interception modes are available in this prototype, namely *Forward and Tap* and *Tap and Drop*. In *Forward and Tap* mode, if a packet matches the search criteria, the packet is forwarded through an output port and a copy of it is also sent to user space for capture. If not, the traffic is simply forwarded transparently to the output port. The *Forward and Tap* mode is intended for a case in which we need to capture in serial mode. This means that the traffic inspector is placed in the middle of the network wire.

In the *Tap and Drop* mode, if a packet matches the search criteria, it is forwarded to user space. If not, it is simply discarded. The *Tap and Drop* mode is the mode that should be used if we want to have a parallel communication interception. In this mode, a copy of the traffic which is being forwarded through the network is sent to the monitoring station. This mode allows to tap more lines than the forward and tap mode because not as many ports are needed to forward the traffic, so the packet inspector has simply to decide if the traffic is to be processed or discarded.

4.3   Design of the Inspector Bloom Filter

This section evaluates the performance of the current implementation of the Inspector Bloom Filter in the NetFPGA. Taking information from a Spanish ISP, we assume that an aggregation metro node concentrates the traffic of about 40000 DSL subscribers producing an average bit rate of 120 Kbit/s each. With these numbers, the average bitrate traversing the NetFPGA:

$$40000 \times 120 \text{ Kbit/s} = 4.8 \text{ Gbit/s}$$

which is close to the maximum input bitrate that the 1G NetFPGA may handle. It should be noted that, although the NetFPGA used for our implementation does not fully support such an input bitrate, our implementation is intended for the validation of our design.

On the other hand, the Bloom Filter implementation comprises $k = 2$ Fibonacci hash functions [29] and a bit array of $N = 65536$ bits. The first hash function h_1 operates directly on the IP address (either source or destination) whereas the second one h_2 performs the hash of a fixed permutation of the bits comprising the IP address. These two hash functions determine which bits have to be set in the Bloom Filter.

Fig. 4 gives the false-positive probability for a number n of IP addresses to be loaded on the Bloom Filter. As shown, for $n = 1000$ suspect IP addresses, the false positive probability equals $9.03 \cdot 10^{-4}$. This value reduces to $9.28 \cdot 10^{-6}$ for $n = 100$ addresses, and to $9.31 \cdot 10^{-8}$ for $n = 10$ IP addresses.

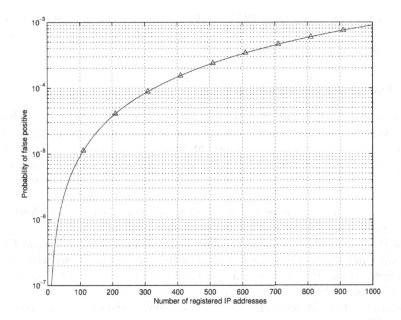

Fig. 4. Probability of false positive in the designed Bloom Filter for k=2, n=65536 bits

These numbers are somehow reasonable since we do not expect more than 1000 suspects in a population of 40000 users. Actually, it is more reasonable to expect 10 to 100 suspects in such a population than 1000 suspects.

Finally, the total incoming traffic arrival at the PCI-X concerns both the actual suspicious traffic plus that traffic due to false positives, i.e.:

$$120 \text{ Kbit/s} \times (n + 40000 \cdot P_{fp}(n))$$

This gives a total data rate of:

$$n = 1000 \text{ Bitrate} = 124 \text{ Mbit/s}$$
$$n = 100 \text{ Bitrate} = 12 \text{ Mbit/s}$$
$$n = 10 \text{ Bitrate} = 1.2 \text{ Mbit/s}$$

In general, we observe that:

$$120 \text{ Kbit/s} \times (n + 40000 \cdot P_{fp}(n)) \approx 120n\text{Kbit/s}$$

since the portion of traffic due to the BF's false positives is very small compared with true positives.

Nevertheless, as we show in the next section the 1G NetFPGA implementation can handle these values without any problem.

5   Prototype Implementation, Benchmarking and Results

This section introduces the FPGA platform used for the development of our prototype and shows the results of a number of benchmarking tests performed to our monitoring station prototype.

5.1   The NetFPGA Platform

Due to its simplicity, versatility, low cost and openness, the NetFPGA [30] framework has been chosen for the implementation of our traffic capture prototype.

The NetFPGA has been developed at Stanford University and provides a basic reference architecture for network hardware implementation, particularly useful in educational and academic environments. There are currently two NetFPGA models operating at different port speeds: 1 Gbit/s and 10 Gbit/s. Both platforms have a stable release. Nevertheless, we have used the 1G NetFPGA for our prototype implementation due to its maturity.

The 1G NetFPGA comes with a Xilinx Virtex II Pro 50 and 4 Gigabit Ethernet copper interfaces. The reference pipeline has a 64-bit word size with a clock speed operating at 125MHz, providing a total raw throughput of 8 Gbit/s. Traffic can be forwarded through the NetFPGA itself and also to/from the server hosting the NetFPGA through a PCI-X bus, allowing the software processing of packets. PCI-X was conceived as an upgrade to prevent certain shortcomings of PCI in servers, as well as improving clock speeds. Nevertheless, in more recent systems, PCI Express (PCIe), with even faster transfer rates, has been the true successor of PCI.

The reference pipeline architecture of the 1G NetFPGA is shown in Fig. 5. This comprises eight reception queues, one Input Arbiter, one Output Port Lookup Module, eight Output Queues and eight Transmission Queues. Concerning the eight transmission and reception queues, four of them belong to the physical ports of the NetFPGA while the other four belong to the virtual ports of the server hosting the FPGA.

Essentially, incoming packets are buffered at the reception queues until the Input Arbiter selects one packet to enter the main pipeline of the NetFPGA. This packet then traverses one or several intermediate modules until it arrives

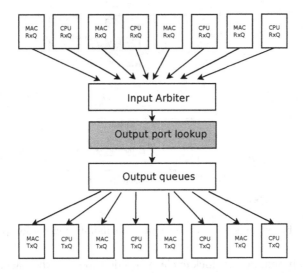

Fig. 5. Reference pipeline architecture of the 1G NetFPGA [30]

at the Output Queues (see Fig. 5). Finally, this packet can go through zero, one or more Ouput Queues at the same time, depending on certain bits of a special control word used internally by the NetFPGA, thus allowing for traffic replication and multicast.

When developing for the NetFPGA, the usual procedure is to take the reference pipeline as a starting point and either add new modules or substitute old ones on top of it. In this light, our design replaces the Output Port Lookup module of the reference pipeline (shadowed box) by a Bloom-Filter-based packet classification module that selects the suspect's traffic. This is depected in 2.

5.2   Benchmarking Scenario

The benchmark scenario can be seen in Fig. 6. The scenario consists of five hosts, four PCs injecting traffic and the server that hosts the NetFPGA. The computer that hosts the FPGA has an Intel Xeon E535 Quad Core CPU running at 2 GHz, with a bus speed of 1333 MHz and 4 GB of DDR2 RAM running at 667 MHz. The other four computers are PCs and servers of heterogeneous features.

To push the monitoring station to its limits, the four PCs connected to our monitoring station inject up to 4 Gbps of traffic. In this configuration, the Tap and Drop mode has been selected with all four ports on the NetFPGA to receive traffic. Four destination IP addresses are trained to a Bloom Filter of size 65536 bits (see section 4.3), one for each connected host. Those packets whose IP address match with any of those trained in the Bloom Filter are copied to the host computer through the PCI-X bus. To run our experiments, several of the connected hosts inject matching traffic at different rates to achieve a total rate inside the NetFPGA pipeline.

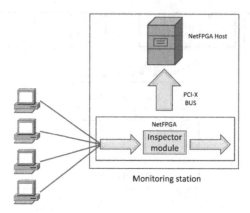

Fig. 6. Benchmarking scenario to evaluate our monitoring station prototype

Since a certain number of clock cycles is needed to store the packet and check the Bloom Filter, the pipeline efficiency is reduced as the packet size decreases. Consequently, three packet sizes have been used in our tests, namely 256, 512 and 1500 bytes, and two capturing modes to promptly identify the bottlenecks in the PC hosting the NetFPGA. In the first mode, packets are written to a file in the hard disk and in the other the packets are also captured but not written to disk. It is worth noting that, due to limitations in the communication between the host and the FPGA, less traffic than is offered to the device is actually captured by the host. But, according to our measurements, the 4 Gbps injectable to it can be processed by the pipeline, which is plausible, as it is possible to attain a raw 8 Gbps bit rate.

In Fig. 7(a), the captured bit rate vs the offered bitrate for the NetFPGA can be seen. For a packet size of 256 bytes, it can be observed that the main bottleneck is given by the PCI-X bus, conclusion which is reinforced by Fig. 7(b), since the maximum number of packets transferable to the host is achieved either if the packets are sent to disk or not. On the other hand, for a packet size of 1500 bytes, it can be seen that, if packets are not sent to disk, the main bottleneck is given by the PCI-X bus bandwidth (but not the transfer rate, since the number of packets per second is lower than the practical limit achieved as can be observed in Fig. 7(b)). If 1500 bytes packets are written to disk, the bottleneck is clearly given by the hard disk, conclusion which is confirmed by the curve of the bitrate captured to disk for a packet size of 512 bytes, which is quite similar in maximum bandwidth. For a 512 bytes packet size, both curves are not very different, because there are neither rate nor transfer rate limitations in the PCI-X bus. The only limit which makes a significant difference is the hard disk bitrate, hence the distance between both the storing and not storing to disk curves. From Figs. 7(a) and 7(b) we see that we have a practical transfer rate limit of $9 \cdot 10^4$ captured packets, a limit of 250 Mbps given by the hard disk and a limit of 400 Mbps in the PCI-X bus bit rate.

The CPU is not a bottleneck in any of the cases, since other captures with different Gigabit Ethernet cards have been performed that reached significantly higher rates due to using a different version of the PCI bus.

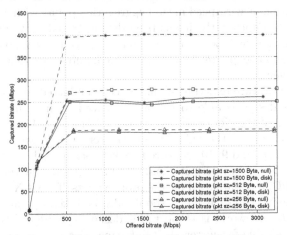

(a) Captured bit rate vs offered bit rate to the monitoring station

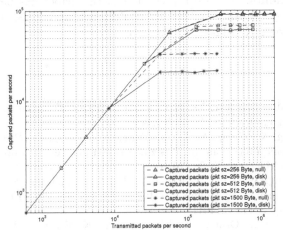

(b) Captured packets per second vs offered packets per second to the monitoring station

Fig. 7. Benchmarking results by bitrate (a) and packets per second (b)

6 Future Work and Conclusions

In this article we have presented a Bloom Filter-based packet monitoring station for Lawful Interception which we have implemented as a prototype on a 1 Gbps NetFPGA.

It has been shown how Bloom Filters allow high speed filtering with low false positive probability for a reasonable number of users. Furthermore, such claims have been supported with aggregation data from a Spanish ISP to show that our design is scalable to be used in network aggregation points, which would allow Lawful Interception at wirespeed in said aggregation points with reasonable cost per suspect. More importantly, it has been demonstrated that, although traffic capturing in aggregation links could be seen as a tall order, it is not only feasible, but also secure and cheaply realisable if realistic numbers are taken into account to face the problem.

Several traffic capture experiments have been conducted to test the limits of our design. Our design is able to run at wirespeed by injecting traffic at full speed in all ports of the NetFPGA (4x 1Gbps). We have achieved the practical limits of 400 Mbps due to the PCI-X bus of the server, approximately 250 Mbps due to the hard disk, and $9 \cdot 10^4$ captured packets per second due to the transfer limit of the PCI-X bus. Finally, it should be understood that these limitations come from the PC hardware used for the prototype itself (PCI-X bus, Hard disk, etc), but not the NetFPGA itself. It should also be taken into account that our intention, as a future work, is to port this design to a 10G NetFPGA, which might be more suitable for current ISP link capacities.

Acknowledgements. The work presented in this paper has been funded by the INDECT project grant number FP7-ICT-218086, and the Spanish CramNet project (grant no. TEC2012-38362-C03-01).

References

1. Broder, A., Mitzenmacher, M.: Network applications of Bloom filters: A survey. Internet Mathematics 1(4), 485–509 (2004)
2. Mu, S., Zhang, X., Zhang, N., Lu, J., Deng, Y.S., Zhang, S.: IP routing processing with graphic processors. In: Design, Automation Test in Europe Conference Exhibition (DATE), pp. 93–98 (2010)
3. Zhao, J., Zhang, X., Wang, X., Deng, Y., Fu, X.: Exploiting graphics processors for high-performance IP lookup in software routers. In: 2011 Proceedings IEEE INFOCOM, pp. 301–305 (2011)
4. Smith, R., Goyal, N., Ormont, J., Sankaralingam, K., Estan, C.: Evaluating GPUs for network packet signature matching. In: IEEE International Symposium on Performance Analysis of Systems and Software, ISPASS 2009, pp. 175–184 (2009)
5. Wang, L., Chen, S., Tang, Y., Su, J.: Gregex: GPU based high speed regular expression matching engine. In: 2011 Fifth International Conference on Innovative Mobile and Internet Services in Ubiquitous Computing (IMIS), pp. 366–370 (2011)
6. Huang, N.-F., Hung, H.-W., Lai, S.-H., Chu, Y.-M., Tsai, W.-Y.: A GPU-based multiple-pattern matching algorithm for network intrusion detection systems. In: 22nd International Conference on Advanced Information Networking and Applications - Workshops, AINAW 2008, pp. 62–67 (2008)
7. Lin, C.-H., Liu, C.-H., Chang, S.-C.: Accelerating regular expression matching using hierarchical parallel machines on GPU. In: 2011 IEEE Global Telecommunications Conference (GLOBECOM 2011), pp. 1–5 (2011)

8. Wu, Q., Wolf, T.: Runtime task allocation in multicore packet processing systems. IEEE Transactions on Parallel and Distributed Systems 23(10), 1934–1943 (2012)
9. Li, Y., Shan, L., Qiao, X.: A parallel packet processing runtime system on multicore network processors. In: 2012 11th International Symposium on Distributed Computing and Applications to Business, Engineering Science (DCABES), pp. 67–71 (2012)
10. Yamashita, Y., Tsuru, M.: Rule pattern parallelization of packet filters on muti-core environments. In: 2011 IEEE 13th International Conference on High Performance Computing and Communications (HPCC), pp. 116–125 (2011)
11. Guo, D., Bhuyan, L.N., Liu, B.: An efficient parallelized L7-filter design for multicore servers. IEEE/ACM Transactions on Networking 20(5), 1426–1439 (2012)
12. Application Layer Packet Classifier for Linux (2013)
13. Huang, N.-F., Hung, H.-W., Tsai, W.-Y.: A unique-pattern based pre-filtering method for rule matching of network security. In: 2012 18th Asia-Pacific Conference on Communications (APCC), pp. 744–748 (2012)
14. Song, H., Hao, F., Kodialam, M., Lakshman, T.V.: IPv6 lookups using distributed and load balanced bloom filters for 100Gbps core router line cards. In: IEEE INFOCOM 2009, pp. 2518–2526 (2009)
15. Dharmapurikar, S., Krishnamurthy, P., Sproull, T., Lockwood, J.: Deep packet inspection using parallel Bloom filters. In: Proceedings of the 11th Symposium on High Performance Interconnects, pp. 44–51 (2003)
16. Dharmapurikar, S., Krishnamurthy, P., Sproull, T.S., Lockwood, J.W.: Deep packet inspection using parallel Bloom filters. IEEE Micro 24(1), 52–61 (2004)
17. Attig, M., Dharmapurikar, S., Lockwood, J.: Implementation results of Bloom filters for string matching. In: 12th Annual IEEE Symposium on Field-Programmable Custom Computing Machines, FCCM 2004, pp. 322–323 (2004)
18. Attig, M., Lockwood, J.: SIFT: snort intrusion filter for TCP. In: Proceedings of the 13th Symposium on High Performance Interconnects, pp. 121–127 (2005)
19. Van Lunteren, J.: High-performance pattern-matching for intrusion detection. In: Proceedings of the 25th IEEE International Conference on Computer Communications, INFOCOM 2006, pp. 1–13 (2006)
20. Tuck, N., Sherwood, T., Calder, B., Varghese, G.: Deterministic memory-efficient string matching algorithms for intrusion detection. In: Twenty-third Annual Joint Conference of the IEEE Computer and Communications Societies, INFOCOM 2004, vol. 4, pp. 2628–2639 (2004)
21. Ho, J., Lemieux, G.G.F.: PERG: A scalable FPGA-based pattern-matching engine with consolidated bloomier filters. In: International Conference on ICECE Technology, FPT 2008, pp. 73–80 (2008)
22. Bando, M., Artan, N.S., Wei, R., Guo, X., Chao, H.J.: Range hash for regular expression pre-filtering. In: 2010 ACM/IEEE Symposium on Architectures for Networking and Communications Systems (ANCS), pp. 1–12 (2010)
23. Cho, Y.H., Mangione-Smith, W.H.: Fast reconfiguring deep packet filter for 1+ gigabit network. In: 13th Annual IEEE Symposium on Field-Programmable Custom Computing Machines, FCCM 2005, pp. 215–224 (2005)
24. Ajami, R., Dinh, A.: Design a hardware network firewall on FPGA. In: 2011 24th Canadian Conference on Electrical and Computer Engineering (CCECE), pp. 000674–000678 (2011)

25. Kayssi, A., Harik, L., Ferzli, R., Fawaz, M.: FPGA-based internet protocol firewall chip. In: The 7th IEEE International Conference on Electronics, Circuits and Systems, ICECS 2000., vol. 1, pp. 316–319 (2000)
26. Park, S.-K., Oh, J.-T., Jang, J.-S.: High-speed attack mitigation engine by packet filtering and rate-limiting using fpga. In: The 8th International Conference on Advanced Communication Technology, ICACT 2006, vol. 1, pp. 6 pp.–685 (2006)
27. Aparicio, R., Urueña, M., Muñoz, A., Rodríguez, G., Morcuende, S.: INDECT Lawful Interception platform: Overview of ILIP decoding and analysis station. Jornadas de Ingeniería Telemática (JITEL) (2013) (accepted for publication)
28. Urueña, M., Muñoz, A., Aparicio, R., Rodríguez, G.: Digital Wiretap Warrant: Protecting civil liberties in ETSI Lawful Interception (review ongoing). Computer and Security
29. Knuth, D.: The Art of Computer Programming, 2nd edn., vol. 3. Addison-Wesley (1998)
30. NetFPGA home page (2013)

Augmented Reality for Privacy-Sensitive Visual Monitoring

Piotr Szczuko

Gdańsk University of Technology, Multimedia Systems Department,
Narutowicza 11/12, 80-233 Gdansk, Poland
szczuko@sound.eti.pg.gda.pl

Abstract. The paper presents a method for video anonymization and replacing real human silhouettes with virtual 3D figures rendered on the screen. Video stream is processed to detect and to track objects, whereas anonymization stage employs fast blurring method. Substitute 3D figures are animated accordingly to behavior of detected persons. Their location, movement speed, direction, and person height are taken into account during the animation and rendering phases. This approach requires a calibrated camera, and utilizes results of visual object tracking. In the paper a procedure for transforming objects visual features and bounding boxes into a script for animated figures is presented. This approach is validated subjectively, by assessing a correspondence between real image and the augmented one. Conclusions and future work perspectives are provided.

Keywords: visual monitoring, privacy, augmented reality, computer animation.

1 Introduction

Augmented reality is a technique of supplementing an image with virtual elements, providing the user with additional elements, important for particular application. The most popular are: location- and compass- based applications with image recognition, resulting in labels and 3D models embedded onto the image, e.g. describing points of interests in the real world [14][19][29]. Marker-based approach requires a known visual pattern, fiduciary marker held by the user or located on the object of interest, which is replaced by a 3D object being located, rotated and scaled accordingly to the marker orientation. Typically a marker position and rotation estimations are enough for almost seamless presentation of the rendered objects [20]. Advanced applications, e.g. television, require also a correspondence between lights and shadows in the real environment (studio) and in 3D virtual space [16]. The author proposes application of AR to a new domain – visual monitoring.

The number of cameras installed in cities increases rapidly, rising numerous privacy concerns. In London a person is captured by cameras a couple of dozen times every day, and recordings can be used as an offense to such individual. Therefore, anonymization methods are being introduced to monitoring systems, automatically obscuring image regions, containing personal identifiable information [5]. Blurring,

A. Dziech and A. Czyżewski (Eds.): MCSS 2014, CCIS 429, pp. 229–241, 2014.

cutting out, mosaicing, are the most common techniques, but can influence the understanding of the image by the observer (e.g. monitoring center operator), making it difficult to determine number of persons, type of activities, etc.   Therefore the author proposes to substitute real image of moving person with a virtual articulated figure, mimicking basic human actions: standing, walking, running. Such modification should work in real-time, to allow live observation, and should take into account number of persons, their exact locations in the image, movement speed and direction. An effort is described to animate 3D figure with accordance to real walking and running motion.

2   Human Pose and Action Acquisition Methods

Considered AR monitoring application assumes that a random person can enter the camera view and his pose / action should be recognized and mapped onto animated figure, displayed on the screen, and obscuring the original image of the tracked person. This approach is similar to a domain of contactless motion capture. The task of acquiring correct body pose and spatial orientation is complex and requires multiple cameras, optimization, and solving for ambiguities [12].

The most popular contactless method is synthesis & matching [11], i.e. creating numerous poses of the virtual model (3D graphic rendering), and then checking correspondence between model and observation edges, regions, biomechanical constrains, plausibility of hypothetic pose, and movement continuity [9][22][23].

In the presented work an assumption was made on accuracy reduction, for the purpose of real-time processing (ca. 25 frames per second are expected). From the image only bounding box coordinates are extracted, to derive other motion features. Therefore small mistakes in pose, speed, and location are allowed, as long as the area occupied by the original image of the person matches the virtual figure location.

3   Augmented Video Monitoring Proposal

Video stream is analyzed to detect areas occupied by moving persons, track their movements, and describe main features: area, orientation, speed. Then, based on provided viewpoint (from camera calibration), human height limits (min, max), and speed limits, a 3D figure is positioned and animated to mimic the person movements (Fig. 1).

In this approach a virtual environment is created, with ground plane on $z=0$ height, with camera orientation mimicking the one of the real camera, with uniform, omnidirectional white light used for rendering. For this purpose a common metric and orientation system is established for the real scene and virtual one. The unit is one meter in the real world. Due to camera calibration, every video image pixel can be translated into x,y,z in meters in the real world [21], and in virtual 3D environment.

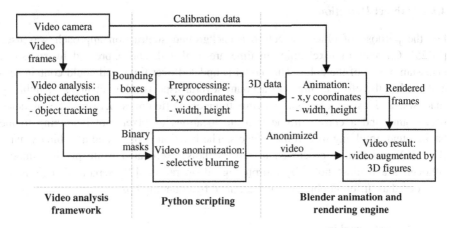

Fig. 1. Data flow, processing blocks and used engines

Video analysis was made in a software framework, providing object detection and tracking implementations, and returning bounding box parameter, and binary masks denoting objects position in every frame. This work was published and documented earlier [6][8][13][24] and is out of the scope of this paper. The novel research has been done utilizing some publicly available datasets and additional software, namely:

- video S1-T1-C3 from PETS2006 [18] - publicly available reference video with walking persons (camera calibration data available), 3020 frames, 120 seconds long,
- 3D graphics rendering and animation software, Blender3D [17], for virtual figure modeling, walking and running actions preparation, rendering of result augmented video.
- Python programming language interpreter, built into Blender 3D [1], for input video anonymization, for camera and ground plane positioning in the 3D space, for translating bounding box parameters into figure animation directives.

For the purpose of this application several assumptions were made:

- Movement must always be in contact with the ground – bottom side of bounding box lies on the floor, and its z coordinate is 0 m in 3D space.
- The ground is flat and positioned on $z=0$ plane
- Video camera is calibrated, its parameters are known, and used for positioning and configuration of virtual camera used for rendering. Camera does not introduce fisheye distortion. Deformations will be considered in the future work.

4   Video Processing

Rendered figures should be positioned, and moved in accordance with persons captured on the video. Therefore, such individuals should be first located, and their movements tracked, to provide input parameters for animation module.

4.1   Object Detection

For the purpose of object detection a background subtraction approach was used [7][25]. Changes of pixel color in time are analyzed, and expressed by statistical Gaussian model of the color. The model is updated over time, and could contain several modes, therefore taking into account several aspects: slow changes of lighting, shadows, and cyclic changes (waving foliage). Differences between the modeled background and a current frame indicate locations of pixels not belonging to the background, implying foreground objects. The location is presented as a binary mask (Fig. 2b), and further processed to remove noise (separated white pixels), smooth silhouettes and close holes by morphological operations [7]. Separated regions are considered as different objects, and described by bounding boxes.

4.2   Object Tracking

Tracking of the objects is based on Kalman filtering [8] of bounding box parameters: *x, y, height, width*, and changes in time: Δx, Δy, $\Delta height$, $\Delta width$. It performs observation of noisy (imprecise) input parameters and estimates correct values, by assuming inertia. When such filtering is applied for the movement it results in more fluent changes of locations and size, and helps in resolving objects collisions, partial obscuration, temporary disappearances [8].

Fig. 2. Object detection and tracking process: a) original frame, b) objects' masks, c) assigned trackers

4.3   Bounding Box Parameterization

Kalman filtering and object tracking process returns: object ID (incremented numeral), frame number, and pixel coordinates of upper left corner of the bounding box (*x,y*), its *width* and *height* (Fig. 3), with assumption that pixel (0,0) is in upper left corner of the image. These data are represented as an XML structure, inspired by common video ground truth description format [27].

Fig. 3. Object bounding box parameterization

From these values other features are calculated and processed by animation module: center of bounding box, speed vector, object location and orientation (Sec. 5.2).

4.4   Image Anonymization Method

Before the virtual figure is rendered onto the video frame, the area occupied by the object is anonymized by selective blurring of image regions. These regions of interest are results of object detection (Sec. 4.1).

Selective blurring is performed by:

1. Blurring binary mask:
   (a) resizing it by factor 1/3,
   (b) filtering (averaging) by 5x5 Gaussian filter, and thresholding to obtain binary values only,
   (c) scaling back (Fig. 4c). This acts as a faster way to close holes, mimicking morphological closing operation (Fig. 4d),
2. Processing image parts containing moving objects:
   (a) extracting by logical AND operation on original frame and blurred masks. The result has the background removed and objects pixels left untouched (Fig. 4e),
   (b) blurring objects pixels (scaled by 1/3, averaged, and scaled back (Fig. 4f),
3. Extracting background by zeroing image pixels where binary mask is equal to one (Fig. 4g),
4. Adding blurred silhouettes image to background (Fig. 4h).

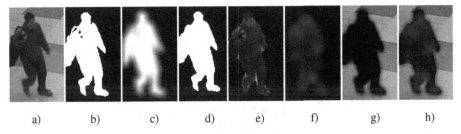

a)   b)   c)   d)   e)   f)   g)   h)

Fig. 4. Results of selective blurring: a) original, b) binary mask, c) blurred mask, d) reference mask from morphological closing of binary mask, e) extracted object, f) blurred object, g) background, h) anonymized result

A comparison was made, assessing performance of presented approach for resizing and blurring of binary mask (step 1. above, Fig. 4c) with morphological closing operation usually applied for mask correction (Fig. 4d). The proposed method is 100 times faster (on the used workstation it takes 8ms for blurring vs. 880ms for closing).

5   Substitute 3D Figures Rendering

For the purpose of augmentation of virtual figures an XLM parsing module was created, extracting object ID, movement history, and then instructing animation and rendering module to pose and render 3D figure accordingly. In the described experiments, the process is offline (operates on video file, sequentially performing steps described in following subsections). Applying the same procedure for real-time processing generally should require caching of $n=3\ldots5$ frames, and therefore providing output images with small delay.

5.1   Coordinate Systems Transformation and Calibration

Results of video processing (Sec. 4) are taken as a rendering module input, and necessary preparations are made, taking into account transformations between image pixels, world coordinates and 3D space coordinates.

A transformation is required between pixel coordinates of objects located in a video frame and virtual world 3D coordinates of figures to be animated. For this purpose a projective model was applied [15], mapping quadrilaterals to other quadrilaterals. Such projection mimics the phenomena of visual perspective, and image acquisition by human eye and video camera [4]. It is described by 3×3 transformation matrix (1).

$$T = \begin{bmatrix} A & D & G \\ B & E & H \\ C & F & I \end{bmatrix} \tag{1}$$

For the purpose of this work it was assumed that fisheye distortions are not introduced. To obtain u, v coordinates in virtual space, following calculations are performed:

$$u = \frac{u_p}{w_p} \tag{2}$$

$$v = \frac{v_p}{w_p} \tag{3}$$

where,

$$\begin{aligned} [u_p \quad v_p \quad w_p] &= [x \quad y \quad 1] \cdot T \\ u_p &= Ax + By + C \\ v_p &= Dx + Ey + F \\ w_p &= Gx + Hy + I \end{aligned} \tag{4}$$

and:

$$u = \frac{Ax+By+C}{Gx+Hy+I}$$

$$v = \frac{Dx+Ey+F}{Gx+Hy+I}$$

(5)

To determine transformation coefficients, sample points must be provided, i.e. at least four pairs of coordinates u,v in meters in real world space, and corresponding x,y in image pixels. Once matrix T is known, the inverse matrix can be derived. Therefore transformations in both ways are available.

For the considered scene 8 pairs of u, v coordinates were available (Fig. 5c), and the same keypoints were located for cameras view and T matrix was calculated. Altering camera orientation, location and zoom influences the transformation coefficients, therefore the process should be repeated in such a case.

a)   b)   c)

Fig. 5. Image and coordinate space transformations: a) original image, b) after transformation from meters to pixel (every 72 pixels represents 1 meter of the ground), c) ground plan keypoints coordinates

For the purpose of correct rendering the virtual camera must be calibrated. Parameters of image distortions, focal length, and position above the ground must be adjusted. For this purpose a well known method of Tsai calibration can be performed [26]. In case of used dataset the real camera calibration was available, therefore the virtual camera was set up with regards to provided parameters. This assured the correct perspective and scaling of rendered objects, to match the one introduced by the real camera.

For the purpose of 3D camera calibration validation four elements of the real scene were recreated as 3D objects, positioned with regards to the floor plan (Fig. 5c), and result x,y coordinates on the rendered image were compared, confirming correct calibration (Fig. 6a).

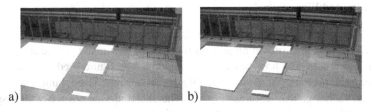

a)   b)

Fig. 6. Recreation of the scene in a virtual environment: a) virtual objects resembling the scene, correct calibration, b) results of incorrect calibration

5.2   Movement Features Processing

For each detected object the sequences of bounding box locations and sizes are processed. First a transformation to real world coordinates is made (3), influencing values of *height, width, x, y*. For the purpose of clarity it is assumed that all following calculations are made in transformed coordinates, i.e. meters in the real world. Due to applied Kalman filtering of moving object features the parameters are considered to be noise-free, and smoothed in time.

The current frame description is processed to determine movement *speed* (in meters per one video frame), *direction*, and object *location* (middle point of bounding box base):

$$V_x(t) = \big(x(t+1) - x(t)\big)$$
$$V_y(t) = \big(y(t+1) - y(t)\big) \tag{6}$$
$$V(t) = \sqrt{V_x^2(t) + V_y^2(t)}$$

$$\theta(t) = \begin{array}{ll} acos\left(\frac{V_x(t)}{V(t)}\right) \cdot \frac{180}{\pi} \cdot sign\left(V_y(t)\right) & \text{for } V_y(t) \neq 0 \\ 0 & \\ 180 & \begin{array}{l} \text{for } V_y(t) = 0 \text{ and } V_x(t) \geq 0 \\ \text{for } V_y(t) = 0 \text{ and } V_x(t) < 0 \end{array} \end{array} \tag{7}$$

$$x_{loc}(t) = x(t) + \frac{width}{2} \tag{8}$$
$$y_{loc}(t) = y(t) + height$$

Object Size Estimation. When a new object enters the scene it usually appears at the screen border (depending on scene configuration). First, the analysis process buffers frames, until the whole object is within the image. The object is assumed to be out of the screen if not all its parts are visible. This is verified by checking if the bounding box is in contact with the screen border: *x*=0 (object still at the left side), *x+width= screen_width* (object still at the right side), *y=screen_height* (at the lower side), *y-height=0* (at the top side). Once none of above is true, it is assumed that current *width* and *height* of bounding box are correct and match real object size. The size is fixed, and buffered frames are processed again.

5.3   Animated Figure

The purpose of the application is not to discriminate between persons, but to offer anonymized monitoring, providing general impression how many people are present on the scene and where, and how fast are they moving. The figure used as a substitute to images of real persons, is modeled in 3D as an average-sized humanoid, without any gender, racial, or age features (Fig. 7). The skeleton was created with respect to BVH standard [3], common in character animation and motion capture. It comprises of

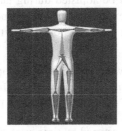

Fig. 7. 3D model and used skeleton

hierarchically connected bones, influencing geometry of the 3D mesh describing model surface. Movement or rotation of the bone higher in hierarchy (called parent), changes locations and orientations of lower hierarchy bones (called children). Bone rotations are limited to biologically correct ranges (e.g. elbow angle from 0 to 180 degrees).

Root bone (pelvis) is attached to the master bone, located on the floor, used only to position and move whole model on $z=0$ plane, matching movement of the real person. Master bone is also scaled to reflect size of the object. It is assumed that proportions are fixed (no difference between child or adult).

Movement Animations. A module called Non-Linear Animation is available in Blender3D, scriptable by the Python language [1]. The created script reads bounding box movements and modifies on the fly values of `action playback scale` (time stretch) to speed up and slow down the action and change walking speed, and degree of `influence` of the action on the character, used to fade one action into other, i.e. smoothly change walking into running or walking into standing still. Those modifications are controlled by values of $V(t)$ (current movement speed in m/s in real world units)(Fig. 8).

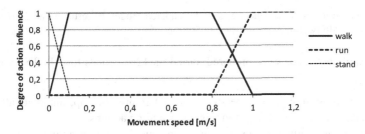

Fig. 8. Type of applied action and its influence, depending on estimated movement speed

It is assumed that movement speed accelerates/decelerates slowly (as a result of applied Kalman filtering), therefore the changes of aforementioned parameters can be made on the fly without decreasing animation quality.

Walk Cycle. The animation for walking human was created by hand, by observing frame-by-frame recorded poses of real walking persons. This technique is known as rotoscopy, and is used for over a century in animation [2]. Whole cycle is 25 frames long, resulting in 1 second of animation. The observed and recreated average gait length is ca. 0.8m [28], and can be adjusted during target animation by action play-back scale parameters. It was experimentally confirmed that short persons' normal walk cycle is 22-24 frames long (880ms-960ms), and tall person walk cycle is 27-29 frames long (1080ms-1160ms).

Run Cycle. The running cycle was created by rotoscopy, and then stretched in time, to last 25 frames, same as walking. This allows for efficient and synchronized fading of one action into other. It was confirmed that short person running cycle is ca. 16 frames (640ms) and tall person running cycle is 18-20 frames (720ms-800ms). For running animation the cycle is shortened by time stretch (action playback scale value).

Standing Animation. For the movement vector V=0 the standing animation is ap-plied. It is also cyclic motion, with the upper body subtle movements (head rotating sideways, arms waving, center of gravity swaying). The length of the cycle is equal to 25 frames as well.

6   Results

Calibrated virtual camera is used to render an animated figure on a transparent back-ground. The result image is embedded on the anonymized video frame (Fig. 9).

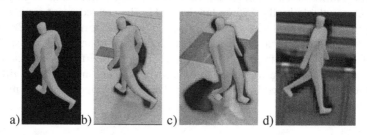

Fig. 9. Frames from result sequence: a) sample rendered model, b) result frame 2567 (walk), c) result frame 0246 (walk), d) result frame 0650 (run)

Three types of sequences were prepared, based on 120 seconds long PETS video S1-T1-C3:

Type A containing anonymized persons, and 3D figures on top, automatically ani-
    mated to reflect walking, running and standing actions,
Type B containing original image of empty scene, and 3D figures acting as above,
Type R as a reference with anonymized persons (no 3D figures).
A subjective assessment was conducted in arranged typical monitoring environment: a desk with two 21 inch LCD monitors 1m distance from the viewer, in daylight, and unlimited access of other stimuli. 10 viewers were asked to focus on the material, and analyze occurring events.

Sequences were presented in following scenarios:

1. Sequence A followed by R to assess loss of intelligibility of A in 5-point scale [10]:

2. Sequence B followed by R to assess loss of intelligibility of B in the same scale:

   1. Very annoying
   2. Annoying
   3. Slightly annoying
   4. Perceptible but not annoying
   5. Imperceptible

3. Sequence A followed by B to assess content understanding, expressed by 3-point scale:

   1. B content is significantly differs from A, and is hard to understand,
   2. B content is slightly different than A, but is understandable,
   3. B and A have the same content, B is easy to understand.

Mean opinion scores for 3 scenarios and standard deviations were calculated (Fig. 10). Decreased intelligibility of 3D-only sequence B is significant, comparing to mixed blurred and 3D augmented video of sequence A. MOS for A is between 3 and 4 points, interpreted as perceptible difference but not annoying, and not impeding the content understanding.

For every sequence also opinions expressed in written form were gathered, pointing out significant drawbacks and future research directions. That allows for identification of key aspects influencing final scores:

- "Abandoned luggage visible in the original recording is not evident in the anonymized videos, version B does not portray this object at all."
- "Person with a trolley is one large object, and positioning of 3D model is incorrect."
- "The period of walk and run cycle is asynchronous with real movement, what is slightly annoying."

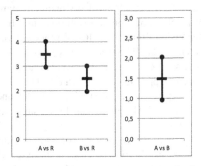

Fig. 10. Mean opinion scores and +/− standard deviations for 3 comparison scenarios

7   Summary and Future Work

The presented work is a proof-of-concept of new method for video anonymization: substituting person image by 3D model, performing the same actions.

The proposed video anonymization method utilizing scaling and blurring for binary mask performed approx.. 100 times faster than typical approach of morphological closing of the binary mask.

Rendering only human figures resulted in decreased intelligibility of the video, because of omission of other objects, such as luggage or trolleys. Therefore, it is planned to introduce generic 3D models for inanimate objects: e.g. bounding box of such object can be represented as a 3D cuboid. Moreover, this can be supported by object shape classification, to increase the accuracy of selection between 3D models of human and luggage.

For mixed anonymized and enhanced videos the animation cycle was reported as asynchronous, therefore future work will focus on parameterization of gait and animation adjustments. A method of 3D object pose assessment is considered, utilizing stereo-cameras for more detailed representation of the scene, simplifying occlusions reconstructions and providing more precise object type information (e.g. human vs. luggage).

Acknowledgement. Research is subsidized by the European Commission within FP7 project "INDECT" (Grant Agreement No. 218086).

References

1. Anders, M.J.: Blender 2.49 Scripting. Packt Publishing (2010)
2. Bratt, B.: Rotoscoping. Focal Press (2012)
3. Biovision Hierarchy,
   http://en.wikipedia.org/wiki/Biovision_Hierarchy
4. Cederberg, J.N.: Projective Geometry. In: A Course in Modern Geometries. Undergraduate Texts in Mathematics, pp. 213–313. Springer (2001)
5. Cichowski, J., Czyzewski, A.: Reversible video stream anonymization for video surveillance systems based on pixels relocation and watermarking. In: 2011 IEEE International Conference on Computer Vision Workshops (ICCV Workshops), pp. 1971–1977 (2011)
6. Czyżewski, A., Szwoch, G., Dalka, P., Szczuko, P., Ciarkowski, A., Ellwart, D., Merta, T., Łopatka, K., Kulesek, Ł., Wolski, J.: Multi-stage video analysis framework. In: Lin, W. (ed.) Video Surveillance, ch. 9, pp. 145–171. Intech (2011)
7. Dalka, P.: Detection and Segmentation of Moving Vehicles and Trains Using Gaussian Mixtures, Shadow Detection and Morphological Processing. Machine Graphics and Vision 15(3/4), 339–348 (2006)
8. Dalka, P., Szwoch, G., Szczuko, P., Czyżewski, A.: Video Content Analysis in the Urban Area Telemonitoring System. In: Tsihrintzis, G.A., et al. (eds.) Multimedia Services in Inteligent Environments, pp. 241–261. Springer, Heidelberg (2010)
9. Deutscher, J., Blake, A., Reid, I.D.: Articulated body motion capture by annealed particle filtering. In: Proc. IEEE Conf. on Computer Vision and Pattern Recognition, pp. 126–133 (2000)
10. ITU-T recommendation P.800: Methods for subjective determination of transmission quality (1996), http://www.itu.int/rec/T-REC-P.800-199608-I/en
11. Kakadiaris, I., Metaxas, D.: Model-based estimation of 3D human motion. IEEE Tran. Pattern Analysis and Machine Intelligence 22(12), 1453–1459 (2000)

12. Kehl, R., Van Gool, L.: Markerless tracking of complex human motions from multiple views. Computer Vision and Image Understanding 104(2-3), 190–209 (2006)
13. Kotus, J., Dalka, P., Szczodrak, M., Szwoch, G., Szczuko, P., Czyżewski, A.: Multimodal Surveillance Based Personal Protection System. In: Signal Processing: Algorithms, Architectures, Arrangements, and Applications (SPA), Poznan, pp. 100–105 (2013)
14. Krolewski, J., Gawrysiak, P.: The Mobile Personal Augmented Reality Navigation System. In: Czachórski, T., Kozielski, S., Stańczyk, U. (eds.) Man-Machine Interactions 2. AISC, vol. 103, pp. 105–113. Springer, Heidelberg (2011)
15. Laveau, S., Faugeras, O.: Oriented projective geometry for computer vision. In: Buxton, B.F., Cipolla, R. (eds.) ECCV 1996. LNCS, vol. 1064, pp. 147–156. Springer, Heidelberg (1996)
16. Moshkovitz, M.: The Virtual Studio: Technology and Techniques. Focal Press (2000)
17. Mullen, T.: Mastering Blender, Sybex (2012)
18. PETS 2006 Bemchmark Data. In: IEEE Conference on Computer Vision and Pattern Recognition 2006 (2006), http://www.cvg.rdg.ac.uk/PETS2006/data.html
19. Rumiński, D., Walczak, K.: Creation of Interactive AR Content on Mobile Devices. In: Abramowicz, W. (ed.) BIS 2013 Workshops. LNBIP, vol. 160, pp. 258–269. Springer, Heidelberg (2013)
20. Schreer, O., Kauff, P., Sikora, T. (eds.): 3D Videocommunication: Algorithms, concepts and real-time systems in human centred communication. Wiley (2005)
21. Szwoch, G., Dalka, P., Czyżewski, A.: Spatial Calibration of a Dual PTZ-Fixed Camera System for Tracking Moving Objects in Video. Journal of Imaging Science and Technology (JIST) 57(2), 1–10 (2013)
22. Szczuko, P.: Hierarchical Estimation of Human Upper Body Based on 2D Observation Utilizing Evolutionary Programming and "Genetic Memory". In: Dziech, A., Czyżewski, A. (eds.) MCSS 2011. CCIS, vol. 149, pp. 82–90. Springer, Heidelberg (2011)
23. Szczuko, P.: Genetic programming extension to APF-based monocular human body pose estimation. Journal of Multimedia Tools and Applications, Multimedia Tools and Applications 68, 177–192 (2014)
24. Szwoch, G., Dalka, P., Ciarkowski, A., Szczuko, P., Czyzewski, A.: Visual Object Tracking System Employing Fixed and PTZ Cameras. Journal of Intelligent Decision Technologies 5(2),   177–188   (2011),
http://iospress.metapress.com/content/m5060n24tk125406/?p=2a
a903da834b4371955e56c56b058b6b&pi=5
25. Szwoch, G., Dalka, P.: Layered background modeling for automatic detection of unattended objects in camera images. In: WIAMIS 2011: 12th International Workshop on Image Analysis for Multimedia Interactive Services, Delft (2011) (Preprint No. 50)
26. Tsai, R.Y.: A versatile camera calibration technique for high-accuracy 3D machine vision metrology using off-the-shelf tv cameras and lenses. IEEE Journal of Robotics and Automation 3(4), 323–344 (1987)
27. University of Maryland, Guide to Authoring Media Ground Truth with ViPER-GT, http://viper-toolkit.sourceforge.net/docs/gt/
28. Uustal, H., Baerga, E.: Gait Analysis. In: Cuccurullo, S. (ed.) Physical Medicine and Rehabilitation Board Review. Demos Medical Publishing, New York (2004), http://www.ncbi.nlm.nih.gov/books/NBK27235/
29. Wikitude, augmented reality platform, http://www.wikitude.com/

Detection of Vehicles Stopping in Restricted Zones in Video from Surveillance Cameras

Grzegorz Szwoch and Piotr Dalka

Gdansk University of Technology, Multimedia Systems Department
Narutowicza 11/12, 80-233 Gdansk, Poland
{greg,piotr.dalka}@sound.eti.pg.gda.pl

Abstract. An algorithm for detection of vehicles that stop in restricted areas, e.g. excluded by traffic rules, is proposed. Classic approaches based on object tracking are inefficient in high traffic scenes because of tracking errors caused by frequent object merging and splitting. The proposed algorithm uses the background subtraction results for detection of moving objects, then pixels belonging to moving objects are tested for stability. Large connected components of pixels that are stable within a sufficiently long period are extracted and compared with the detected moving objects. Therefore, detection of stationary objects which were previously moving is possible and if the object has stopped in a designated area, the event is declared. The algorithm was evaluated using a real traffic monitoring camera and performance of the algorithm is discussed. The algorithm may be used for automatic detection of potentially dangerous traffic events in video acquired from surveillance cameras.

Keywords: object detection, event detection, traffic monitoring, video surveillance.

1   Introduction

Video traffic monitoring systems have become a necessity in modern urban environments. A surveillance system with video cameras allows for detection of violations of the traffic law, such as stopping in forbidden places, passing the red light, wrong-way driving, changing a lane where it is not allowed, driving a private car on a bus lane, etc. However, most of the currently used systems do not allow for automatic detection of complex events in online mode. They are used for tasks such as traffic counting, congestion detection, etc. [1-4], as well as for the post factum detection which allows for fining offending drivers, but do not provide the possibility to react in time. Some traffic law violations may constitute a serious security threat. For example, stopping a vehicle on the pedestrian crossing is only the law violation, while stopping it in the middle of a busy intersection may lead to a collision and stopping on tramway or railway tracks can cause a serious accident. Therefore, automatic detection of specific traffic events is an important aspect in the modern automated video surveillance systems.

A. Dziech and A. Czyżewski (Eds.): MCSS 2014, CCIS 429, pp. 242–253, 2014.
© Springer International Publishing Switzerland 2014

This paper focuses on detection of one of the abovementioned traffic law violations, namely stopping a vehicle in a restricted zone. The problem may be formulated as follows: one of more sections of the camera view are designated as the detection areas (e.g. the middle of the street intersection, a pedestrian crossing, tracks) and the task of the algorithm is to detect any moving vehicle that stops in one of these zones. The same rule may be used for detection of vehicles parking in forbidden areas, the additional condition is that the vehicle has to remain motionless for a defined time. Most of the approaches to this problem are based on object tracking. Each moving object is tracked and if its tracker's velocity is near zero, it is declared stopped. There are two main methods used in such algorithms. The first method finds image changes on the pixel level, in order to detect local movements. A typical example of such approach is with the optical flow algorithm [5]. The second group of methods detects moving object by means of background subtraction, then the detected results are tracked with Kalman filters [4, 6, 7] or similar methods. Both approaches have main drawbacks. The former is computationally complex and it is not possible to achieve online processing without incorporation of expensive and power consuming parallel systems. The latter is able to process the video in online mode. However, tracking with Kalman filters is efficient only in simple, low traffic scenarios [7]. In busy areas, where objects are constantly merging and splitting, stopping and moving, this approach results in high rate of tracking errors which does not allow for efficient event detection. Methods for solving the splitting trackers problem (assigning trackers to proper objects) with the approaches based on color or texture descriptors [8] often fail in case of traffic monitoring where different vehicles often have similar appearance.

The approach proposed here is based on the background subtraction, but it eliminates the tracking algorithm in favor of testing stability of the pixels belonging to the detected moving objects. Section 2 presents details of the algorithm and the results of tests performed in a real world scenario are discussed in Section 3.

2   Description of the Algorithm

The main idea behind the proposed algorithm is that if a previously moving object stops, it is still detected as a moving object by the background subtraction algorithm (it may be incorporated into the background model after some time), but the values of pixels belonging to the object will vary only within small limits due to camera noise and light changes. The algorithm may be divided into four functional stages (Fig. 1).

1. *Background subtraction* and *object detection* identify pixels belonging to moving objects and group them in clusters representing moving objects.
2. *Detection of stable pixels* examines pixels belonging to moving objects and tests their stability in time. It is assumed that in case of a stopped object, its pixels values will remain within a narrow range.
3. *Detection of stationary objects* groups foreground pixels which are stable for longer than a defined threshold into clusters.

4. *The decision system* finds relations between the detected moving objects (stage 1) and the stationary regions (stage 3); if a moving object is sufficiently 'filled' with stable pixels and it is situated in a detection zone, an alarm is raised.

The details of each stage are presented in the following subsections.

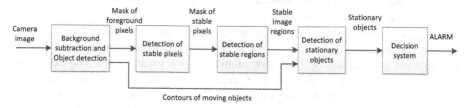

Fig. 1. Block diagram of the proposed algorithm

2.1   Background Subtraction and Object Detection

The task of background subtraction is to divide image pixels into foreground (belonging to moving objects) and background ones. The requirement for the background subtraction algorithm is that it has to detect pixels of stopped objects as a foreground for a defined period. It may be achieved with any algorithm based on background learning that requires objects to remain motionless for some time before they are blended into the background. In the proposed algorithm, a standard approach: the Gaussian Mixture Models (GMM) [9] is used. The result of background subtraction (a binary mask image) is post-processed with a shadow removal algorithm and morphological cleaning [10]. Detection of moving objects is performed by finding connected components in the processed mask. An additional advantage of this stage is that the number of pixels to process in the next step is limited to the foreground pixels which reduces the amount of computations and the risk of detection errors in the background areas (which is possible in the methods based on the optical flow). Moreover, since there is no need to perform pixel analysis outside the detection areas, such pixels are excluded from the background subtraction (they are treated as the background) which further reduces the amount of necessary computations.

2.2   Detection of Stable Pixels

The next stage processes the cleaned background subtraction result and searches for foreground pixels with values that are stable within a defined period. Let I denote the currently analyzed camera image and G be the binary mask image created in the previous stage, with non-zero values for pixels belonging to the detection areas and classified as the foreground, and zero for all other pixels. The image I is downscaled by a factor s using the bilinear interpolation algorithm, and mask G and is downscaled by the same factor using the nearest neighbor algorithm. The downscaling is optional and is introduced in order to reduce the computational load of the algorithm and the influence of object details with small sizes on the detection results. The value of the scale factor should be adjusted to the typical size of the detected objects in a given area, which depends on the camera resolution and the perspective effect of the camera view. Additionally, a Gaussian blur filter with a 5×5 aperture is applied to the downscaled image $\mathbf{I}$ in order to smear small variations of pixel values due to camera noise.

The detection of pixels with values stable in time is realized by constructing a model of stable pixel values and by comparing the current pixel value with the model. The proposed algorithm was inspired by the Codebook algorithm proposed by Kim for background subtraction in video [11]. Each pixel of $\mathbf{I}$ is represented in the model by a set of vectors $\mathbf{v}$ describing the color, brightness and statistical properties of the pixel:

$$\mathbf{v}_i = \left[\overline{R}_i, \overline{G}_i, \overline{B}_i, \check{I}_i, \hat{I}_i, f_i, p_i, q_i \right], \tag{1}$$

where $\left(\overline{R}_i, \overline{G}_i, \overline{B}_i \right)$ are the averaged pixel values in the RGB color space, $\left(\check{I}_i, \hat{I}_i \right)$ define the permitted range of brightness variations, f_i counts the number of matches of this vector, and p_i and q_i are the times (actually, the frame numbers) of the first and the last vector match, respectively.

Each pixel $\mathbf{I}_{(x,y)}$ is processed independently of the other pixels (so the computation may be parallelized). If the pixel belongs to the background in the current frame ($\mathbf{G}_{(x,y)}$ is zero), all vectors representing the current pixel are removed from the model and the processing of this pixel is complete. Otherwise, the current value (R, G, B) of the pixel is compared with the vectors representing this pixel in the model until a matching vector is found or all vectors are processed. Each vector represents a possible color and brightness of the pixel and these values are allowed to vary within a defined range. In the camera image, the value of the pixel belonging to a stationary object may change on frame-by-frame basis because of camera noise, variations in scene lighting, automatic exposure of the camera, etc. However, as long as these changes are small enough, the pixel value may be considered stable. Therefore, the vector matches the current pixel value if a difference in both the color and the brightness is smaller than the threshold. Similarly to the Codebook algorithm, the color difference has to fulfill the condition:

$$\sqrt{\left(R^2 + G^2 + B^2 \right) - \frac{\left(R\overline{R} + G\overline{G} + B\overline{B} \right)^2}{\overline{R}^2 + \overline{G}^2 + \overline{B}^2}} \leq \varepsilon, \tag{2}$$

and the brightness difference condition is:

$$\alpha \hat{I} \leq \sqrt{R^2 + G^2 + B^2} \leq \frac{\check{I}}{\alpha}, \tag{3}$$

where ε and α are the maximum allowed differences in color and brightness, respectively. In order to find a match between the vector and the pixel, both conditions have to be met, therefore it is recommended to test the brightness condition (Eq. 3) first, as it requires fewer operations. If this condition is not met, a more complex color condition (Eq. 2) does not need to be computed.

The next processing step depends on whether any of the vectors **v** matched the pixel. If a match is found, the matched vector is updated according to the formula:

$$\mathbf{v}_i = \left[\frac{\overline{R}_{i-1} + f_{i-1}R}{f_{i-1}+1}, \frac{\overline{G}_{i-1} + f_{i-1}G}{f_{i-1}+1}, \frac{\overline{B}_{i-1} + f_{i-1}B}{f_{i-1}+1}, \min(I,\breve{I}), \max(I,\hat{I}), f_{i-1}+1, p_{i-1}, i \right], \quad (4)$$

where i is the index of the current frame and I is the current brightness of the pixel, calculated as:

$$I = \sqrt{R^2 + G^2 + B^2}, \quad (5)$$

If none of the vectors matches the pixel or there are no vectors for this pixel in the model, a new vector is created and initialized by values:

$$\mathbf{v}_i = [R,G,B,I,I,1,i,i], \quad (6)$$

This part of the algorithm is completed by removing vectors that were not matched for a defined time (vectors for which the difference between the current frame index i and value q_i is larger than the threshold). This operation reduces the computation time by removing old vectors that matched the pixels of objects that are no longer present in the observed area. The value of this threshold should be large enough to allow for short-term occlusions of the object and small enough to ensure that vectors are removed when the object leaves the area.

It should be noted that although the procedure of matching pixel values with vectors and vector updating is similar to the Codebook algorithm, the proposed procedure is not a direct implementation of the Codebook method, in which separate stages of the model training, pruning and background subtraction are required [12]. In the algorithm presented here, the vectors are added to the model and removed from it when needed on a frame-by-frame basis. It is also worth noting that the proposed model may be considered as an additional layer of the background model used for object detection. Theoretically, this procedure could be implemented in the background subtraction module. However, implementing this operation within the separate processing stage allows for logical separation of different image processing operations and makes it independent of the algorithm used for background subtraction.

2.3   Detection of Stationary Regions and the Decision System

After processing of all pixels of the image **I**, pixels with stable values have to be located. For this task, a binary result image **R** of the same size as the image **I** is constructed. Let the matrix $\mathbf{V}_i$ represent a model of pixels values in the image frame $\mathbf{I}_i$. Each pixel $\mathbf{I}_{i(x,y)}$ is represented by a set of $N_{i(x,y)}$ vectors:

$$\mathbf{V}_i(x,y) = \left\{ \mathbf{v}_i^k : k = 0...N_i(x,y) \right\}, \quad (7)$$

where k is the vector index. The pixel value is considered stable in the frame i if, and only if, there is a vector that was matched to the pixel in the current image and the 'age' of this vector exceeds the defined threshold T expressed in the number of frames:

$$\mathbf{R}_i(x, y) = \begin{cases} 1, \exists k : (i - p_i^k) \geq T, k = 0...N_i(x, y), \\ 0, \text{otherwise} \end{cases} \tag{8}$$

If the above condition is fulfilled, the pixel is marked as stable: $\mathbf{R}_{i(x,y)} = 1$. Note that the time p_i of the vector creation is used for comparison, so the pixel will be correctly marked as stable if a short-term occlusion occurred during the analysis.

If the resulting mask $\mathbf{R}$ has zero values only, the processing ends for the current frame. If there is at least one non-zero value, connected components are extracted from the morphologically cleaned mask $\mathbf{R}$ using the same method as in the stage 1. As a result, clusters of stable pixels are found. Individual stable pixels do not provide information on whether the object has stopped, the pixel value will also be stable when an uniformly colored object passes through the pixel. However, large groups of connected stable pixels indicate that a region of the image contains pixels of almost constant value and, since these pixels do not belong to the background, these pixel groups allow for the detection of objects that have stopped.

In the final decision stage, a relationship between the objects detected in stage 1 and stable regions extracted in this stage is established. A detected object matches a stable region if the overlap of bounding boxes of both contours is sufficiently large. Next, a coverage of the detected object with stable pixels is calculated. Because of variations of pixel values (e.g. due to the camera noise), some pixels may not reach the stability. Therefore, it is usually sufficient to fulfill the condition that approx. 90% of the pixels belonging to the object have to be stable in order to detect the object as a stopped one. Additionally, a threshold is imposed on the minimal area of the detected pixel group in order to exclude small objects from the detection (which also allows limiting the detection to vehicles and omitting objects such as people walking, animals, trash moved by the wind, etc.).

Fig. 2 illustrates the process of detection. In order to visualize the current state of the model $\mathbf{V}$, the age of the vector matched in the current frame is represented by a gray level intensity, from bright (a recently created vector) to dark (vector with age approaching the threshold T). Stable pixels are marked with the darkest shade of gray – these are the non-zero values in the resulting mask $\mathbf{R}$. Vectors created in the current frame are marked with the white color and the black color indicates that the pixel belongs to the background. Initially, all the objects are moving (frame 1118). The vehicle stops, while other objects (people) continue moving (frame 1160). As the vehicle remains stationary, the codes of its pixels progress towards the darker shades, while the other (moving) objects are represented by the white and bright gray colors (frame 1181). Finally, most of the pixels representing the vehicle are marked as stable (matched vector ages exceed the threshold), which results in detecting a sufficiently large connected component in the resulting mask **R** (frame 1200). Note that different pixels of the vehicle become stable at different moments and that not all parts of the vehicle are correctly detected by the background subtraction procedure. However, these aspects do not prevent the detection of the stopped vehicle.

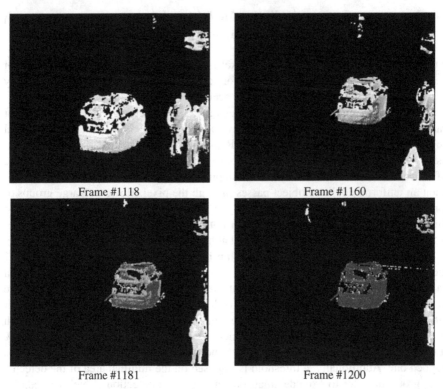

Fig. 2. Example of detection of a stopped vehicle – shades of gray indicate the age of a matched vector, dark gray shade marks pixels with stable values

3   Experimental Results

For the purpose of evaluation of the developed algorithm, a test setup was installed in Warsaw, Poland. The Axis IQeye 702 camera (1600×1200 resolution, 10 fps, MJPEG codec with a minimal compression ratio) monitored a large intersection in the city centre. The detection algorithms described in this paper were implemented as a C++ code, using the OpenCV library. Video processing and event detection operations were performed online using a computer that acquired camera images and processed them using the proposed algorithm. For testing purposes, the video stream was recorded from the camera without introducing additional compression. A ground truth data for the recordings was prepared manually by reviewing the recorded material and denoting the timestamps of the actual events. All events detected by the algorithm were validated by checking them against the ground truth data.

A total of 26 hours of video material recorded on two consecutive days were analyzed. Originally, the intent was to detect vehicles stopping in the middle of the intersection. However, not a single event of this type was observed. Therefore, in order to verify the algorithm, another area situated near the left image border was selected for detection (Fig. 3). Vehicles going straight through the intersection are obliged to stop at the red signal that is situated before the pedestrian crossing (outside the left image border). Vehicles turning right are allowed to pass the conditional traffic light. It was observed that many vehicles stop within the area between the pedestrian crossing and the intersection (probably passing the "late yellow"). The aim of the experiments was to detect such events, 189 of which were observed in the recorded material and indexed in the ground truth data. The detection time (minimum period of stopping inside the area) was set to 6 seconds, the minimum size of a stable region was experimentally set to 7500 pixels in order to filter out small artifacts, the minimum coverage of the object with stable pixels was 90% and the image was downscaled for the analysis by a factor of 8.

Fig. 3. Definition of the area for detection of stopping vehicles used in the experiments (a cropped section of the full camera frame is shown)

Fig. 4 shows examples of successful detections in the described scenario. The results of the tests, expressed in the numbers of true positive, false positive and false negative results, as well as standard performance measures (precision, recall and accuracy) were calculated and presented in Table 1. Additionally, incorrect decisions of the algorithm were analyzed and classified according to their cause (Table 2). It can be observed that all the performance measures exceed 76%. A relatively large number of false positives was observed. One FP occurred c.a. every 12 TPs or, on average, every 43 minutes. However, as it may be concluded from Table 2, exactly half of them were caused by the inefficiency of the background subtraction procedure. When light in the scene changed rapidly (for example, the sun was covered or uncovered by clouds), the background model needed some time to adjust, and during this period a large part of the observed area was detected as a stable foreground region, leading to false alarms. Additionally, a number of false negatives caused by background subtraction errors was observed, mainly after the background model was readjusted due to light changes, which caused large parts of moving vehicles to be assigned to the background. As a result, a more efficient procedure for backlight compensation has to be implemented in the object detection procedure in order to avoid such errors. If these 26 false positives due to background subtraction errors were eliminated, precision would be increased to 94.5% and accuracy to 86.9%.

Considering the errors occurring in the stopping detector itself (stages 2 to 4), some FPs were due to detection of the top parts of large vehicles (mainly buses) that stopped in the bottom lane (below the detection area) while turning right. Such errors could be avoided by performing a separate detection of stopped vehicles in the right turn lanes and discarding alarms that occur in both areas. However, such a solution would increase the computational load of the algorithm. A small number of FNs was observed, mainly due to occlusion of the stopped vehicle by other vehicles moving alongside it (this was mainly observed when a vehicle was stopped for a short time, barely exceeding the limit), and three cases were not detected despite the data from the background subtraction algorithm being correct – they were probably caused by variations in pixel values, so the amount of stable pixels was too small to form a stable region.

Table 1. The results of performance evaluation of the algorithm in a real world scenario

Measure	Count
Number of events	189
Correct detections (TP)	173
False negatives (FN)	16
False positives (FP)	36
Recall: TP / (TP + FN)	91.5%
Precision: TP / (TP + FP)	82.8%
Accuracy: TP / (TP + FP + FN)	76.9%

Table 2. Statistics of incorrect decisions of the proposed algorithm

Error type	FP	FN	FP + FN
Background subtraction errors	26 (50.0%)	10 (19.2%)	36 (69.2%)
Objects occluded by other moving objects	0	3 (5.8%)	3 (5.8%)
Detection of objects moving in another lane	9 (17.3%)	0	9 (17.3%)
Incorrect decisions of the detector	1 (1.9%)	3 (5.8%)	4 (7.7%)
All errors	**36 (69.2%)**	**16 (30.8%)**	**52 (100%)**

Fig. 4. Examples of successful detection of stopping vehicles

4   Conclusions

The proposed algorithm achieved the goal of a satisfactory rate of correct decisions in the test setup. The main advantage of the algorithm is that it is able to perform online analysis of video streams from cameras, therefore live automatic event detection is possible. This is an important implication for the traffic monitoring systems that are currently used mainly for offline, post factum "manual" detection. With the proposed approach, traffic events related to vehicles stopping in forbidden zones, which may indicate a potential serious accident (e.g. when a vehicle stops on the tracks) may be detected as soon as they occur. Although such a scenario was not discussed here, the algorithm may be easily adapted to detect vehicles that park in forbidden zones, it only requires testing the time that the vehicle remains stopped and testing if the object is still present in the scene after it is incorporated into the background model. It may be used for detecting potential security threats (e.g. a vehicle stopping for a prolonged time near a bank office may be a getaway car).

Compared to the optical flow methods, the algorithm provides good computational performance, although the computational time depends on the number of pixels in the detection areas. In high resolution cameras it is possible to downscale the image without sacrificing the detection accuracy. The proposed algorithm significantly outperforms the Kalman tracker method which works sufficiently well only in case of a very low traffic. A quantitative comparison of the proposed algorithm with the Kalman-based one was not performed because the latter was rejected from the experiments after processing a small part of the test recordings. A very large number of FPs were caused by false trackers occurring due to the inability of the algorithm to cope with frequent merging and splitting, and, in the same time, this algorithm was unable to detect most of the actual events because of tracking errors. Therefore, analysis of the reference Kalman algorithm by testing it on the full 26 hours of recordings was concluded to be pointless.

It should be noted that the proposed algorithm is able to detect only a single type of traffic events. Other events that are not related to stopping vehicles require alternative approaches. Development of such algorithms will be a topic of further research and all these algorithms together will constitute an universal, automatic traffic events detector.

Acknowledgements. Research is subsidized by the European Commission within FP7 project INDECT, Grant Agreement No. 218086.

References

1. Zhu, Z., Yang, B., Xu, G., Shi, D.: A Real-Time Vision System for Automatic Traffic Monitoring Based on 2D Spatio-Temporal Images. In: Proc. 3rd IEEE Workshop on Applications of Computer Vision, Sarasota, pp. 162–187 (1996)
2. Zhu, Z., Xu, G., Yang, B., Shi, D., Lin, X.: VISATRAM: A Real-time Vision System for Automatic Traffic Monitoring. J. Image and Vision Computing 18, 781–794 (2000)
3. Zhou, J., Gao, D., Zhang, D.: Moving Vehicle Detection for Automatic Traffic Monitoring. IEEE Trans. Vehicular Monitoring 56, 51–59 (2007)
4. Tai, J.-C., Tseng, S.-T., Lin, C.-P., Song, K.-T.: Real-time Image Tracking for Automatic Traffic Monitoring and Enforcement Applications. Image and Vision Computing 22, 485–501 (2004)
5. Krausz, B., Bauckhage, C.: Analyzing Pedestrian Behavior in Crowds For Automatic Detection of Congestions. In: IEEE Int. Conf. Computer Vision Workshops (ICCV Workshops), Barcelona, pp. 144–149 (2011)
6. Czyżewski, A., Szwoch, G., Dalka, P., et al.: Multi-Stage Video Analysis Framework. In: Lin, W. (ed.) Video Surveillance, pp. 147–172. InTech, Rijeka (2011)
7. Dalka, P., Szwoch, G., Ciarkowski, A.: Distributed Framework for Visual Event Detection in Parking Lot Area. In: Dziech, A., Czyżewski, A. (eds.) MCSS 2011. CCIS, vol. 149, pp. 37–45. Springer, Heidelberg (2011)
8. Jiang, Z., Hyunh, D.Q., Moran, W., Challa, S., et al.: Multiple Pedestrian Tracking using Colour and Motion Models. In: Int. Conf. Digital Image Computing: Techniques and Applications (DICTA), Sydney, pp. 328–334 (2010)
9. Stauffer, C., Grimson, W.E.: Adaptive Background Mixture Models for Real-time Tracking. In: Proc. of IEEE Conf. on Computer Vision and Pattern Recognition, Fort Collins, pp. 246–252 (1999)

10. Dalka, P.: Detection and Segmentation of Moving Vehicles and Trains Using Gaussian Mixtures, Shadow Detection and Morphological Processing. Machine Graphics and Vision 15, 339–348 (2006)
11. Kim, K., Chalidabhongse, T.H., Harwood, D., Davis, L.: Real-time Foreground-Background Segmentation Using Codebook Model. Real-Time Imaging 11, 167–256 (2005)
12. Kim, K., Harwood, D., Davis, L.S.: Background updating for visual surveillance. In: Bebis, G., Boyle, R., Koracin, D., Parvin, B. (eds.) ISVC 2005. LNCS, vol. 3804, pp. 337–346. Springer, Heidelberg (2005)

Improving of Speaker Identification from Mobile Telephone Calls

Radosław Weychan, Agnieszka Stankiewicz,
Tomasz Marciniak, and Adam Dabrowski

Poznan University of Technology, Chair of Control and Systems Engineering,
Division of Signal Processing and Electronic Systems,
ul. Piotrowo 3a, 60-965 Poznań, Poland
{radoslaw.weychan,agnieszka.stankiewicz,
tomasz.marciniak,adam.dabrowski}@put.poznan.pl
http://www.dsp.org.pl

Abstract. The paper examines issues related to proper selection of models used for quick speaker recognition based on short recordings of mobile telephone conversations. A knowledge of the encoder type used during the transmission of speech allows to apply an appropriate model that takes specific characteristics of the encoder into account: full rate (FR), half rate (HR), enhanced full rate (EFR) and adaptive multi-rate (AMR). We analyse both proper model selection and automatic silence removal. Analysis of time of processing is also a part of this study.

Keywords: speaker identification, GSM, Gaussian mixture models.

1 Introduction

Automatic speaker recognition with contemporary computer systems is an attractive functionality, which can be used e.g. in various types of call-center systems to verify identity of speakers. In case of the public switched telephone network (PSTN) and the typical pulse-code modulation (PCM) bitstream of 64 kbit/s (8-bit quantization with sampling rate equal to 8000 samples per second) the speaker verification performance is about 95 % [10]. An inseparable use of the speech codecs applied in mobile networks decreases efficiency of the speaker identification [7,8,13]. Direct application of the encoder parameters seems to be impractical according to [7], since such approach can be realized only in the systems implemented by the operators of the cellular network.

In case of crossing the signal through several base stations and base station controllers in the cellular network the GSM-type coding of speech may be applied to the signal multiple times. Such occurrence is referred in this article as the effect of tandeming on speech signal.

Based on our research [8] we propose speaker verification system presented in Fig. 1. First step of signal processing is automatic removal of silence in the speech signal based on voice-activity detection (VAD) algorithm as discussed in [3,10]. For each of the speakers we have developed models incorporating different types

A. Dziech and A. Czyżewski (Eds.): MCSS 2014, CCIS 429, pp. 254–264, 2014.

of speech coders. The model that is the best match for identification process can be used in the phase of speaker verification. The modeling algorithm used during this stage is the Gaussian mixture model (GMM).

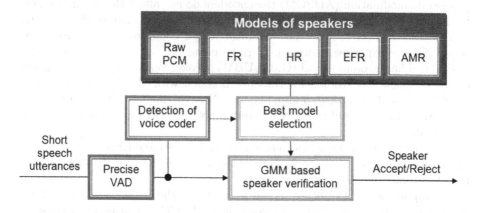

Fig. 1. Speaker verification with automatic selection of speaker models

Short discussion of encoders used in the experimental studies is given in [8]. Detection of the encoder type based on the mel–frequency cepstral coefficient (MFCC) parameters and the mean square error (MSE) [2]. In [11] an extended 85 dimensional feature vector was proposed to detect the encoder type, which includes also LPC coefficients, energy per frame, zero-crossing rate, Hilbert envelope, its variance and dynamic range, importance weighted signal to noise ratio (ISNR), pitch period estimate and estimate of the long term acoustic channel by blind channel estimation (BCE) algorithm. A classification and regression tree (CART) method was used. Results obtained in [2,11] show that detection of the transcoded speech, encoder type and even the bitrate can be used as the first step of the GSM-based speaker recognition.

In our application two end-point detection (EPD) algorithms were used for VAD and futher for silence removal. Applied method are: energy analysis and Jang HOD algorithm, both analyzed in [8]. In this study we propose the enhanced verions of those method, by detection and removal of silence in the beginning, middle, and at the end of each sentence. Therefore we are calling them "middle energy" and "middle Jang HOD" algorithms.

2   Related Work

Research on the analysis of the effects of speech coding on the quality of speech and speaker recognition are conducted for about 20 years. Such publications began to appear primarily at the development of the mobile communication techniques.

In the paper [9] it is shown that the speech signal coding reduces quality of the speech recognition (only the GSM full rate (FR) coder was investigated and the speaker recognition was not tested). An important issue is the analysis of multiple encoding (called tandeming). While in case of the adaptive differential pulse-code modulation (ADPCM) the encoders do not affect the recognition effectiveness, the GSM codecs reduce speech recognition performance significantly.

The tests related to matched and mismatched conditions can be found in paper [5]. The experiments were performed using the Gaussian mixture model – universal background model (GMM-UBM) speaker verification. Identification of the speakers was studied for the speech coded with G.729 (8 kbps), GSM (12.2 kbps), and G.723.1 (5.3 kbps) codecs. No experiments related to the half rate (HR), enhanced full rate (EFR), and adaptive multi-rate (AMR) encoders were made.

However, the above-mentioned encoders, i.e., FR, HR and EFR (except AMR) have been tested in the paper [7]. During this research the TIMIT database and its 8 ksps downsampled version was used.

An importance of the fitted model is shown in the paper [12]. Its authors compared linear predictive cepstral coefficients (LPCC), mel-frequency cepstral coefficients (MFCC), real cepstral coefficients (RCC). Results for the PCM training and the matched training only, were reported.

Studies on the influence of speech coding on the speaker recognition, reported in the literature, are so far quite limited. For example in the paper [4] the database ARADIGIT was tested only the matched conditions were only examined.

3   TIMIT Database

During the experiments the standard TIMIT database [6] was used. It contains recordings of the speech signal of 630 speakers presenting eight main dialects of English, each of them uttering 10 sequences. This gives 6300 speech files in summary. The average time of each sentence is about 3 s. This database is used primarily to test the efficiency of speech recognition algorithms. The sequences of speech were recorded with a resolution of 16 bits and sampling rate 16000 samples/second. In our experiments, the sampling rate was converted to the value of 8000 samples/second with the use of the same processing technique as the previous one.

In order to achieve the proper transcoding with the use of the GSM encoders, all files have been normalized to 0.9 of their maximum amplitude.

4   SNR After GSM Speech Coding

The degradation of signal quality can be measured by calculating the signal to noise ratio (SNR). In [9] the authors proposed a method that used only linear-prediction based GSM algorithms, making the SNR calculation much easier. We applied this coefficient for short utterances as described in [8].

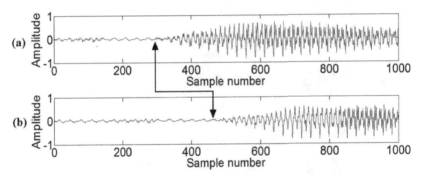

Fig. 2. Subset of frames of original speech (a) and once transcoded by FR encoder (b) (black line with arrows describes a delay between the encoder input and output — about 160 samples/20 ms)

Table 1. SNR values computed for tandems in case of TIMIT database

Encoder type	SNR [dB]			
	1 coding	2 codings	3 codings	4 codings
FR	27.211	27.1127	27.0195	26.8455
AMR	22.3673	19.2768	17.1698	15.6038
EFR	34.7623	31.5058	29.5246	28.3428
HR	25.2108	23.6957	22.6965	21.9322

The SNR values have been computed for the TIMIT database. This database has been transcoded four times by four main GSM encoders: full rate (FR), enhanced full rate (EFR), half rate (HR), and adaptive multi-rate (AMR). The last three encoders use adaptive and fixed codebooks.

It can be noticed that the calculation of the SNR values sample by sample may give incorrect results if large differences occur between the corresponding samples. The EFR and HR encoders give very similar results. In the case of the FR encoder, which uses predictive algorithms, the corresponding transcoded frames are more similar to the original ones (the use of the correlation function gives better results than those presented in [9]).

Fig. 2 presents the transcoding effects that occur during the FR coding. The SNR values for subsequent tandems (multiple subsequent transcodings) are presented in Table 1 and Fig. 3, which contains SNR values for subsequent tandemings in case of the TIMIT database. Subsequent tandems affect the signal less and less but the SNR values decrease nonlinearly. The transcoding operation most degrades the speech in the case of AMR encoder, and for FR coder / decoder the SNR coefficient decreases the least, as could be expected. For GSM encoders that use CELP algorithm, the length of the file seems to be very important in case of comparison between subsequent recordings.

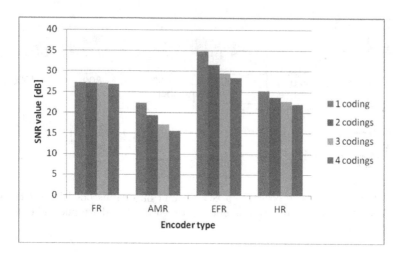

Fig. 3. SNR values computed in tandems for the TIMIT database

5   Speaker Recognition from GSM-Coded Speech

In order to determine the influence of GSM coders on speaker recognition accuracy, we tested four GSM coders (AMR, EFR, FR, and HR) and the unprocessed by EPD (raw) speech in the matched conditions. This means that the speaker

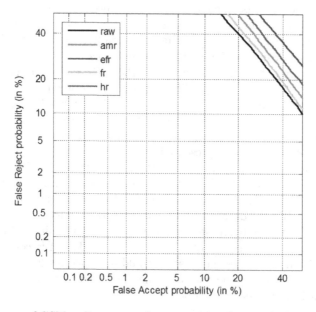

Fig. 4. Influence of GSM coding on speaker recognition for matched conditions in case of the TIMIT database

model and the speaker sentence used for tests were taken from the same database, thus coded with the same coder.

As it can be seen in Fig. 4 and 5, coding of speech decreases accuracy of the speaker recognition, which was expected. The coders in the order from the best to the worst result are: FR, EFR, AMR, and HR. The equal error rate (EER) values for this experiment are presented in Table 2 in bold.

6   Analysis of Tandeming Effect

Every cellular phone call comes through the base station and the base station controller. There can be several switches between the sender and the receiver. Every operation of coding and decoding has an impact on the signal quality. An idea of tandeming (transcoding the speech several times) is to check how it influences the speaker recognition accuracy.

Table 2 show EER values for matched and mismatched conditions for four GSM coders. Speech samples used for the test and the training part were

Table 2. EER of speaker recognition for transcoded speech (in %) in case of TIMIT database

Test vs. Model	Raw speech	Speech transcoded 1 time				Speech transcoded 4 times			
		AMR	EFR	FR	HR	AMR	EFR	FR	HR
Raw speech	**28.6**	31.1	34.3	32.9	35.0	37.3	40.6	34.5	41.9
AMR	32.6	**31.9**	38.0	33.2	34.6	37.3	44.6	34.7	41.4
EFR	35.2	36.0	**37.9**	35.8	37.9	39.5	41.7	36.1	42.4
FR	34.6	34.0	35.9	**30.0**	33.9	38.1	42.4	30.3	41.4
HR	38.0	36.3	41.2	35.4	**34.4**	39.1	45.8	35.7	40.2

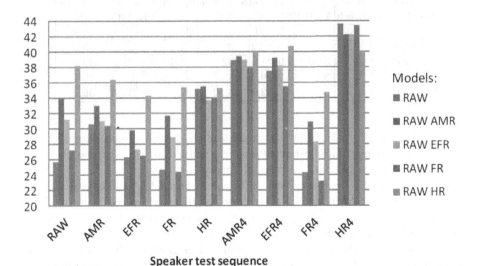

Fig. 5. EER of speaker recognition system for transcoded speech in case of TIMIT database

transcoded 1 and 4 times. It can be observed that in cases of AMR, EFR, and HR encoders EER value increases with the number of tandeming.

In case of TIMIT database, for single transcoding two models give the best result: raw speech and FR encoded. For four transcodings, the proper choice of model is much more significant to increase speaker recognition accuracy.

Fig. 5 present bar chart of values included in Table 2. The abscissa axis is described with the tested sequence transcoded by a specific encoder, while the ordinate axis shows the EER value. Colors of the bars correspond to the used models. As it can be observed, the full rate encoder gives better results even than the raw data in case of TIMIT database.

7   Analysis of Silence Removal

A comparison of the Tables 3 and 4 shows that removing silence has a significant influence on the speaker recognition system. In case of TIMIT database, the result is better (up to 6 %), but amount of speakers uttering various sentences once and different recording conditions make EER values higher.

7.1   Middle Energy Algorithm

Table 3 show results for matched and mismatched conditions with the use of four GSM coders and middle energy algorithm.

Table 3. EER of speaker recognition for transcoded speech with removed silence by middle energy method (in %) in case of TIMIT database

Test vs. Model	Raw speech	Speech transcoded 1 time				Speech transcoded 4 times			
		AMR	EFR	FR	HR	AMR	EFR	FR	HR
Raw speech	29.9	31.2	30.9	35.0	36.2	36.5	32.9	37.3	43.3
AMR	31.4	30.2	29.8	32.2	32.5	32.4	30.3	34.5	39.5
EFR	32.7	31.0	29.9	31.6	32.3	33.6	30.8	33.5	40.2
FR	35.7	34.1	32.2	29.2	32.5	36.9	33.7	29.5	40.4
HR	37.8	35.3	33.9	32.8	32.0	34.7	32.8	33.3	36.1

Removing silence, both from the model and the tested speech, improved the recognition efficiency. The best results were obtained for the test speech coded only once regardless of coder and model applied.

In case of TIMIT database, best EER values trend to be diagonal. Almost the same results for AMR and EFR encoders are dictated by used type of CELP algorithm. In both cases, single and four times transcodings, speech encoded with FR encoder as a model and for test stage give best results.

Fig. 6 illustrate the obtained EER values. Designation ME stands for the model processed with the middle energy algorithm, and coloured bars represents speaker model tested against the speaker test sequence listed on the horizontal axis.

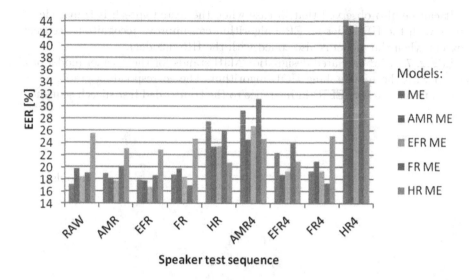

Fig. 6. EER of speaker recognition system for transcoded speech with removed silence with use of middle energy method in case of TIMIT database

Testing the TIMIT database, model speech encoded with encoder related to test stage gives a result which can be better distinguished from any other in case of single transcoding.

7.2   Middle Jang HOD Algorithm

It can be observed based on Table 4 and Fig. 7, that the middle Jang HOD algorithm, used for removing unvoiced parts of speech, shows significant improvement of the speaker recognition accuracy. It brings a very similar effect to that of the previously studied middle energy method. The differences between them are almost unnoticeable.

Table 4. EER of speaker recognition for transcoded speech with removed silence by Jang HOD method (in %) for TIMIT database

Test vs. Model	Raw speech	Speech transcoded 1 time				Speech transcoded 4 times			
		AMR	EFR	FR	HR	AMR	EFR	FR	HR
Raw speech	30.8	31.7	31.7	35.1	35.9	35.7	32.3	36.5	42.2
AMR	32.9	31.4	30.9	33.5	32.9	32.7	30.5	35.2	39.8
EFR	33.5	31.7	30.7	32.3	32.4	33.4	30.8	34.1	39.9
FR	37.0	35.2	33.6	30.6	33.1	37.3	34.1	30.5	40.5
HR	38.4	36.1	34.9	34.1	32.9	35.1	33.2	34.4	36.2

It can be also observed that in case when the tested speech is transcoded 4 times with the HR coder no EPD algorithm can improve recognition accuracy (except when the model is also coded with the HR encoder).

In Fig. 7 the abbreviated designation MJH stands for the speaker model processed with the middle Jang HOD algorithm. The corresponding graphs show recognition accuracy (EER) in reference to the transcoded test speech sequence.

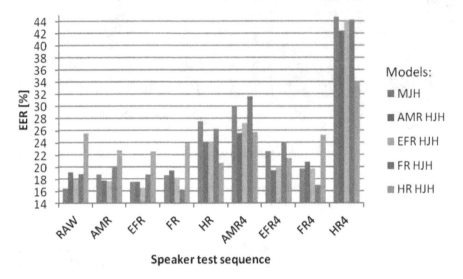

Fig. 7. EER of speaker recognition system for transcoded speech with removed silence with use of middle Jang HOD method in case of TIMIT database

8   Time of Processing

The average times of computations for each part of the speaker recognition system are shown in Table 5 and Fig. 8. The tested stages are: silence removal, feature extraction, creation of model, and verification of one particular speaker with one model.

The performance of tested algorithms is adequate to their complexities – removing silence with middle Jang HOD algorithm takes more time than computation of the signal energy.

Even though detection of silence is time consuming, speech recordings containing only voiced parts enables to create the speaker model faster (because of much smaller amount of the samples left). Therefore, in case of the middle energy algorithm the sum of the time spent on detecting silence and creating the speaker model is shorter than for the unprocessed speech. When the middle Jang HOD method is used the computational time is longer.

The experiments were performed in the Matlab environment working in Linux operating system. The hardware used for tests involved Xenon Quad Core E5405 2.0 GHz CPU and 2 GB RAM.

Table 5. Time of processing of TIMIT database (in [ms])

	Raw speech	Speech with removed silence	
		Middle energy	Middle Jang HOD
Silence removal	—	27.5	158.4
Feature extraction	5.1	2.8	2.8
Model creation	71	42.5	42.1
Verification of speaker	2.2	1.3	1.3
Overall	78.3	74.1	204.6

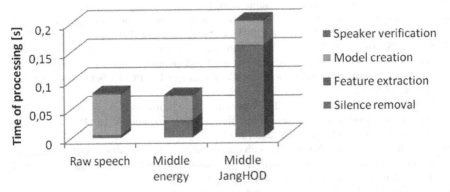

Fig. 8. Time of processing raw speech and speech with removed silence in case of TIMIT database

9   Conclusions

In this paper we analysed speaker verification based on short utterances of phone conversations. We examined model selection for FR, HR, EFR and AMR encoderd and effect of tandeming. Results shows that selection of the appropriate model improves verification of the speaker (up to 6 % of EER). Verification with the use of silence removal algorithms improves results up to 9–16 % of the EER, but it is closely linked with the dedicated model. The computation time for cutting silence by the middle energy method is shorter than for the unprocessed speech. The low complexity of proposed system – voice activity detection, encoder detection and also simplified GMM algorithm, give the possibility of an implementation in embedded systems, which are not able to work with the use of effective but complex and time-consuming algorithm like Alize [1].

References

1. Bonastre, J.F., Wils, F., Meignier, S.: Alize, a free toolkit for speaker recognition. In: Proceedings of the IEEE International Conference on Acoustics, Speech, and Signal Processing (ICASSP 2005), vol. 1, pp. 737–740 (March 2005)

2. Dabrowski, A., Drgas, S., Marciniak, T.: Detection of gsm speech coding for telephone call classification and automatic speaker recognition. In: International Conference on Signals and Electronic Systems, ICSES 2008, September 14-17, pp. 415–418 (2008)

3. Dabrowski, A., Marciniak, T., Krzykowska, A., Weychan, R.: Influence of silence removal on speaker recognition based on short polish sequences. In: Proc. of Signal Processing SPA, September 29-30, pp. 159–163 (2011)

4. Debyeche, M., Krobba, A., Amrouche, A.: Effect of gsm speech coding on the performance of speaker recognition system, pp. 137–140 (2010)

5. Dunn, R.B., Quatieri, T.F., Reynolds, D.A., Campbell, J.P.: Speaker recognition from coded speech in matched and mismatched conditions. In: A Speaker Odyssey-The Speaker Recognition Workshop (2001)

6. Garofolo, J.S., et al.: Timit acoustic-phonetic continuous speech corpus. Linguistic Data Consortium, Philadelphia (1993), http://catalog.ldc.upenn.edu/LDC93S1

7. Grassi, S., Besacier, L., Dufaux, A., Ansorge, M., Pellandini, F.: Influence of gsm speech coding on the performance of text-independent speaker recognition. In: Proc. of European Signal Processing Conference (EUSIPCO), September 4-8, pp. 437–440 (2000)

8. Krzykowska, A., Marciniak, T., Weychan, R., Dabrowski, A.: Influence of gsm coding on speaker recognition using short polish sequences. In: Proc. of Signal Processing SPA 2012, pp. 197–202 (2012)

9. Lilly, B., Paliwal, K.: Effect of speech coders on speech recognition performance. In: Proceedings of the Fourth International Conference on Spoken Language, ICSLP 1996, October 3-6, vol. 4, pp. 2344–2347 (1996)

10. Reynolds, D.: Robust text-independent speaker identification using gaussian mixture speaker models. IEEE Trans. Speech Audio Proc. 3(1), 72–83 (1995)

11. Sharma, D., Naylor, P., Gaubitch, N., Brookes, M.: Non intrusive codec identification algorithm. In: 2012 IEEE International Conference on Acoustics, Speech and Signal Processing (ICASSP), pp. 4477–4480 (2012), doi:10.1109/ICASSP.2012.6288914

12. Vuppala, A.K., Sreenivasa Rao, K., Chakrabarti, S.: Effect of speech coding on speaker identification. In: 2010 Annual IEEE India Conference (INDICON), pp. 1–4 (2010)

13. Vuppala, A., Sreenivasa Rao, K., Chakrabarti, S.: Effect of speech coding on speaker identification. In: Annual IEEE India Conference (INDICON), pp. 1–4 (2010)

Author Index